# LANDSCAPES OF THE CHINESE SOUL

# LANDSCAPES OF THE CHINESE SOUL

## The Enduring Presence of the Cultural Revolution

Edited by

*Tomas Plänkers*

**KARNAC**

First published in 2010 in German with the title *Chinesische Seelenlandschaften. Die Gegenwart der Kulturrevolution.*
© 2010 Vandenhoeck & Ruprecht GmbH & Co. KG, Göttingen


First published in English in 2014 by
Karnac Books Ltd
118 Finchley Road, London NW3 5HT

British Library Cataloguing in Publication Data

A C.I.P. for this book is available from the British Library

ISBN 978 1 78049 093 9

Translated by John Hart
Cover artwork by Cheng Yun Wang, 2008

The translation of this work was funded by Geisteswissenschaften International – Translation Funding for Humanities and Social Sciences from Germany, a joint initiative of the Fritz Thyssen Foundation, the German Federal Foreign Office, the collecting society VG WORT and the Börsenverein des Deutschen Buchhandels (German Publishers & Booksellers Association).


Edited, designed and produced by The Studio Publishing Services Ltd
www.publishingservicesuk.co.uk
e-mail: studio@publishingservicesuk.co.uk

Printed in Great Britain

www.karnacbooks.com

# CONTENTS

CHAPTER THREE

CHAPTER FOUR

CHAPTER FIVE

CHAPTER SIX

# ACKNOWLEDGEMENTS

We are grateful to the Foundation for Psychosomatic Disorders in Stuttgart, Germany, for its support of the research on the psychic consequences of the Chinese Cultural Revolution that is the focus of this book. See the contribution of T. Plänkers, "The Cultural Revolution in the mirror of the soul" (pp. 83–120).

We thank Cheng Yun Wang for the cover artwork, *Sunrise* (2008). Cheng Yun Wang, born 1959, is Professor at the Sichuan Music and Art Academy in Chengdu, China. He says,

> The Cultural Revolution was going on throughout my childhood. It is the first thing I remember. Neither then nor now have I been able to understand this event or to explain it in philosophical terms. Sunrise is my attempt, through painting, to bring these childhood experiences to some kind of closure.

We also thank Contact Press Images (Paris) for allowing us to print pictures from Li Zhensheng's book *Red Colour News Soldier* (Phaidon Press, 2003). Furthermore we thank the "Börsenverein des Deutschen Buchhandels" for the financial support for the translation of the German original.

**Natascha Gentz**, PhD, is a sinologist and Professor of Chinese Studies, Dean International (China), Head of Asian Studies, Director of the Confucius Institute for Scotland at the University of Edinburgh, and Director of the Scottish Centre for Chinese Studies.

**Rolf Haubl**, PhD, is Professor of Sociology and Psychoanalytic Social-Psychology at the University of Frankfurt/Main, Director of the Sigmund Freud Institute (SFI), a group training analyst and group analytical supervisor, organisational adviser (DAGG, DGSV), and Leader of the Research Focus on Psychoanalysis and Society at SFI.

**Friedrich Markert**, MD, is a specialist in psychiatry, neurology, and psychosomatic medicine and has been in private practice in Frankfurt since 1981 as a psychiatrist and psychoanalyst (DPA, IPA), group analyst (SGAZ Zürich), supervisor and Balint group leader. Since 2008, he has taught at the Shanghai Mental Health Center in China, training Chinese psychiatrists and psychologists in analytic group therapy.

**Tomas Plänkers**, PhD, is a member of the Sigmund Freud Institute in Frankfurt (Research Institute for Psychoanalysis and its Application), and is in private practice. Since 2000, he has been teaching psychoanalytic psychotherapy and psychoanalysis in China, and is a Consultant Member of the IPA China Committee. His main scientific work is in the fields of clinical and social psychoanalysis. He is editor and author of many clinical and social-psychological publications, including books on the psychological consequences of East German totalitarianism.

**David E. Scharff**, MD, is the Co-Founder, Board Chair, and Former Director and Supervising Analyst of the International Psychotherapy Institute, Chevy Chase, Maryland. He is the Clinical Professor at Georgetown University Medical School, and a teaching analyst at Washington Psychoanalytic Center. He serves as Chair of the IPA's Work Group on Family and Couple Psychoanalysis, and is Chair of the Continuous Training Program in Couple, Family and Child Therapy of the Beijing Mental Health Association. He is the author and editor of thirty books and numerous articles, including, with Jill Savege Scharff, *The Interpersonal Unconscious* (2011) and *Psychoanalytic Couple Therapy* (2014).

**Liying Wang**, PhD, is a post-doctoral student and teaching assistant at the Institute for Non-European Languages and Cultures at the University of Nuremberg-Erlangen. She was born in Shenyang in China. She has participated in the research project "Forms of Biographical Processing of Social Upheavals" as research associate at the Foundation for Psychosomatics in Stuttgart.

*PREFACE*

*David E. Scharff*

This volume, by members of the Sigmund Freud Institute in Frankfurt and co-operating sinologists and psychoanalysts, documents the research project on the trauma of the Cultural Revolution in China and its intergenerational effects. It describes direct examples of trauma inflicted during that period, and it also gives the larger cultural context in which we can begin to comprehend the extent and impact of national trauma in modern China. The scope of the book also allows us to view this trauma through the perspective of 2,500 years of Chinese thought, and in the light of Chinese social history and governmental policy in the past 100 years. Its wide ranging content encompasses much that a Western student of psychoanalysis, of history, and of comparative thought needs in order to see the magnitude of the impact of the Cultural Revolution on Chinese individuals and on China as a country, as we all witness the return of China as one of the most influential cultures on the world stage. It is incumbent on us to take on board the intellectual developments of Chinese history if we are going to try to understand issues of mental health and treatment in China. It might seem to the psychoanalyst and psychotherapist that such cultural history is not especially relevant to the core issues of dealing with patients, but the contributors to this book do not think so. Imagine if psychoanalysis as a field were to decide that the study of the Holocaust was irrelevant to our field! Not only would it be a loss concerning the capacity of analysis to contribute to understanding the most devastating events that happened in Europe and the West in the past 100 years, but we would be unable to help thousands of patients who were directly or indirectly affected by the Holocaust. In addition, we would be denied those lessons that continue to apply to understanding and treating widespread trauma in our own time.

Even if we acknowledge the historical and social-political differences from the Holocaust, this is precisely the point that cries out for understanding the history and consequences of the Cultural Revolution. Its impact on China was at least as far reaching as that of the Holocaust on Europe and the Middle East. As this volume shows, the trauma to those involved was both immediate and long lasting. The case for transmission to a current generation of Chinese adults is just as compelling as the transmission of Holocaust trauma to families of the victims and children of survivors.

However, there is a crucial difference that, for me, makes this volume even more compelling and timely: the Chinese government's successful policy of suppression of information, its imposed censorship of discussion about the Cultural Revolution, stands in stark contrast to the openness of Germany and other European governments that have encouraged examination of the legacy of Nazi terror.

The history of official "blind eye" on the impact of the Cultural Revolution in the West can be seen beginning in the 1970s. When Nixon went to China for his historic visit that opened relations between China and the USA, little was understood of the devastation occurring there at the time. Then, since the end of the Cultural Revolution, concurrent with Mao's death, the arrest of the Gang of Four, and the opening up that began in 1978, the revisionist history promulgated by the Chinese government has built and maintained a curtain of silence about most facts and effects of the years between 1966 and 1976. It is as though the West had blotted out essential facts of Hitler's entire reign of terror from 1933 to 1945. This silencing of thought in China has been perpetuated by the Chinese Communist Party's official version of the causes of the Cultural Revolution, reprinted as the final entry in Plänkers' volume. This Party statement is a remarkable document, beginning with what *seems* to be a frank admission of the errors of the period of the Cultural Revolution that might at first surprise the reader for its apparent openness concerning errors perpetrated on the Chinese people. But the document then proceeds to deflect blame away from Mao and on to the persons of Mao's wife, Jiang Qing, and the Gang of Four. Others who were in favour at the time the document was written are excused for their errors in the light of their contributions to the state. While it is admitted that Mao made errors, he is exonerated in view of the overall wisdom of his leadership over the years.

Westerners visiting China today can still witness the sturdiness of this position almost thirty-five years on, despite the radical changes that are visible everywhere in industry, transportation, urban development, and social issues. In Chinese cities, there are signs of industrial boom, including a crush of cars and high rises sprouting in large cities. Smog of a kind not seen in the West in a generation, and other signs of pollution, such as tainted water supplies, are the result of rapid and unchecked industrial development, and rapid population migration from the rural, agricultural areas into cities. Indeed, the Chinese are building large cities at a rate unprecedented in human history. Economically, they will continue to need to do so. China needs its new cities to support industrialisation and its shift from an agrarian to an industrial world economy. But as it does so, seeds of erosion of progress are sown, too. This rapid in-migration has created a class of non-citizens in the cities, workers needed by the economic shift who are effectively stateless, lacking identification cards that would legitimise them in the cities, lacking health care, family support, and economic security. We can add to this the insecurity built by thirty-five years of the one child policy in a country with millennia of tradition of large families, with family loyalty as a supreme value. China now faces a completely new family structure. In the absence of large-scale social security structures, these only children will be the sole support of their parents and grandparents in years to come. The demographics in China of an aging population with inadequate numbers of younger family members and workers to support them make the economic problems of aging in the West seem insignificant by comparison.

These social issues are relevant to the psychoanalytic clinician. I summarise some of them because I believe they constitute a significant part of the context into which this book needs to be integrated: the culture of intergenerational trauma that cannot be spoken adds up to a national culture of trauma, as Tomas Plänkers has written. While the concept of "national trauma" is perhaps not completely validated sociologically, it certainly makes sense to us clinically. The fact that the Cultural Revolution terrorised so much of the country, that it destroyed artefacts, traditions, and embedded ways of thought, that it deprived an entire generation of students of their education and sought to eradicate the educated class of professionals and academics, and that it directly terrorised, humiliated, and killed thousands, could not fail to put a black mark on China's hope for modernisation. My point is that this legacy of trauma continues to affect modern Chinese culture and the patients we might see, or whom our students see, and that it is insidiously intertwined with these other social changes. It becomes almost invisible, but its effects smoulder on like an underground fire that only finds its way to the surface periodically, but that then ignites whatever it touches. I believe that modern disruptions caused by escalating social forces will recall and reignite the legacy of the trauma from the Cultural Revolution.

Talking to Chinese colleagues today, however, I run into puzzling attitudes. First, it is not easy to have conversations, especially if I am clumsy enough to invoke questions about Mao himself. There is an unwritten rule that one does not criticise Mao, and that extends to being wary of criticising the Cultural Revolution. This means that the Cultural Revolution itself and, therefore, its effects, remain largely unspoken. It is hard to know how much discussion of these issues goes on in situations of trust behind closed doors, but it seems to me to be unusual and to be undertaken with a certain sense of risk. This means that a current culture of silence has moved from being a deliberate stifling of discussion by the Communist Party to being a self-censorship that is even more effective. It is only recently, for instance, that a native Chinese reported from first hand investigation on the scope and effect of the famine that Mao caused in the period beginning in 1958 with the agricultural and communal policies of the Great Leap Forward. That the largest famine in human history in which between 35 and 45 million died (Yang, 2012) had never been reported on by a Chinese journalist until Yang Jisheng's 2012 publication of *Tombstone: The Great Chinese Famine 1958–1962*, says a great deal about the effects of internal censorship. When I spoke about the magnitude of the famine in Shanghai in 2012, one young doctor in the audience rose to say that no one had told them how many people died at that time.

There is another obstacle to understanding that results from the lack of discussion about the Cultural Revolution and that of the Great Leap Forward that preceded it. When I have spoken to Chinese colleagues, there is frequently scepticism about the importance of discussing these traumas. Some have said, in effect, "Do we really need to worry about these things? It was long ago, and China has rebounded. How do you know that the scars of these times are still important for us now? Look around at all that is happening."

This is not so easy to answer directly. We can quote the literature on intergenerational effects of trauma, drawn from research on the Holocaust in Europe and on the continuing effects and transmission of childhood trauma such as physical and sexual abuse, but the scepticism we meet can be profound. From our point of view, this is a direct effect of the official national pattern of silence. From a psychoanalytic point of view, therefore, we need the kind of evidence offered by this book, the hard data of research done in China rather than Europe, that shows that the trauma of those Chinese who now constitute the older generation has already been passed on to their children, and that the psychological effects of those direct participants in the traumatic epoch have influenced their treatment of, and attitudes towards, their children. We need the kind of evidence this book gives that the trauma of the Cultural Revolution has made a substantial imprint on those children in their own adulthood. This lets us surmise with considerable confidence that the seeds of this trauma will continue to ripen in sure but quiet ways in generations to come.

*Landscapes of the Chinese Soul* is a treasure: it has harvested a wealth of understanding from the research initiated by the Sigmund Freud Institute. It has made it available so that others can continue to explore the legacy of trauma in China, and can continue to work towards mitigating suffering in a part of the world that psychoanalysis has only begun to study. We are all indebted to the Institute and to the contributors for the opportunity this book affords.

## Reference

Yang Jisheng (2012). *Tombstone: The Great Chinese Famine, 1958–1962*, S. Mosher & G. Jian (Trans.). New York: Farrar, Straus & Giroux.

# Introduction: Cultural Revolution and cultural regression

*Tomas Plänkers*

The Great Proletarian Cultural Revolution gives a shape to Chinese history under Communist rule, forcing its division into three phases: before, during, and after. The first period extends from the founding of the People's Republic of China in 1949 to the beginning of the Cultural Revolution in 1966. Historians disagree about the duration of the Cultural Revolution. Some identify it with the years 1966–1969; others include the whole decade between 1966 and 1976, ending only with the death of Mao Zedong (1893–1976). The official resolution of the Communist Party of China concerning the Cultural Revolution (adopted 1981, see pp. 175–191) uses the broader definition. The third period, which continues today, began in 1978 under the leadership of Deng Xiaoping. It is the era of continuing economic reforms, the turn away from centralised economic planning and towards capitalistic economic structures.

Before the Cultural Revolution came the disastrous famine of 1958–1962, in which thirty to forty million people died. This debacle, associated with the "Great Leap Forward", could have cast doubt on the leadership competence of the Party. Thus, it was kept secret not only from the outer world, but also to a large extent within China itself; even the elites in Beijing heard only selective reports. After a period of withdrawal in the post-famine years, Mao took the helm again with the Cultural Revolution. This new upheaval was required, as he thought, to break up the inertia of established political relationships. As a sequel to the 1949 revolution and its political consolidation in ensuing years, the cultural superstructure must now be transformed. To produce a profound renewal of a society whose ways of thought go back millennia, this new movement took aim at "the Four Olds": old ways of thought, old cultures, old habits, and old customs. An atmosphere of paranoia arose, in which many political leaders fell under suspicion of supporting the "capitalist road". Suddenly, society was split into "true revolutionaries", "supporters of Mao Zedong thought", and reactionary forces, "demons and serpents", against which the harshest measures were justified. This led to an orgy of violence, together with the destruction of physical cultural treasures on an unprecedented scale, all in accord with Mao's doctrine of "no development without destruction"—though the process usually stopped with the destruction. A bizarre cult of personality arose around Mao. The song "The East is Red" became a religious hymn:

The east is red, the sun is rising.
China has brought forth Mao Zedong.
He plans happiness for the people,
Hurrah, he is the great Redeemer of the people!
Chairman Mao loves the people,
He leads us,
To build the new China
He leads us on.

Swept away by love for their new god, the masses went on a witch-hunt against anyone they disliked. Political justifications were not far to seek. Revolutionary goals—proclaimed in an endless stream of pamphlets, meetings, speeches, wall newspapers, and books—gave a progressive disguise to what was, in fact, a deeply regressive group process, acknowledged as a catastrophe even by the Communist Party of China in its 1981 resolution. Psychoanalysis designates individual and social relationships as regressive when they reanimate early, infantile forms of relationship. Regression was now the norm in China: regression in relationship form (the highly idealised Chairman–Father with millions of "children"); regression in the affective situation (symbiotic elation, destructive hate); regression in the level of psychic integration (dominance of splitting and projection: thinking in terms of black and white, friend and enemy). The practical results were the annulation of inhibitions against violence and an extensive collapse of government structures: an anomic condition of society.

Although these were terrible events—the 1981 Party resolution speaks of "many crimes . . . bringing disaster to the country and the people" (see p. 176)—the Cultural Revolution did have a genuinely revolutionary impact on the traditions of the nation and the Party. In former years, the expression of personal opinion was suppressed: now anyone could be criticised, anyone could write an opinion in a wall newspaper; political authorities were no longer untouchable. The political heritage of the Cultural Revolution is Janus-faced. In today's

*Photograph 1.*   Young Pioneers greet representatives of the Conference of Progressive Work Groups and Model Workers in the auditorium of the North Plaza Hotel in Heilongjiang, Harbin, Heilongjiang Province, 10 February 1973.

China there is no subservient mentality towards the Party leadership. Functionaries are obeyed because they have power, but they are not honoured. A break with the Confucian world-view (though this is once again being promoted) seems really to have been initiated. As a youth movement directed against "the Olds", the Cultural Revolution took up where the Cultural Movement of 4 May (1919) left off. The youth of 1919 had sought to connect to enlightened Western intellectual currents. In 1966, the object was "socialist man"—but this was also, at the time, a Western ideological vision.

Germans are all too familiar with processes like these. Although the twelve disastrous years of Nazi rule did not produce a socially anomic condition, they led to individual and social regression and the unleashing of destruction, with trauma to victims, perpetrators, and witnesses alike. These traumas have been the subject of intensive study in Germany, Israel, and the USA, with research directed to their character, the personality changes they produced, their transmission to later generations, and their psychoanalytic treatment. This background is useful for a consideration of the Chinese Cultural Revolution (see, for instance, the researches of Gänßbauer, 1996; Kogan, 1990, 1998). Of course, the two catastrophes differ socially, culturally, and politically (compare Schwarcz, 1996). The victims of the Holocaust and the Second World War are not to be equated with the victims of the Cultural Revolution. Yet, psychic traumatisations, whatever their origin, can have identical structural, dynamic, and also (as we now know) neurobiological characteristics. Similarly, larger groups, even whole societies, may deal with their traumatised members in ways that help recovery, or hinder it.

With each war and social catastrophe since 1945, the field for traumatological study has broadened. Thus, the Vietnam War yielded studies of the war's effects on its American veterans (who received very much more attention than its Vietnamese victims). However disparate the events that give rise to them, psychic consequences, it has become clear, have much in common. This commonality is reflected in the international acceptance of the diagnosis of post traumatic stress disorder (PTSD), however subject to criticism the label might be as a limited conception of psychic traumatisation.

The road to scientific recognition and study of the psychic traumatisations of the Holocaust, the Second World War, the Vietnam War, and the wars in the Middle East and in Africa was all too long; the analogous investigation of the psychic consequences of the Chinese Cultural Revolution has yet even to begin. The history of twentieth century China can be seen as a series of catastrophes endured and inflicted, a chain of dramatic social events with an enduring influence on great segments of Chinese society. A few historical reference points: after the end of the Qing Dynasty in 1911 and the birth of the Chinese republic, a power struggle among rival groups ensued, leading to civil war from 1927 to 1945.[1] These years also saw the Second Sino-Japanese War, 1937–1945,[2] which killed three million soldiers and over eighteen million civilians (over nine million in crossfire and more than eight million from other causes). Ninety-five million people fled or were displaced. The Communist victory in 1949 and the foundation of the People's Republic of China brought the country only a new series of catastrophes. Mao Zedong and the Communist Party of China were responsible for the deaths of seventy million people (according to Chang and Holiday, 2005a, p. 17). The aforementioned "Great Leap Forward" of 1958–1962 produced the greatest famine in human history, with an estimated thirty to forty million deaths.

Then came the so-called Great Proletarian Cultural Revolution, 1966–1976. It was officially justified as a fight against the internal enemies of socialism in China. Pointing with scorn at so-called revisionism in the contemporary Soviet Union, leaders called for battle against "reactionary bourgeois authorities". In the name of safeguarding the power of the proletariat, war was declared on enemies in the Communist Party and in the population at large, especially among the educated and intellectual classes. The Soviet Union had seen a similar persecution under Stalin. There, too, accusations of treason against the revolutionary cause had been used to neutralise political foes and to reinforce the rule of the Party chief. The movement in China began as an intra-Party purification campaign, but quickly spread to all segments of the population. The process gained its own momentum; the political leadership lost control of it for a time.

The movement began in 1966 in universities and schools. At public meetings and in the posters called "wall newspapers", accusations were levelled against professors and other instructors. The campaign quickly spread to other social institutions, to the party apparatus, the army, and the whole economy, and soon produced a state of permanent persecution.

The resulting violence is captured in iconic images: for instance, of professors paraded through the streets with dunce caps on their heads and placards around their necks proclaiming their crimes, on their way to being beaten, tortured, and perhaps killed. Not a few such individuals committed suicide. There was looting; there were arbitrary arrests. In one Beijing suburb over three hundred people were tortured to death by Red Guard members. Thousands of homes were searched, plundered, and destroyed by Guards. Political and personal undesirables were tortured and killed. There were cases of cannibalism (Schwarcz, 1996, p. 3, citing reports by Zheng Yi).

Officially, these groups were battling the "Four Old Evils" mentioned above: old ways of thought, old cultures, old habits, and old customs. These abstract linguistic wrappings disguised the pursuit of personal advantage, influence, and power, and the settling of old scores. Violent and bloody confrontations between rival groups sometimes amounted to military battles, with thousands of deaths.

Sometimes, and with increasing frequency as time went on, persecutors and persecuted switched places. Political and institutional power devolved more and more from the official organs of the Party and the state to locally dominant groups of Red Guards, rebels, military men, or Revolution Committees, leading finally to the collapse of the Party and state institutions. Armed conflicts among rival groups produced almost wartime conditions. For a time, the Red Guards ran an independent justice system with its own prisons. All over the country universities, schools, and factories closed. By the end of 1968, the whole society had reached an anomic condition. This was alleviated by the so-called Rustication Campaign, in which 12–17 million urban youths and former Red Guards were sent to the countryside, but the following years saw further waves of violence and persecution as the most various groups pursued their ends.

The number of lives lost in the Cultural Revolution is unknown; estimates vary between a few hundred thousand and several million. Chinese officials, for example, placed the figure at twenty million (Li Hou-cheng, 1981, cited in Pye, 1986, p. 597). The whole intellectual class was largely eliminated. There was a regular campaign to erase evidence of China's traditional culture. In Tibet, too, most religious institutions were destroyed and their representatives executed, with large parts of the population confined in re-education camps and, in some cases, tortured. It is estimated that more than a million people died in Tibet in this period. If it is difficult to arrive at a valid number

*Photograph 2.*   School children march through the streets on the national
holiday, carrying spears with red tassels and wearing the armbands of the
Red Guard. In the background is a department store with architectural
similarities to Russian buildings.

of deaths, it is harder still to assess the psychic damages inflicted by
social regression, a climate of persecution that lasted for years, the
brutalisation of social intercourse, torture and murder, constant
danger, and the loss of autonomy over personal life choices. As with
the physical effects of nuclear radiation, the psychic consequences
continue, silent and unrecognised, for generations. Only Holocaust
research has produced scientific models and concepts that allow us to
grasp these catastrophic long-term effects.

After Mao's death in 1976, the 1980s brought a certain critical
engagement with the Cultural Revolution. There arose the so-called
Wound, or Scar, literature (*shanghen wenxue*), in which victims bore

witness to their experiences. The name derives from a narrative whose title is variously translated "The Scar", "The Wound", or "The Wounded", by the author Lu Xinhua, published in 1981 (after Saechtig, 2005, p. 35). Such publications gave the afflicted people their first chance to be heard. Their most prominent representative was Ba Jin (1904–2005),[3] himself a victim of the Cultural Revolution. After 1980, he chaired the Chinese affiliate of PEN and came to be seen as a moral authority. He dealt with the Cultural Revolution in many of his writings, and eventually proposed the founding of a museum dedicated to it (Ba Jin, 2005). This demand is to be understood symbolically as a call for an open confrontation with this part of the Chinese past. Our experience with long-term psychoanalysis teaches us all too well how the failure to confront the past leads to psychic illness and dysfunction. The remark of American philosopher George Santayana, often cited in the context of German history, has obvious application to recent Chinese history as well: "Those who cannot remember the past are condemned to repeat it" (2009, p. 217).

Who in Germany will not think of the struggle to come to terms with the Nazi era? Although many in China have supported the search for self-understanding, this has not become a social norm. There has been no official engagement with the Cultural Revolution since, at the latest, 1989, when the democracy movement was bloodily suppressed, but we know from our psychoanalytic experience that official silence does not banish events from the human unconscious. The "ten year catastrophe" (Ba Jin, 1985, p. 14) lurks in latency in the social psyche, a presence whose conscious manifestation is apparently still feared. Of course, it took Germany several decades—under much more favourable political and cultural conditions—to begin its internal confrontation its own "twelve year catastrophe", and we should not forget how many Germans of the revolutionary-minded 1968 generation were bedazzled by the Cultural Revolution. Geographical distance and cultural remoteness allowed the news from China to be idealised. People thought the dawn of true socialism was at hand. Anyone who pointed to the real circumstances was assumed to belong to the bourgeois, anti-revolutionary camp. In this matter, too, we sought to evade reality for quite a while.

If we at the Sigmund Freud Institute are making the attempt to examine these historical and psychic realities more closely, to make them an object of a psychoanalytic, social-psychological and sinological investigation, it is not with any pejorative idea of exposing China's "old wounds". Rather, in the spirit of Ba Jin, we see the attempt to penetrate the past as meaningful and clarifying for the present—and as an aid to preventing any future repetition of such events.

> A while ago, someone complained to me about the narrative "Scar" and about what people call "Scar Literature" in general. He said that these works, by exposing our own wounds and showing our weak points, damage the reputation of the State. I discussed this problem with Professor Yang Zhenning. I expressed the thought that scars that are not fully healed are still worse and more terrible than the so-called Scar Literature. We must look the truth in the eye and not hide our sickness out of fear of the treatment. (Ba Jin, 1980, after Saechtig, 2005, p. 37, translated for this edition)

Chinese officialdom—which speaks with many voices—has also called for truth-telling about the past. On the occasion of China's appearance at the 2009 Frankfurt Book Fair, Wu Shulin, Deputy Minister for the General Administration for Press and Publications (the national censorship office), had this to say about Chinese history:

> . . . being loyal to historical facts should be valued more than individual lives. The editing rule of 'being a transmitter and not a maker', which was proposed by Confucius, has been adhered to among serious publishers till today. (Wu, 2009, p. 15)

If contemporary China is, none the less, defensive about this part of its history, this reflex might have to do with both aspects of the Janus-faced Cultural Revolution: on the one hand with the scarcely bearable traumatic experiences, and on the other with the uncomfortable fact that this was China's first youth revolt, which swept like a storm across the country and taught fear to many of the rulers of the day.

This investigation of the psychic consequences of the Chinese Cultural Revolution is one of a series of so-called "Eastern Projects" through which, beginning in 1989, the Sigmund Freud Institute set out to look into the psychic implications of social systems in the former East Bloc countries. We researched psychic changes and continuities in schools in Prague and eastern Germany after the fall of the Berlin Wall (Kerz-Rühling & Plänkers, 2000), explored the unconscious motivations of unofficial collaborators with the Stasi police in the German Democratic Republic (Kerz-Rühling & Plänkers, 2004), and looked into the psychic consequences of child-raising in communal crèches, as practised in the German Democratic Republic (Israel & Kerz-Rühling, 2008).

Much has been published since 1976 in China and abroad about the history, background, and consequences of the Cultural Revolution. These publications tend to privilege either objective or subjective facts. That is, they either portray historical developments (see "Selective chronology of events", pp. 165–174) or they report personal experience (compare Feng, 1991). In the context of known history, our investigation focuses on the reports of persons who were, statistically viewed, less impacted than others, and derives characteristics of personality structure. This involves psychodynamic structures, as expressed in perception, judgement, and behaviour, social-psychological structures resulting from the experience of violence, and narrative patterns.

This book is divided into six chapters reflective of the multi-disciplinary nature of the investigation. It does not attempt a historical portrayal of the Cultural Revolution (for that, see, for instance, Yan and Gao, 1996). We begin with a sinological paper as a theoretical introduction to our empirical project. Natascha Gentz discusses the problems of collective memory and the individual processing of experiences in the Cultural Revolution against the background of various narratives found in documents of the Communist Party, in literature, and in the products of the media and especially on the Internet. She then applies her analysis to the narratives of the Chinese individuals of the first and second generation whom we interviewed for this project. She shows how the experiences of the period—chaos, the overturning of all values, the collapse of secure structures—left the victims with a feeling of contingency, of being exposed to random forces, that challenges all understanding. In our second chapter, Ling Wang investigates how this particular experience of contingency was dealt with and how typically Chinese concepts of fate came into play. Among these contingencies, as seen in our interviews with informants and their children, was exposure to violence. Rolf Haubl explores the effects of such exposure, showing how the past experience of violence induces a latent potentiality for violence in the present. Next, I present our actual research project, its methodological approaches and content, and its results. There follows a consideration of the concept of trauma against the background of psychoanalytic concepts and in the specific cultural context of China. In particular, I will suggest that the trope of "collective trauma", often encountered in discussions of the Cultural Revolution, is questionable. Finally, Friedrich Markert presents at length interviews with a father and his son, in order to give a clear impression of the kind of material we gathered and to demonstrate its psychoanalytic interpretation, with the intercultural problems this undertaking presents.

This international, multi-disciplinary project could not have been carried out without the unflagging co-operation and participation of German and Chinese colleagues. It was a group undertaking in the truest sense of the expression. First of all, I am grateful to the direct participants in the project: the authors in this book, as well as Gertrud Reerink, Ulrich Ertel, and Dr Hermann Schultz, all of whom took part in the time-consuming psychoanalytic evaluation of the material. Dr Liying and Chunqiu Li made a basic and essential contribution with their translations of the Chinese interviews, and I thank them warmly. For well-known reasons, our Chinese co-workers in China must remain unnamed. It is precisely on these grounds that I feel such solidarity with them and such gratitude to them for conducting the interviews. I also thank Dr Antje Haag und Professor Doctor Alf Gerlach (both members of the German-Chinese Academy for Psychotherapy, DCAP), who, through their writings and our conversations, helped me arrive at a better understanding of China in general and of the Cultural Revolution in particular. Special thanks go to the Foundation for Psychosomatic Disorders, which generously provided the means for the conduct of our investigation. And last, but not least, I thank the two Directors of the Sigmund Freud Institute, Professor Marianne Leuzinger-Bohleber and Professor Rolf Haubl. In carrying out this project, I could always count on their support.

## Notes

1. The Chinese Civil War was the struggle for the political leadership of China following the end of the Qing Dynasty in 1911–1912. Its main component was the conflict between the nationalist Kuomintang under Chiang Kai-shek and the Communist Party of China under Mao Zedong, which began after Chiang's northern campaign of 1927 and ended with the flight of the Kuomintang to Taiwan in 1949.
2. The First Sino-Japanese War was 1894–1995.
3. Ba Jin is a pseudonym that the writer adopted in 1928 while studying in France. It fuses the names of two men he admired, BA-kunin and Kropot-KIN (Martin, 1985, p. 199).

## References

Ba Jin (1985). *Gedanken unter der Zeit.* Cologne: Eugen Diederichs.

Ba Jin (2005). Gedanke 145. In: Jiang zhen hua de shu. Chengdu: Sichuan Renmin Chubanshe, A. Saechtig (Trans.). *Mut: Forum für Kultur, Politik und Geschichte, 449*: 38–41.

Chang, J., & Halliday, J. (2005a). Mao: Das Leben eines Mannes, Das Schicksal eines Volkes. Munich: Blessing.

Feng, J. (1991). *Voices from the Whirlwind: An Oral History of the Chinese Cultural Revolution.* New York: Pantheon Books [reprint of: *One Hundred People's Ten Years.* Beijing: Foreign Languages Press, 1990].

Freud, S. (1921c). *Group Psychology and the Analysis of the Ego. S.E., 18:* 67–143. London: Hogarth.

Gänßbauer, M. (1996). *Trauma der Vergangenheit. Die Rezeption der Kulturrevolution und der Schriftsteller Feng Jicai.* Dortmund: Projekt.

Israel, A., & Kerz-Rühling, I. (Eds.) (2008). *Krippenkinder in der DDR.* Frankfurt: Brandes & Apsel.

Kerz-Rühling, I. & Plänkers, T. (Eds.). (2000). *Sozialistische Diktatur und Psychische Folgen.* Tübingen: edition diskord.

Kerz-Rühling, I. & Plänkers, T. (2004). *Verräter oder Verführte. Eine Psychoanalytische Untersuchung Inoffizieller Mitarbeiter der Stasi.* Berlin: Links.

Kogan, I. (1990). Vermitteltes und reales Trauma in der Psychoanalyse von Kindern von Holocaust-Überlebenden. *Psyche—Zeitschrift für Psychoanalyse, 44*: 533–544.

Kogan, I. (1998). *Der stumme Schrei der Kinder: Die zweite Generation der Holocaustopfer.* Frankfurt: Fischer.

Martin, H. (1985). Ein Nachwort zu Ba Jin. In: *Ba Jin, Gedanken unter der Zeit* (pp. 195–203). Köln: Eugen Diederichs.

Pye, L. W. (1986). Reassessing the Cultural Revolution. *China Quarterly, 108*: 597–612.

Saechtig, A. (2005).Verarbeitung statt Verdrängung. *Mut: Forum für Kultur,Politik und Geschichte, 449*: 34–37.

Santayana, G. (2009). *The Life of Reason* (Volume 1). Ort: BiblioBazaar.

Schwarcz, V. (1996). The burden of memory: the Cultural Revolution and the Holocaust. *China Information, 11*(1): 1–13.

Wu, S. (2009). Remarks at Global Chinese Publishing Forum, Frankfurt International Bookfair 15 October 2009.

Yan, J., & Gao, G. (1996). *Turbulent Decade: A History of the Cultural Revolution,* D. W. Y. Kwok (Ed. & Trans.). Honolulu: University of Hawai'i Press.

Beginning in September 1966, under threat from "the directorate of the rebels" (or the directorate of the whip), I changed the way I used my brain. If everyone roared "Down with Ba Jin!" I raised my right hand and joined in the chorus. Thinking now about my conduct back then, I can't understand it. But it wasn't that I was lying; I was expressing an honest wish to be crushed by the others, so that I could make a new beginning, become a new person. (Ba Jin, 1981, cited in Saechtig, 2005, p. 36, translated for this edition)

Thus the main characteristics of the individual submerged in the mass are the loss of the conscious personality, the dominance of the unconscious personality, the alignment of thoughts and feelings in one direction through contagion and suggestion, and the tendency to put suggested ideas into immediate action. The individual is no longer himself, he has become an automaton without will. (Gustave Le Bon, 1895, cited in Freud, 1921, p. 71)

# CHAPTER ONE

# Negotiating the past: narratives of the Cultural Revolution in party history, literature, popular media, and interviews

*Natascha Gentz*

The following contribution concerns the reasons why the processing of the traumatic experiences of the Chinese Cultural Revolution has been so difficult for the country in political, social, and cultural contexts. The working through of such experiences generally depends on a supportive social environment that acknowledges the experience of trauma and, thus, permits traumatised persons to emerge from amnesia and confront what they have been through. Such a social consensus has not existed in China since the Cultural Revolution. On the one hand, the political edicts of a socialistic dictatorship have defined the permissible ways of dealing with the past. On the other hand, due to the complexity of the circumstances, there is no consensus to date as to whether a confrontation with the past is even necessary or important. As the following discussion will show, political guidelines have not only had a restrictive effect but have also put their own definite stamp on understanding and interpretation of the events of the Cultural Revolution: a stamp reflected in culture, literature, film, and scientific debate. The effects extend beyond mainland China. In the West, too, many of these *données* have been absorbed and have influenced conceptions of this phenomenon.

The last part of this chapter offers a linguistic and content analysis of interviews with contemporary witnesses and their children (see the contribution of Plänkers, pp. 83–120) from these cultural, political, and social-historical perspectives. It will be clear that most of the interviewees have not arrived at a substantive political consideration of the events.

This gap is partly explained by the fact that open debate about the Cultural Revolution has been discouraged, both in its immediate wake and our own day. Thus, heightened censorship was imposed in 2006 to block any unofficial presentations, activities, or publications marking the fortieth anniversary of the Revolution's onset. Nevertheless, the Cultural Revolution has been dealt with over the years in numerous unofficial publications, in literature and film, and even in public debate.

Discussions about how to interpret the Cultural Revolution and its effects take place in many forms and media and are often quite controversial. Scientific researchers, too, disagree about what triggered the "ten catastrophic years" and what the enduring consequences have been. Having gathered collective and individual voices in various media, I shall attempt to characterise this gamut of opinions and assessments and so to clarify the cultural background of our interview texts. Even though individual publications on the Cultural Revolution are restricted, even though public debate is discouraged and departures from the officially sanctioned interpretation might bring reprisals, the period is the subject of wide-ranging discussions in which distinct individual processing strategies are revealed. The Chinese Internet, which, in recent decades, has developed into an alternative realm for public debate and the articulation of dissent, offers an important forum. Despite the fact that the concept "Cultural Revolution" is taboo and supposedly subject to Internet censorship (Xiao, 2004), the abundance of search results shows that full control is lacking or impossible.

Whether and how historical accounts help shape cultural identity is a question that has been much discussed of late. Assmann's distinction between cultural and communicative memory (Assmann, 2001) has been particularly influential. Communicative memory extends perhaps a century back and concerns events that have been directly witnessed, at least in part; it is nourished by personal experience and by the reports of others. Collective memory, on the other hand, is established by texts that have the status of Holy Writ and attain universal acceptance. The Chinese Party leadership's attempt to crystallise the events of the Cultural Revolution in an untouchable political document (see text of the resolution of 1981, pp. 175–191) can be understood as a bid to establish a collective memory, and with it a unified political identity. The strategy was a partial success; many of the Party's findings have entered into collective memory and also turn up in our interview transcripts. However, since the events are too recent to have left the realm of personal experience, a whole series of alternative reports, communicated in other forms, exists, constituting part of a communicative—that is, still negotiable—memory.

The attempt to establish a universally valid interpretation of the political turbulence of the Cultural Revolution was embodied in the "Resolution on Certain Questions in the History of Our Party Since the Founding of the People's Republic of China", approved at the Sixth plenary meeting of the Eleventh Central Committee (Resolution, 1981). With its publication on 1 July of that year in the *People's Daily* (*Renmin Ribao*), it became the established study text for Party cadres and the masses. It presents the orthodox interpretation of the events and the sanctioned vocabulary ("ortholalie", correct speech) for discussion of the events and their connections. A counterproposal was offered a few years later, in 1986, by historians Yan Jiaqi and Gao Gao, a husband-and-wife team; this document circulated only in samizdat, and brought house arrest for Yan Jiaqi during the campaign against "bourgeois liberalism". Published in English as *Turbulent Decade*, the work appeared in Chinese in 1990 under the neutral title *The Ten Years of the Cultural Revolution in China*, and quickly became a best seller in Hong Kong and Taiwan (Yan & Gao, 1996). As we shall see, Yan Jiaqi actually did not stray far from the paradigm set by the Party. It is the historical writings of the Red Guards that openly challenge the Party's interpretation.

Beginning in 1976, writers took up the events of the Cultural Revolution in the so-called Scar Literature, which was officially supported by the Party and the propaganda apparatus, so long as it remained within the limits set in the resolution (He, 1992). Deviant representations, such as Zhang Xianliang's reports from labour camps, could only circulate underground (Kinkeley, 1991). After the end of the 1980s came a flood of autobiographical narratives of the Cultural Revolution, a bibliography of which would fill many pages. These

accounts certainly reflect a strong urge to share and to process experiences, especially traumatic ones. At the same time, the narratives
exhibit an astonishing conformity, showing the strong imprint of
social and cultural context—the communicative memory.

The greatest variety of individual interpretations and processing
strategies is found on the Internet, which (especially since that start of
the twenty-first century) has become the dominant means of communication in China. The penultimate section of this chapter will deal
with the ways this medium allows Chinese "net citizens" to gather
information, argue, or work through grief.

## Communist Party historiography

### The Official Party Resolution

The "Resolution on Certain Questions in the History of Our Party
Since the Founding of the People's Republic of China" establishes the
framework within which the causes, events, and consequences of the
Cultural Revolution are to be assessed. Such Party resolutions serve to
legitimise leadership changes and to portray these as the logical
consequences of historical progress. The assumption is that the march
of history, dictated by economic processes, leads to ever more evolved
social forms. The model text for the drafting of such historically
minded resolutions is the 1939 Soviet curriculum, "The History of the
Communist Party of the Soviet Union (Bolshevik), Short Course"; this
circulated in China in millions of copies for decades and was, to some
degree, the model for the first Chinese Party Resolution of 1945. Just
as the Soviet course of study served to consolidate Stalin's position
after the "Great Purges", the "Certain Questions" resolution of 1981
marked the definitive triumph of Deng Xiaoping over the Old Maoists
around his predecessor, Hua Guofeng. In the Soviet curriculum, intra-
Party conflicts were always defined as the struggle between "two
lines": a correct one, represented by the great leader Lenin and his
follower Stalin, and the erroneous line of Party enemies; this pattern
would be reproduced in explaining the Cultural Revolution.

The interpretative model of the "struggle between two lines"
pervades all of the Chinese Party's historical writing, including its
explanation of the Cultural Revolution. Such a bipolar model

naturally leaves no room for political debates and competing ideas. Since the resolutions are always written from the winners' viewpoint, deviant opinions or alternative political strategies are cast as unsuccessful plots against the Party by its enemies.

Such Party documents are themselves the result of lengthy discussions and debates within Party committees. In this case, the deliberations lasted more than a year and involved over a thousand Party cadres and historians. The document was adopted in July 1981, approximately the sixtieth anniversary of the founding of the Chinese Communist Party (Brady, 2008; Schoenhals, 1992). (Before Deng Xiaoping's rehabilitation, Hua Guofeng and his so-called "Whateverists", who maintained that whatever Mao Zedong had said and done was correct, had had their own interpretation to offer. They had blamed the Cultural Revolution on the "erroneous line" of Liu Shaoqi, Lin Biao, and, later, Deng Xiaoping: an attempt, under cover of leftist rhetoric, to reintroduce capitalism.) The resolution of 1981 brought a fundamental change in that it assigned the central role in the Cultural Revolution to Mao Zedong. At the famous Third Plenary Meeting of the Eleventh Central Committee, in December 1978—still regarded as the turning point in Chinese politics—the way was paved for this development: "leftist" errors made before and during the Cultural Revolution were corrected, and the concept of class warfare was de-emphasised in favour of the programme of the "Four Modern-isations". An important practical consequence was that class status was no longer noted in individual identification papers. The so-called "Gang of Four" were cast as the principal perpetrators; their trial began (four years after their arrest) in November 1980. Also called to account were other high-ranking cadres who had been involved in the Lin Biao coup of 1971, an attempted *putsch* against Mao that had led to Lin Biao's death in a plane crash, though the exact circumstances are murky to this day.

It was against this background that the orthodox interpretation of the Cultural Revolution was fashioned and adopted. The main problem was how to assign blame for the era now known as the "ten catastrophic years". Since Deng Xiaoping's leadership was, above all, concerned to establish social order and stability in order to guarantee the efficient implementation of his reforms, it was deemed unwise to probe too deeply into the causes of complex factional battles and their roots in society and the population as a whole. Neither could Mao

Zedong be assigned the role of chief culprit, as Jiang Qing tried to do in her defence at the trial; the dethronement of this absolute leader, the Founder of the People's Republic, the creator of Mao Zedong Thought, would also endanger social stability. A carefully calibrated solution was arrived at, one that indeed acknowledged leftist errors on Mao's part during the Cultural Revolution, but offered the excuse that Mao, at the end of his life, could no longer distinguish right from wrong. This was described tellingly as a "tragedy", and Mao's overall contribution to social progress was assessed with the formula "70% positive, 30% negative". Even this early, the Communist Party of China suggested that Mao be identified as a "tragic hero". As demonstrations in 1975 against the "Gang of Four" had shown, there was widespread discontent about the excesses of the left-wing leadership, implicitly including Mao. The resolution attempted to shield Mao from popular resentment by acknowledging his errors but assessing them as marginal in relation to his achievements.

The Cultural Revolution was now interpreted primarily as a power struggle within the political elite. This was also a way of denying or papering over real social conflicts. The crude division into "good" and "bad" was also applied to the population at large. People in general — that is, the masses — had been misused and manipulated by the leadership; they were innocent and belonged to the Good. By freeing individuals from personal responsibility, this interpretation secured people's solidarity with the government and their active co-operation in the modernisation project. In the process, the "manipulated" masses were once more deprived of a voice — especially the young generation of the Red Guards, who never appear in the document under that name.

The greatest simplification in this picture is this: it portrays the Chinese population as a unified, immature mass, blatantly contradicting the then still formally acknowledged division of people into classes with specified backgrounds. Yet, it was just these differing class backgrounds (boiled down during the Cultural Revolution into two labels: "Red" and "Black") that had provided the basis for the battles of Red Guard subgroups with one another, and of the Red Guards with different governmental power centres. The division of society into classes that competed with one another for prestige, positions, and privileges — incipient in the 1950s — was continued in an extreme form in the Cultural Revolution; the Red Guards themselves split into Rebels and Conservatives, who respectively attacked older leaders or their newer replacements. As Anita Chan has persuasively described in various publications on the Guards, the camps recruited their members from all segments of society, disregarding the boundaries of schools, universities, work units, cities, rural collectives, counties, and provinces (compare Chan, 1985, 1992; Chan, Stanley, & Unger, 1980). That serious social conflicts had arisen through the competition of interest groups, leading finally, with the support of a divided elite incapable of governing, to violent confrontations—this was not a story deemed advisable to tell.

Still more politically charged—and simply ignored in the retrospective political accounting—was the role of the Red Guards in general and of the Rebel group within them in particular. The Cultural Revolution began above all as the expression of a battle between the underprivileged classes (represented by the Rebel Guards) and the privileged classes (represented by the conservative Guards). Among the Rebel Guards were groups that understood themselves as independent social movements, and which, for the first time in the history of the People's Republic, were in a position to act autonomously: to conduct political meetings, to publish pamphlets, and to lead public discussions. An example of the mature, political mind-set of the young generation is the text "Whither China" (He, 1996; Unger, 1991), a 1968 pamphlet that earned Red Guards member Yang Xiguang ten years in prison. For Yang, the great problem in China lay not in a conflict among different classes but in the alienation of Party and government from the masses, in the accumulation of power and privileges by the Party, and in the development of a "red class" of powerful bureaucrats. Thus, blind worshippers of Mao had turned into the sharpest critics the system had ever had. Most of them went on to be prominent in the first democracy movement in the early 1980s.

The political explosiveness of these activities is reflected in the fact that in 1983, seven years on from the official end of the Cultural Revolution and over a decade after the peak period of Rebel activism, campaigns against former Red Guards were still going on. It is echoed again in the way the government equated the student demonstrations of 1989 in Tiananmen Square with the activities of the (Rebel) Red Guards.

Even the temporal definition of the Cultural Revolution as "ten catastrophic years" is significant. From the people's perspective, the

Cultural Revolution took place in the years 1966–1969, the years of mass rampage. Mao's directives began to apply the brakes in 1968, and Lin Biao declared the official end of the Revolution at the Ninth Party Congress in 1969. By redefining the Cultural Revolution as a ten-year affair, the new Party leadership around Deng Xiaoping de-emphasised the independent activity of the masses and reduced the events to a power struggle within the elite. Indeed, it was the arrest of the "Gang of Four" in 1976 that marked a decisive turn in this power struggle, culminating in the triumph of Deng Xiaoping.

I have gone into the resolution's interpretation of the Cultural Revolution to this extent because a whole series of its findings are accepted even now as unexamined facts, both in China and by Western researchers. We shall see how the aforementioned interview texts (see the contribution of T. Plänkers, pp. 83–120) repeat many of these formulae.

Why was this interpretation, constituting a pretty clear distortion of historical facts and motivated by a patent political agenda, accepted so readily and for so long? Despite the strong effect of propaganda and censorship on collective perception and memory, scepticism toward political propaganda was in fact at its strongest just after the Cultural Revolution. Yet, the official explanation of events was proba-bly not only the most comfortable, but also pragmatically the only realistic one. It is difficult to distinguish perpetrators and victims in the Cultural Revolution; the multifarious campaigns and political reversals had flipped the roles so many times that a real exploration of old cases would have risked stirring up an unfathomable deposit of internal battles and conflicts. Needless to say, the new basic agreement on stability and unity did not get rid of social tensions, and neither did it prevent competing interpretations of the events from arising.

## Unofficial Party history

The most prominent example of an unofficial alternative version has already been mentioned: *The Ten Years of the "Cultural Revolution" in China*, by the historians Gao Gao and Yan Jiaqi (a couple), published first in 1986 in Tianjin and in English in 1996 under the title *Turbulent Decade: A History of the Cultural Revolution* (Yan & Gao, 1996). Although the book was banned and pulled from the market in China

*Photograph 3.* National conferences like this one on "Schooling in and Application of Mao-Zedong Thought" were a widespread method of propagating Mao's ideas. Workers' Stadium, Beijing, 21 October 1966.

shortly after it appeared, it continued to circulate among Chinese intellectuals, and the edition published in 1990 in Taiwan and Hong Kong became a best-seller in the Chinese diaspora, probably because it was the first unofficial narrative of the political events by a participant.

Yet, this presentation did not differ very significantly from the official version described above. The authors, themselves members of the political and intellectual elite, contemplated the events mainly from the perspective of the political centre. Even their title shows their acceptance of the paradigm of "ten years". In this representation, too, the masses figure more or less as a herd of sheep that willingly followed the shepherd of the moment. Moreover, the origins of the Cultural Revolution are traced to the "Battle between Two Lines". This focus on the elites is also discernible in the discussion of the Red Guards, especially concerning the relationship of the Guards to political sponsors in the leadership.

The book's popularity stemmed most of all from its attempt to provide the first complete chronology of events which readers, and, indeed, most people, knew without context and in a fragmentary way. In addition, the historians provided excerpts from countless documents and pamphlets published by the Red Guards. In their foreword, the authors expressed the hope of probing more deeply in further studies. This hope was not fulfilled. Yan Jiaqi, who had, meanwhile, risen to become an adviser to Zhao Ziyang, fell out of favour in the spring of 1987 and was placed under house arrest during the campaign of "criticism of bourgeois liberalism". In 1989, after taking a prominent role in the student protests, he fled to exile in the USA. Since then, he has been strongly engaged on behalf of the Chinese democracy movement.

This case shows how difficult it was to publish unofficial interpretations, even relatively conformist ones, of political battles and national conflicts. Nevertheless, there are numerous examples of independent attempts to throw more light on a dark era. One of the most prominent early researchers was the Shanghai author Ye Yonglie. Since 1988, he has published a series of popular biographies of Mao Zedong, Jiang Qing, and other political leaders of the Cultural Revolution, as well as the first independent monographs on important political topics such as the crisis year of 1957, the "Anti-Rightist Campaign" or a "secret history" of the Communist Party of China (e.g., Ye, 1988, 1992, 1993a,b). Because he never strayed far enough from the official line to be vulnerable, Ye was able to get access to high and even hostile Party members. Nevertheless, his project of taking on specific political–historical subjects one at a time was daring by nature and attracted a great deal of attention.

In recent decades, a strong research community has developed in China, producing a multitude of studies on the subject both at Party-linked research institutes and at universities. In the first years after the Cultural Revolution, researches of this sort served mostly didactic purposes and hewed closely to the lines of the resolution. Today, however, researchers deal with more sensitive themes, such as the role of the Red Guards (see Esherick, Pickowicz, & Walder, 2006). Also, most of the well-known non-Chinese studies, as, for example, MacFarquhar's penetrating four-volume investigation of the Cultural Revolution (1997), have been translated into Chinese and are on sale in bookstores.

The reception of alternative accounts from the viewpoint of the masses involved in the struggles, especially from that of politically active Red Guards, has been much cooler. Witness the case of Liu Guokai's *A Brief Analysis of the Cultural Revolution* (Liu, 1987).

What the presentations of Yan Jiaqi and Liu Guokai have in common is a disdain for Mao and a harsh verdict concerning his policies. While Yan Jiaqi compares Mao with Stalin and especially criticises his arrogant brushing aside of the legal fundamentals of the Constitution, Liu goes a step further and describes the first years of the Cultural Revolution as a fascistic military regime under Mao's sole control, dedicated purely to consolidating his absolute power. Liu had already secretly written the first draft of his manuscript in 1971, shortly after the official dissolution of the Red Guards. His portrayal of the activities of the Guards is clearly conditioned by his own political background. For Liu Guokai, as for other activists named above, the central conflict that led to the excesses of the Cultural Revolution was not within the Party elite but, rather, between that elite as a whole and the masses. This is very much the view of the aforementioned Yang Xiguang and the politically mature generation of the Guards, who saw the Cultural Revolution as the result of social conflict between the politically disenfranchised masses and a privileged class of leaders equipped with total, arbitrary power. In this telling, only the first three years of the Cultural Revolution were the real thing, a moment in which—for the first time in Chinese history—mass democracy was really put into effect and decisions made at the base, in the manner of the Paris Commune. In this view, the Cultural Revolution was an attempt, albeit a failed one, to solve the problem of the existence of this privileged class (He, 1996, pp. 19–21).

Although this interpretation reflects a particular political agenda, it must be noted that it has arisen repeatedly. As we shall see, more recent popular portrayals of the Revolution in literature and film emphasise exactly this aspect—the historically unique liberation of youth from parental or political authority.

## Representations of the Cultural Revolution in fictional and autobiographical literature

Artistic treatments of the experiences of the Cultural Revolution are many and various. In literature, the so-called Scar Literature shows the first attempts at reflection, while numerous autobiographical accounts (often published abroad) amplify the record. Although works of these two sorts rarely depart from the sanctioned political guidelines, they are widely read in China and elsewhere and have strongly influenced the collective assessment of this historical period.

### Scar and autobiographical literature

So-called Scar Literature began appearing immediately after the end of the Cultural Revolution and dominated the literary scene from 1977 to 1979. The first publications, such as Liu Xinwu's "The class teacher", had great shock value for a reading public that had seen nothing like this degree of social criticism for two decades (Liu, 1981). Lu Xinhua's "Scar", also translated as "The wounded", appeared in 1981 and would be read by millions, giving its name to this whole literary current. It and similar books had a cathartic effect, profiling the blind, senseless destruction of family structure and emotional ties.

Scar Literature, it is true, generally followed the Party line in assigning blame to the "Gang of Four", and many of the works seem superficial and rather didactic. None the less, the numerous "scar stories" took the stance of wanting to "tell the truth", meaning, in this case, the truth as experienced by the victims. Many of these works have been criticised for their poor style and their self-pitying or self-righteous tone. As McDougall and Kam (1997, p. 370) note, the novelty of this writing lay mainly its choice of subject. Few of these products survived the next decades as literary works. Yet, they shaped public opinion. According to Mobo Gao, Scar Literature began the process of public judgement of the Cultural Revolution both inside and outside China (Gao, 2008, p. 32). Even without straying from the interpretations established in the Party resolution, this literature did a service in focusing attention on individuals and their fates. In their attention to, and rehabilitation of, such themes as love, personal relationships, and the humanistic worldview, these works sought to establish common, binding values; they also restored a certain human dignity to the masses, which had been dismissed as apolitical and voiceless.

The young people who had been sent from the cities to the countryside, and who were now returning, were especially disinclined to accept the Party resolution's view of the people as a manipulated mass. While the leadership and older intellectuals were quite ready to write off Red Guards and exiled youth as "a lost generation" and leave them to their fates, the young people themselves were striving to find meaning in what they had gone through. Refusing the "lost generation" label, they styled themselves the "mature", the "enlightened", the "thinking", or the "awakened" generation. Their renewed battle for recognition (and jobs) is especially well captured in the play WM, treating the different life perspectives of youth during the Rustication period and in the post-Cultural Revolution era of "stability and unity". Of course, the work proved too explosive and was banned (Vittinghoff, 2002).

This effort to wrest meaning from these sufferings also contributed to the widespread "nostalgia wave" of the middle 1990s. This looked back not so much to the early years of the Cultural Revolution as to the Rustication phase in the 1970s. In metropolises such as Peking and Shanghai, restaurants opened that served simple, coarse peasant meals in rooms adorned with heroic photographs, propaganda posters, and other memorabilia. The returnees, now well established in life, published their own newspapers and set up websites in which those years—actually marked by want, deprivation, and existential threat—were glorified.

Most of the autobiographical recollections by young Red Guards or prominent victims resemble Scar Literature in mode and tone. Interestingly, autobiographies published in China and abroad take broadly similar, often overlapping, narrative lines; we look in vain for much in the way of individual voice, diversity, or ambiguity.

An investigation of fifty such autobiographies published in China has revealed four principal themes common to the works: narratives of good people who become the victims of bad ones; morality stories, showing how one overcomes the experience of evil; portrayals of the absurdity of events and developments; tales of misunderstandings and blunders (Xu, 1998). Zarrow (1999) similarly discovers consistent narrative and thematic structures in autobiographies published abroad. The protagonists enjoy a peaceful, happy youth as promising, politically aware students; they are seduced and manipulated; they are shockingly awakened from their dream, or nightmare, by the Lin Biao incident; finally, they find salvation and freedom by fleeing to the West, where they write down their stories. Zarrow duly notes how such narratives cater to the expectations of Western audiences. The happy *denouement* of arrival abroad, he argues, reinforces the orientalist image of a despotic East contrasting with the free democratic West, and this fact accounts for much of the popularity of these reports.

The most prominent example of this genre is Jung Chang's autobiography, *Wild Swans*, which has appeared in translation throughout the world. It is hard to think of another Chinese book that has attained such sales figures and ubiquity. Its appearance in the English book market in 1991 marked a breakthrough for Chinese autobiographical literature in the UK and the USA. Such autobiographies are read as factual reports by "authentic voices" (Gentz, 2006, p. 122). *Wild Swans* in particular has had a lingering influence on public opinion about modern Chinese history.

Jung Chang describes the Cultural Revolution from the perspective of a privileged daughter of the Communist elite whose family falls into disfavour, making her a victim of tragic events under a brutal regime. Strikingly absent is any thought of potential responsibility for these occurrences on her part or that of her father, a high-ranking propaganda official. Characters are simply good or simply evil, with no shades of grey. Jung Chang, too, managed a "flight" to the West by means of a prestigious government scholarship for studies in Britain. She has become still more famous through her most recent publication about Mao Zedong, presented as a work of historical research (Chang & Halliday, 2005). The success of *Mao: The Life of a Man, the Fate of a People* is hard to fathom, since the book has been panned in numerous academic reviews as riddled with contradictions and useless as history (see Gao, 2008, Chapter Four). Chang ascribes all the responsibility for various crises and catastrophes of modern Chinese history to Mao alone.

So, there is an abundance, even in China, of literature on the Cultural Revolution; yet the subject remains on the censors' list of fifteen "important topics", publications concerning which must be pre-approved by GAPP, the General Administration for Press and Publications (CEEC China, 2009). Since the literature we have discussed is mostly from the victims' perspective, it necessarily focuses on the portrayal of violence, outrages, and personal suffering.

This right to relate personal travails is not, however, accorded to all participants in the Cultural Revolution. Neither those who were convicted as "perpetrators" after the Lin Biao Incident or after the end of the Cultural Revolution nor the radical students (now dubbed "reactionaries") who had remained true to Mao's convictions were allowed to write autobiographies and to present their own, necessarily very different, views of the events. Exceptions were made for a few accounts that were published under particularly strict censorship (Gao, 2008, p. 52).

In post-Maoist China the voices of the radical Left (which is again showing signs of life) are no longer welcome and attempts to glorify Mao are discouraged. In 1985, a young worker in remote Shaanxi province posted a wall newspaper in his shoe factory with the slogan: "The Cultural Revolution was good". He was sentenced to ten years imprisonment, soon cut short by his unexplained death (Gao, 2008, pp. 46–47). The authorities' ferocity in this case shows that the ban on discussion is not aimed merely at arguments about past guilt but also at still unresolved or newly emerging debates about the future. Dirlik (2003) points out the paradox: Mao was led to launch the Cultural Revolution by an anxious presentiment that capitalism could yet regain its ascendancy – a prognosis that time has only confirmed (p. 158).

The sole permissible portrayal of the Cultural Revolution – one-sidedly from the victims' point of view – obscures the complexity of the real struggles, and also makes it harder for individuals to examine their own roles in, and perhaps partial responsibility for, the things that occurred. Take the exiled writer and Nobel prize recipient Gao Xingjian, whose view of China is exceedingly critical: in his *Das Buch eines Einsamen Menschen* ("One man's bible") (2004), he acknowledges his part in events without, however, accepting any guilt. Thus, Gao describes his participation in "struggle meetings" on the side of the radicals, but attributes it to fear of retaliation against anyone who withdrew. He still places himself on the side of the Good, those who tried to de-escalate or who were able to get around the authorities. What distinguishes this novel from many others, however, is the subliminal presence of a traumatic experience, initially suppressed through amnesia, but surfacing in the course of the story through clearly identifiable post trauma syndromes (Gentz, 2006).

This phenomenon is described in a similar, sometimes even clearer, manner in other works, for example, in the figure of the literature professor in Ha Jin's novel *The Crazed* (written abroad), or in Huang Jianxin's film *Who Cares?* (*Shui shuo wo bu zaihu*, 2001). The latter takes up, with a certain dry humour, the themes of amnesia, schizophrenia, and psychosis in socialism; in a hospital scene, for instance, a neurotic patient continually re-enacts ballet scenes from the model operas of the Cultural Revolution.

## Subversiveness and humour

This humorous or ironic–satirical tone prevails also in a series of literary works that are very controversial in China, being dismissed by some as sensational, crowd-pleasing trash and embraced by others in cultish fashion.

The best-known exemplar of this quite different perspective on the Cultural Revolution and its effects on youth is Wang Shuo, one of the most popular and controversial authors of contemporary China. He has written over twenty best-sellers since the early 1980s, with a combined sales of some ten million copies, and a dozen of his books have been filmed. Wang's writing, which has influenced a whole generation of artists, authors, and filmmakers (Barme, 1999), is pervaded with irony, subversiveness, and "boorishness"; some critics call the movement he unleashed "Hooligan literature". His fame became international with the filming of *In the Heat of the Sun*, which concerns the adventures of a youth gang during the Cultural Revolution. His other novels also deal with the effects of the Revolution on succeeding generations. He takes a distanced view of political events, focusing instead on the daily life of the youngsters: their unwonted freedom from the authority of parents, teachers, and sanctioned youth organisations, their (sexual) frustrations and romantic longings, and their attempts to navigate adolescence without instruction.

The protagonists of his novels do not begin as victims, but as privileged Red Guard members—like the author himself—accustomed to an almost aristocratic lifestyle, taking privileges for granted, and looking forward to a secure future. The coming of the Cultural Revolution changes all this drastically; well-trodden paths of social advancement become uncertain and well-learnt patterns of behaviour no longer bring the expected rewards. However, it is precisely their elite status that emboldens these young people to break social taboos and to experiment with new relationships (Yao, 2004). For Wang Shuo, this experience generates a youth subculture within socialism, which, in the absence of guides to behaviour, can also lead to disappointment and aggressiveness. Thus, Wang almost deliberately avoids any judgement, especially any political judgement, of the Cultural Revolution. Instead of condemnation or disillusionment, he takes a stance of disdain and irony, sometimes crossing the line into sarcasm.

The film *In the Heat of the Sun,* in which the freedom of youth (including freedom from restrictive morality) is most clearly and positively portrayed, drew strong official criticism, but Wang Shuo is especially popular with young people who see their attitudes and lifestyle reflected in these works. His narrative style, characterised by wordplay and by ironic distortions of political slogans and propaganda statements, has infused the language of the young—so much so that the prominent literary critic Li Tuo declared that Wang and his works had revolutionised the way people spoke, thought, and wrote.

## The Cultural Revolution on the Internet

The best evidence that the Cultural Revolution is still very much on people's minds and alive in their debates is found on the Internet. Entering "Cultural Revolution" in the most popular Chinese search engines, such as yahoo.com.cn, sohu.com.cn, sina.com.cn and google.com.cn, yields more than a million results, a volume that in itself presents a methodological challenge. Since the average age of most Internet users in China lies between twenty-five and thirty-five, an age group that has no direct experience of the Cultural Revolution, this level of interest is quite surprising. Yet, there are rather few websites devoted exclusively to the subject; these include the "Virtual Museum of the Cultural Revolution" (Huaxia wenzhai), an American site, and such Chinese sites as "Network for Research on China's Cultural Revolution" (Zhongguo wenge yanjiu wang). Many of these sites (some of which have, meanwhile, disappeared) have featured reminiscences, photo collections, and original documents: examples are the sites "Turbulent years of the Cultural Revolution in China" (Zhongguo wenhua da geming huangtan suiyue), "Memories of the Cultural

Revolution" (Wenge jinian), or "Rusticated Chinese youth" (Huaxia Zhiqing). More numerous entries on the subject are found buried in subsections of large web portals, or in the electronic message centres called bulletin board systems (BBS). The popularity of BBSs is seen, for example, in the website "Rusticated Youth". Just two years after it went up, the site was voted the fifteenth most popular Chinese BBS site, receiving more than 700 contributions a day (Yang, 2003, p. 467). Even the BBS forum "Strengthening the nation", owned by the *People's Daily* in Beijing and considered conservative, contains numerous entries having to do with the Cultural Revolution.

At first glance, the main function of the Cultural Revolution websites, whatever their focus, is to keep memory alive. The call to remember, lest history repeat itself, occurs again and again. Many sites take the form of virtual museums or memorials, while safely reflecting the officially sanctioned portrayal of events.

As early as 1983, the author Ba Jin petitioned for the establishment of an official museum dedicated to the Cultural Revolution. The idea proved controversial, however, and never bore fruit. Two kinds of substitutes have arisen: virtual museums modelled on Holocaust museums and memorialising the dead, and physical collections of texts, photographs, and memorabilia. The latter, more commercial, reflect a new fad for Mao.

The first private "Cultural Revolution Museum" was opened in 1999 in Sichuan. Consisting mainly of period porcelain ware, it drew criticism online as quite contrary to the spirit of Ba Jin's suggestion. In April 2004, Fan Jianchuan, a rich entrepreneur, proposed a large museum complete with dining hall and a reception hall; here again the vision was rather a kind of Disneyland than a setting for real confrontation with the past. Another initiative came from the veteran cadre Pen Qu'an in Guangdong. He first proposed to develop an existing, rather remote, cemetery for Cultural Revolution victims into a memorial site. According to Internet reports, the author Feng Jicai spoke up to support building a Cultural Revolution museum at this spot. In March 2005, after long negotiations with local authorities, the plan was realised (see The first Chinese Cultural Revolution Museum is born, 2005).

Numerous virtual museums are based outside China, and especially in the USA. The largest and best known of these is the "Virtual Museum of the Cultural Revolution", maintained in Maryland by

Chinese dissidents and pro-democracy exiles and explicitly based on Ba Jin's idea. The website itself cannot be accessed in China, but many contributions to the associated Internet journal *Huaxia Wenzhai* can be found on websites within the country. We should also mention the prominent activist Wang Youqin, who for years has been gathering names and biographies of Cultural Revolution victims and publishing them in her "Chinese Holocaust Memorial" at the University of Chicago.

Similar efforts have been undertaken inside China. In 2004, for instance, Chen Xianqing published a collection of "Fatalities in the Cultural Revolution"; another website titled "A young girl's Hall of Memories" was set up like the entry to a columbarium and contained stories of the destruction of whole families. Both sites have disappeared, or, at least, are no longer accessible.

The Internet also yields some individual statements that deal with shame, regret, and personal guilt: for instance, a report of a visit to the single cemetery for Red Guard members in Chongqing.

An additional platform for anonymous personal griefwork is offered by virtual cemeteries on the Internet, for example NETOR, where users can enter names of the departed, lay down flowers or candles, and write expressions of sorrow. An example is this entry concerning the middle-school teacher Chen Yuanzhi, who was beaten to death by her students in August 1966 at the age of forty-two. Hundreds of contributions discuss the case, speak of sadness and pity, express best wishes, or enquire about the guilty and responsible parties. One comment reads: "I didn't know Teacher Chen and did not experience the Cultural Revolution myself, yet I live surrounded by guilt and shame". Political implications are sometimes raised alongside expressions of grief: "Who is it that brings so much misfortune so often to the Chinese nation? The glorious Party!", or "Why do the victims of the Japanese aggression approach the Japanese government with demands for compensation, while none of the victims of the Cultural Revolution demands compensation from our government? Why were the people who used brutal force never brought to justice?" (NETOR, 2009).

Elsewhere, there are demands for an official memorial day for the Cultural Revolution, to be on 15 May (Ma, 2000), but the formulaic insistence that this chapter of Chinese history should not be forgotten is by no means universally shared. Ba Jin's proposal for an official museum was rejected not only by the government, but also by intellectuals in China and abroad; they feared a revival of cultural-revolutionary activities if young people were exposed to the rhetoric and realities of the period.

On the Internet, too, it is a matter of argument whether the crimes of the Cultural Revolution should be confessed and regretted. The best example is the well-known debate between the prominent cultural critics Yu Jie and Yu Qiuyu, which began in the year 2000 and continued for years. The opening shot was a public challenge to Yu Qiuyu by the very young (and controversial) Yu Jie, titled "Yu Qiuyu, why aren't you sorry?" Yu Jie asked Yu Qiuyu how he could write about a series of prominent personalities without ever offering an opinion of his own, and why, for instance, he concealed his work at a literary magazine connected with the "Gang of Four". Yu Quiyu rejected all these accusations as calumnies, but the incident launched an agitated debate among Chinese authors. Defenders of the older man accused the younger one of adopting a Red Guard-like pose himself by demanding public self-criticism. It is suggested that Yu Jie's probes into Yu Qiuyu's past echo the cultural revolutionary practice of bringing accusations against innocent people with evidence exhumed from their pasts.

According to this line of argument, it is neither possible nor desirable to engage with or process the past; such labour is itself seen as revival of the methods of the Cultural Revolution. This short-sighted perspective is challenged by others, including the author Yi Hong. Yi explains that questions of guilt and remorse are valid, and not only for the Cultural Revolution. One must distinguish, he says, between the need to have guilt acknowledged on the one hand and the desire for personal revenge on the other (Yi, 2000).

The critically minded website, "Fengkuang suiyue", adopted a similar position, making the Yu Quiyu case the banner of the entire site, which opens with the following statement:

> For the present Chinese the Cultural Revolution was so terrible that it cannot be forgotten. Yet hence this painful history is approached with a numb onlooker mentality customary to our compatriots . . . Yu Jie asks Yu Qiuyu, why he doesn't repent. Yet who comes to ask: Why are we as a nation not repenting. (Fengkuang, 2005)

Quite aside from this particular debate, Internet users are trying to identify the psychodynamic factors that make it so difficult to face the revolution. A contribution titled "China must confront the Cultural Revolution" identifies three psychological obstacles. First is the fact that the movement affected the entire nation, involving every individual somehow; most people now feel shame for their past behaviour and tend to repress memories of it. Second, there is an unconscious reluctance to meddle with the image of Mao as the great leader and hero. Finally, there is a lack of role models. Since not even leadership figures and intellectuals have revealed their complex relationships to the Cultural Revolution, why should ordinary people do so (Lin, 2000)?

One argument recurs among the countless postings on this subject: since everyone was both victim and perpetrator, public confessions would uncover nothing useful. At the same time, there is disagreement about what may be properly remembered and who among the participants has the right to pass judgement on the Cultural Revolution. Thus, one contributor was attacked for his statement that his childhood in the Cultural Revolution period was happy. Only those who experienced the Cultural Revolution themselves, one contention goes, have the right to pronounce a verdict upon it.

The sheer mass of postings on the Cultural Revolution makes it clear that the official dogma set in the 1981 resolution has long since lost its persuasiveness. A piece titled "Was the Cultural Revolution really just a chaotic rebellion?" states this plainly:

> Can the resolution published in 1981 ... survive a trial by History? How is it that these problems have not been discussed since the resolution? How is it that, a whole historical period having been repressed, one can no longer express the thought that what really happened is the criterion for truth? Why do journalists concerned with the recent past get no answers when they pose questions that go beyond the bounds of the resolution? Can such a complicated history be summarised in a handful of conclusions? (Xiao, 2002)

While published autobiographies and virtual museums emphasise negative aspects of the Cultural Revolution (the brutality of the Red Guards, the dictatorial system), the Internet provides a place (the only place) for more positive assessments of that time and sunnier accounts of personal experiences in it. A great variety of portrayals and viewpoints is available; information can be had from many sources. Silence is by no means the rule. Nevertheless, when it comes to print publications, the Party and national leadership still try to limit public discussion to a few perspectives, in essence those of the 1981 resolution: that the Cultural Revolution was mounted by the "Gang of Four" in a power struggle over Mao's succession, that the paradigm of "ten chaotic years" still holds, and that the epoch is simply to be deplored.

## Discussion of the interviews

The processing of traumatic experiences requires a supportive environment in which, first of all, the existence of the trauma is recognised. To come to terms with what was a shattering sense of powerlessness in the face of life-threatening forces, and with a collapse of existing systems of values and norms, there must be consensus concerning who did what to whom. The 1981 Party resolution, by assigning all blame to a small group, gives the survivors little help in interpreting the events that traumatised them.

Judging by the interviews we conducted (see Plänkers, pp. 83–120), our witnesses have not thought much about the political and social background of the Cultural Revolution, or availed themselves of the abundant information the Internet offers on the subject. Events are narrated in random clumps, causal connections are traced on a strictly personal level, and the experiences are processed on a purely individual basis. Striking, too, is the manner in which the events of the Cultural Revolution are described: in the language and jargon of the revolutionary era. These political phrases and slogans have not only stuck in memory but also appear to be the sole means of expression these persons have at their disposal. Informants from the first generation, especially, provide historical context by baldly naming political campaigns and events, without attempting to explain their content and interconnections.

Unsurprisingly, there is a distinct difference between the political vocabularies used by the first and second generations of those who experienced the Cultural Revolution. The older generation of interviewees draws on more than 500 political concepts and clichés; the second uses only about 150, which are much more simplistic and relate to simple political contexts.

The language used, especially by the first generation, suggests no distance from, or real confrontation with, events; rather, political clichés and titles of campaigns are used metonymically as if they explained the whole context. Slogans and rubrics such as "Smash the Gang of Four", "The May 16 Circular", "The Three Main Rules of Discipline", "Eight Points for Attention", "The Revolution Makers", "Great Government, Great Leader", "Hold High the Banner of Marxism–Leninism", etc. are part of the normal vocabulary of the interviewees, not used with implicit inverted commas around them. It is also striking how often the chronology of personal events is presented in terms of these slogans and campaigns. Thus, for example, interviewee Mr Li (4A) recalls his wedding as occurring in the year of the May 16 Circular. Mr Zhao (6A) links the year of his mother's death with the "Event of November 19". And, although he cannot remember the years of his wedding or the births of his children, he can specify the years of his induction into the People's Liberation Army, his arrest, and his stay in the labour camp.

Recognising that memory is no mere reproduction of stored elements but, rather, an active assembly of episodes into a coherent life story, we must ask what cultural, collective, and individual factors determine the selection, organisation, and narrative viewpoint of that story. Literary critics seek structure in narratives. The writers of autobiographies draw on memories to build meaning and coherence. Might similar patterns be reflected in the interviews? The interplay of language and subjectivity, underlined in post-structuralist literature, is evident here.

The particular political and social complexities of the Cultural Revolution might make it simply impossible to reach a social consensus about it: witness the contemporary debates about, and attempts to create, a museum or memorial. Evidently, the processing of events has come to no conclusion. This fact is only partially attributable to the complex and shifting roles of perpetrators and victims. The marked conventionality of political vocabulary in the interviews suggests that subjects, of the first generation especially, test and build up their stories with the aid of the propaganda concepts they grew up with, never achieving a distanced perspective.

The many ideological U-turns that characterised the Cultural Revolution, the tectonic shifts in the political landscape, also impede the building of a coherent narrative line. Events and experiences are neither given in chronological order nor related by meaning. In case after case, the participants, whether active or passive, say that they did not know why something happened, against what background, why a new political line had been declared, etc. For example, interviewee Ms Song (5A), seeking to find out what led to her husband's arrest, does not dare confide in other people but waits for the final verdict of the Party. She says again and again that she did not know or understand what had occurred.

This inability to trace reasonable connections also determines the narrative mode of the texts, which generally take the form of stream of consciousness. Thought processes are reflected in associative leaps in syntax and grammar and in ready access to political vocabulary. The interviews jump again and again from general contexts to very specific examples, which are repeated and placed metonymically to stand for the whole experience. No informant offers a grand narrative that brings the components into relation. Instead, events have an impact on the participants as if guided by supernatural powers or like natural catastrophes that require no explanation (see the contribution of Wang, pp. 35–56).

Ignorance of actual happenings during the turmoil of the Cultural Revolution is hardly surprising; an objective view of events was not to be had. However, it is astonishing that later, with an abundance of literature accessible, the participants apparently lacked interest in tracing the real events and seeking explanations for them. Instead, the phenomenon was absorbed as a tragic catastrophe, just as in the official version, and filed away as ancient political history.

One possible explanation for this mind-set lies in the interviewees' long experience of campaigns, violence, persecution, and the battle for survival. The Cultural Revolution (this important statement recurs) was not the worst period the informants had endured. For many, the years before the Cultural Revolution, with land reform, the persecution of large landowners, famine, and existential struggle, seemed worse. Thus, the victims have no reason to regard this one phase of the history of the People's Republic as particularly significant. One first-generation witness summarises her experience of the Cultural Revolution like this:

"The Cultural Revolution ran from '66 to '76, but to be honest, it lasted ten more years for us, the school graduates from '66 to '68. Why? The phase in which the rusticated youth were fighting to return to the cities was even more painful."

In general, explanatory attempts adhere closely to a supposed Party line. So, Mr Zhao (6A):

"How shall I deal with all these things? I want to talk about this here, how I should deal with my experiences. How a revolutionary should deal with them. The Party desires that I live my last years in peace. How can I fulfil this assignment of the Party? I've thought about this from time to time and have come to no conclusion. I think that what I experienced was only episodes in a revolutionary process. Such things necessarily happen in a time like ours. This process doesn't always unfold as we expect. What is the underlying problem? I think the underlying problem is private property."

In another interview, we learn that the Cultural Revolution was discussed among classmates at a recent class reunion and explained as a "phenomenon of feudalism in China". The informant came to the conclusion that the determined continuation of present reforms is the country's only way out.

Another general explanation, again reflecting the model of the Party resolution, sees the issue as a power struggle between the two lines of Liu Shaoqi and Mao Zedong. So, for instance, Mr Hong (7A) says, "The Cultural Revolution was really made because Chairman Mao wanted to take action against Liu Shaoqi". Ms Song (5A) likewise confirms that people were simply unaware and did not recognise the power struggle. Mr Zhang (1A) sees the Cultural Revolution as the biggest error of Mao Zedong. This assignment of guilt to Mao and the leadership is repeated in the second generation. Ms He (6B) summarises,

"I still consider the Cultural Revolution as, how shall I put it — when I deny it, I deny it completely. I think it's just a political battle, and I believe, I simply can't understand it, that Mao Zedong . . . people followed you into the Revolution, they all risked their lives, gave up their families and professions, for so many years, and now you've sent them to their deaths. . . . For that reason I think, if . . . Even now I don't know, if he knew about such things or not, had he no feeling at all?" (translated for this edition)

In this bit of an interior monologue, the informant even engages in a pretended exchange with Mao Zedong.

All these attempted explanations remain within the prescribed political parameters: one was naïve and passive; one had had no notion what was going on politically. No responsibility for personal actions is taken; if the course of events is felt to be tragic, there are no expressions of guilt feelings or reflections about one's own possible collaboration in evil.

Stating repeatedly that such a political catastrophe must not be repeated, the informants offer no thoughts of their own as to how to prevent a repetition, or how they themselves might have acted differently in the past. One informant accuses himself of "cowardice", without explaining how and why he might have shown more courage, or what, in the context of the Cultural Revolution, real courage might have been. The trope of heroism might have its source in public education, in which much has been made of role models, collective morality, and singular acts of courage.

Even in imperial China, the moral upbringing of the people was considered a task of a good and successful government. Exemplary heroes and role models played an important part in propagating correct thinking and right behaviour. This educational model persisted in the People's Republic and was used to mobilise the population in support of political campaigns. The norm of self-sacrifice for the group, even to the point of death, was drilled into people from childhood on through stories and pictures of heroes and it was repeatedly enacted, memoirs make clear, in the Cultural Revolution (Chan, 1985). Even though their lives almost always end tragically, these heroes serve as models for personal success. From its beginning, the hero's life demonstrates that self-fulfilment is to be seen in sacrifice for the collective. This faith in the value of exemplary life and death helped buffer the shocking experiences of the Cultural Revolution period: the death of classmates in cities gripped by something like civil war; the catastrophic conditions during the later Rustication period; the threats to personal survival (Bergman, 1984).

Knowing this background, we asked witnesses, in questionnaires and, in some cases, through more detailed interviews, to tell us what role models (a) were known to them and (b) had made a strong impression on them. Both generations confirmed that they had heard, seen, and read a great deal about such models. Surprisingly, three of the older witnesses categorically deny any influence from role models, while the younger generation affirms such influence, with only one young interview partner siding with the elders.

There is more unanimity in the names mentioned than about their supposed influence. Most often listed are Lei Feng, Huang Jiguang, and Dong Cunrui, all heroes promoted particularly often and for many years as examples of self-sacrifice and service to society. Also mentioned were An Yemin, Zhang Side, and Norman Bethune, other representatives of this type.

The story of Lei Feng, the best-known model hero of all, is worth telling by way of example. It should be noted that the historical facts are controversial, with some even doubting that the man existed. In the official version, Lei Feng was born in Hunan in 1940. After his father was murdered by the Japanese and his mother killed herself in order to escape the attentions of a large landowner, the Party took the orphan in. As a soldier in the Liberation Army and a Party member, he distinguished himself by good deeds, which, though unspectacular, add up to the ideal picture of a decent, self-sacrificing, and perfectly functioning "cog" in the socialist system. His case embodies the still-popular image of the Party as the parents and the People as the devoted children. Lei Feng died in 1962 after an unspecified accident while installing rural power lines. His fame is due to his diary, which became a text for the whole nation in 1963 when Mao issued the call "to learn from Lei Feng".

Lei Feng's high name recognition among the interviewees also reflects the fact that the Party re-emphasised his role as model hero after the student protests at Tiananmen (1989) in order to promote a unified, positive attitude toward the leadership. Today, Lei Feng's face can even be seen on commercial posters and billboards.

The other two heroes most cited, Dong Cunrui and Huang Jiguang, were soldiers who gave up their lives for the cause. During the civil war between Communists and Nationalists, Dong thwarted a dangerous Nationalist offensive by blowing up the bridge on which he stood. Huang Jiguang died in the Korean War; having tossed his last hand grenade, he made a stand in front of a bunker, in the face of a hail of bullets from American machine guns, and made it possible for Chinese troops to advance.

The two were proclaimed as heroes of the People's Liberation Army in 1963 and celebrated as late as the 1990s as models to be imitated (Bonin, 1996; Landsberger, 2001).

Although these were the heroes who came first to our informants' minds, they were not—with the exception of Lei Feng—cited as the figures most worthy of imitation. The "most influential" list included names such as Minister-President Zhou Enlai, who was known for having spared or hindered the execution of many victims of the Cultural Revolution (one of the interviewees had benefited from his intervention); Norman Bethune, a Canadian surgeon and Communist who saved the lives of numerous soldiers during the civil war in Yan'an, or Zhang Side, who died in an accident in a coalmine.

During the 1950s, when foreign literature was quite accessible, the new socialist generation also found heroic figures in best-selling foreign novels such as the Soviet story, *Wie der Stahl gehärtet wurde* ("How the Steel Was Tempered") (Ostrowski, 1977), and the Polish work, *Die Stechfliege* ("The Gadfly") (Voynich, 1979). These protagonists, too, were mentioned as influential models.

"How the Steel Was Tempered" epitomises the literature of Socialist Realism. Written by Nikolai Alexejewitsch Ostrowski, the novel tells the story of Pawel Kortschagin, who, though blinded and fettered to his bed, never gives up his martial determination to serve the Communist Party and the Red Army. "The Gadfly", written by Ethel Lilian Voynich, concerns the life and struggles of Arthur Burton in mid-nineteenth century Italy; it became one of the most popular novels in China, as in the Soviet Union. Combining the themes of romantic heroism, self-sacrifice, and the will to resist, it was required reading for young members of the Pioneers.

While the Party succeeded in lodging the names of its chosen heroes in the collective memory, it is also true that our interviewees have distanced themselves from these models and focused on others. Generally, figures from the professions have taken the place of the heroic war martyrs. It is noteworthy, too, that only one hero, Lei Feng, was named as influential more than once, and this by two generations of the same family. So, we see some individualisation in the choice of model.

Yet, the idea of orientating one's life by such model figures has not lost its validity for our interview partners, and the alternative heroes, whether or not they belong to the latest official canon, are all names celebrated at some point in Chinese socialist propaganda. Both "The Gadfly" and "How the Steel Was Tempered" were recommended as examples for the young by the youth league in the People's Republic during the liberal phase of the "Hundred Flowers Campaign" of 1956. Even after thirty years of exposure to Western literature and films featuring quite different leading figures and approaches to living, our informants found their choices limited to heroes from the socialist pantheon. A single informant named figures from classical Chinese literature as influential and worthy of imitation.

The behaviour exemplified by the models always involves self-sacrifice for the collective in accordance with the Party line of the moment. No support is offered for the notion of heroism *in resistance to* the Party. The kind of confrontation with history that might actually prevent it from repeating itself has not taken place among our informants. Although exemplars for such engagement are no longer hard to find in China, the Party sanction that might make such a confrontation seem useful and important is lacking.

## Conclusion

The Party's "Resolution on Certain Historical Questions" was an attempt not only to legitimise the new leadership, but also to bring an end by fiat to internal social conflicts. The explanation of the "ten chaotic years" as a conflict within the Party elite that devastated the masses was so convincing that it is perpetuated in popular histories, in Scar Literature, and in autobiographical works. This picture was also readily accepted in the West, confirming, as it did, Western assumptions about the nature and inevitable failure of socialism, as well as the older, and lingering, "orientalist" picture of the "despotic East".

The process of working through the traumas of the Cultural Revolution in China has been delayed and prolonged not only because government prescriptions make open discussion more or less taboo. It is also the case that a social consensus about basic questions, the necessary starting point for an open confrontation with the past, does not exist. Because the Cultural Revolution saw so many complications and political reversals among the elites, the Red Guards, and mass organisations, it is hard to distinguish perpetrators from victims.

All this confirms what Perry stated in the opening sentence of her path-breaking study of the Cultural Revolution in Shanghai: "China's Cultural Revolution looms as one of the most important, yet least understood milestones of the twentieth century" (Perry & Li, 1996).

Given this difficult starting position, it becomes a matter of controversy—with the positions transparently dictated by group interests—just who may speak of these events and in what manner. On one side stands the older generation of the Cultural Revolution, people who, having been rehabilitated and restored to high position, want nothing less than an analysis of old conflicts; preferring to leave their own past roles in obscurity, they also fear a renewal of tensions and a rekindling of the desire for revenge. On the other side are participants who were young in those times and now seek validation for their political ambitions—who refuse, at least, to be written off as a lost, passive generation. The Chinese government is especially disturbed by views like those of the "Losers from Modernisation", who are inclined to justify the Cultural Revolution and emphasise its positive aspects; these opinions arise in zones of society where socialist promises have given way to capitalistic practices, just as Mao once feared. These voices are heard today on the Internet, a medium that, though not free of political control, also cannot be entirely tamed by it.

Missing in all these politically focused discussions are the central questions: why the Cultural Revolution occurred in the first place, and what led it to take such violent forms. Since most of the personal accounts are written from the standpoint of the victims (and eventual winners), since possible rebuttals by perpetrators are silenced, there can be no real exploration of what made people so ready to use force or what led to particular acts. Instead of being content with the simplistic "explanation" on offer ("chaotic outbreaks of an amorphous mass"), one could wish for an investigation of the internal mechanisms of the regime and society, leading to specific programmes for the prevention of future violence. However, for the reasons detailed in this chapter, such a debate—the very thing that might really help to prevent a repetition of history—is scarcely to be imagined.

## References

Assmann, J. (2001). *Das Kulturelle Gedächtnis: Schrift, Erinnerung und Politische Identität in Frühen Hochkulturen*. Munich: C. H. Beck.

Barme, J. (1999). The apotheosis of the Liumang. In: J. Barme (Ed.). *In the Red: On Contemporary Chinese Culture* (pp. 62–98). New York: Columbia University Press.

Bergman, P. (1984). *Paragons of Virtue in Chinese Short Stories During the Cultural Revolution*. Göteborg: Graphic System AB.

Bonin, M. (1996). When the saints come marching back. *China Perspectives*, 5(May/June): 10–19.

Brady, A.-M. (2008). *Marketing Dictatorship: Propaganda and Thoughtwork in Contemporary China*. Lanham, MD: Rowman & Littlefield.

CEEC China. Freedom of expression, speech and the press. www.ceec. gov/pages/virtualAcad. Accessed on 4 May 2009.

Chan, A. (1985). *Children of Mao: Personality Development and Political Activism in the Red Guard Generation*. London: Macmillan.

Chan, A. (1992). Dispelling misconceptions about the Red Guard movement: the necessity to re-examine cultural revolution factionalism and periodization. *Journal of Contemporary China*, 1(1): 61–85.

Chan, A., Stanley, R., & Unger, J. (1980). Students and class warfare: the social roots of the Red Guard conflict in Canton. *The China Quarterly*, 83(September): 397–446.

Chang, J. (1991). *The Wild Swans: Three Daughters of China*. London: HarperCollins.

Chang, J., & Halliday, J. (2005). *Mao: The Untold Story*. London: Cape.

China's first Cultural Revolution Museum is born. Zhongguo shouzuo wenge bowuguan de dansheng. Waitan huabao. www.bundpic.com/pap/20050505/15.htm. Accessed 25 May 2005.

Chinese Holocaust Memorial. http://humanities.uchicago.edu/faculty/ywang/history/. Accessed 27 April 2004.

Commission of the Central Committee of the C. P. S. U. (Eds.) (1939). *History of the Communist Party of the Soviet Union* (Bolshevik): Short Course. Moscow: Foreign Languages Publishing.

Dirlik, A. (2003). The politics of the Cultural Revolution in a historical perspective. In: K. Law (Ed.), *The Chinese Cultural Revolution Revisited* (pp. 158–183). New York: Palgrave Macmillan.

Esherick, J. W., Pickowicz, P., & Walder, A. G. (2006). *The Chinese Cultural Revolution as History*. Stanford, CA: Stanford University Press.

Fengkuang S. http://china1966.vip.sina.com/index.html. Accessed 26 May 2005.

Gao, M. (2008). *The Battle for China's Past: Mao and the Cultural Revolution*. London: Pluto Press.

Gao, X. (2004). *Das Buch eines Einsamen Menschen*, N. Vittinghoff (Trans.). Frankfurt: Fischer.

Gentz, N. (2006). How to get rid of China: ethnicity, memory and trauma in Gao Xingjian's novel *One Man's Bible*. In: N. Gentz & S. Kramer

(Eds.), *Globalization, Cultural Identities, and Media Representations* (pp. 119–142). Albany, NY: State University of New York Press.

He, B. (1996). *The Democratization of China.* London: Routledge.

He, Y. (1992). *Cycles of Repression and Relaxation: Politico-literary Events in China, 1976–1989.* Bochum: N. Brockmeyer.

Huaxia wenzhai wenge bowuguan [CND Museum of the Cultural Revolution]. www.cnd.org/CR/. Accessed 12 September 2009.

Kinkeley, J. C. (1991). A Bettelheimian interpretation of Chang Hsien-liang's concentration camp novels. *Asia Major, 3*(4): 91–113.

Landsberger, S. (2001). Learning by what example? Educational propaganda in twenty-first-century China. *Critical Asian Studies, 33*(4): 541–571.

Lin, M. (2000). Zhongguo ying miandui "wenige" [China must confront the Cultural Revolution]. http://www.xys.org/xys/ebooks/others/history/contemporary/culture_revolution/mianduiwenge.txt. Accessed 25 September 2009.

Liu, G. (1987). *A Brief Analysis of the Cultural Revolution.* Armonk, NY: M. E. Sharpe.

Liu, X. (1981). Der Klassenlehrer. In: J. Noth (Ed.), *Der Jadefelsen: Chinesische Kurzgeschichten 1977–1979* (pp. 11–34). Frankfurt: Sendler.

Lu, X. (1986). The wounded. In: R. F. Dernberger, K. J. DeWoskin, & S. M. Goldstein (Eds.), *The Chinese: Adapting the Past, Building the Future* (pp. 591–604). Ann Arbor, MI: Center for Chinese Studies, University of Michigan.

Ma, Q. (2000). Jianyi jianshe wenge jinianri [Proposal to institute a Cultural Revolution memorial day]. http://blog.sina.com.cn/s/blog_609f25eb0100ehr8.html. Accessed 25 September 2009.

MacFarquhar, R. (1997). *The Coming of the Cataclysm, 1961–1966: The Origins of the Cultural Revolution, 3.* Oxford: Oxford University Press.

McDougall, B., & Kam, L. (1997). *The Literature of China in the Twentieth Century.* New York: Columbia University Press.

Memories of the Cultural Revolution. Wenge jinian. http://dfh1966.nease.net/. Accessed 15 April 2005.

NETOR. www.netor.com/m/box200104/m5863.asp?BoardID=5863. Accessed 25 September 2009.

Ostrowski, N. A. (1977). *Wie der Stahl gehärtet wurde.* Berlin: Verlag Neues Leben.

Perry, E. J. & Li, X. (1996). *Proletarian Power: Shanghai in the Cultural Revolution.* Boulder, CO: Westview.

Reemtsma, J. P. (2001). *"Wie Hätte Ich Mich Verhalten?" und Andere Nicht Nur Deutsche Fragen: Reden und Aufsätze.* Munich: C. H. Beck.

Rusticated Chinese youth (Huaxia zhiqing). http://q.163.com/hxzqq/. Accessed 25 September 2009.

Schoenhals, M. (1992). *Doing Things with Words in Chinese Politics: Five studies.* Berkeley, CA: University of California Institute of East Asian Studies.

Turbulent years of the Cultural Revolution in China. Zhongguo wenhua da geming huangtan suiyue. http://dfh1966.nease.net/. Accessed 15 April 2005.

Unger, J. (1991). Whiter China: Yang Xiguang, Red Capitalists and the social turmoil of the Cultural Revolution. *Modern China, 17*(1): 3–37.

Virtual Museum of the Cultural Revolution. www.cnd.org/CR/. Accessed 25 September 2009.

Vittinghoff, N. (2002). China's generation X: rusticated Red Guards in controversial contemporary plays. In: Woei Lien Chong (Ed.), *China's Great Proletarian Cultural Revolution: Master Narratives and Post-Mao Counternarratives* (pp. 285–318). Lanham, MD: Rowman Littlefield.

Voynich, E. L. (1979). *Die Stechfliege.* Reinbek: Rowohlt.

Xiao, Q. (2004). The words you never see in Chinese cyberspace. http://chinadigitaltimes.net/2004/08/the-words-you-never-see-in-chinese-cyberspace/. Accessed 30 April 2009.

Xiao, Y. (2002). Wengezhende shi dongluanma? [Was the Cultural Revolution really a chaotic upheaval?] http://mwjx.3322.org:8080/bbs/show_txt.php?fid=2783. Accessed 16 March 2004.

Xu, Z. (1998). *Dangdai xiaoshuo yu jiti jiyi: Xushu wenge* [Contemporary literature and collective memory: Narratives of the Cultural Revolution]. Taipei: Maitian chubanshe.

Yan, J., & Gao, G. (1996). *Turbulent Decade: A History of the Cultural Revolution,* D. W. Y. Kwok (Ed. & Trans.). Honolulu: University of Hawai'i Press.

Yang, G. (2003). The internet and civil society in China: a preliminary assessment. *Journal of Contemporary China, 12*(36): 453–475.

Yao, Y. (2004). The elite class background of Wang Shuo and his hooligan characters. *Modern China, 30*(4): 261–286.

Ye, Y. (1988). *Chenzhong de 1957* [The difficult year 1957]. Hongkong: Mingxing chubanshe.

Ye, Y. (1992). *Lishi xuanzele Mao Zedong* [History has chosen Mao Zedong]. Shanghai: Shanghai renmin chubanshe.

Ye, Y. (1993a). *Zhonggong milu* (Geheime Aufzeichnungen zur KPCh). Hongkong: Liwen chubanshe.

Ye, Y. (1993b). *Jiang Qing zhuan* [A Biography of Jiang Qing]. Beijing: Zuojia chubanshe.

Yi, H. (2000). Wenge yu chanhui [The Cultural Revolution and remorse]. www.cnread.net/cnread1/net/zpj/y/yihong/000/013.htm. Accessed 26 September 2009.

Zarrow, P. (1999). Meanings of China's Cultural Revolution: Memoirs of exile. *Positions*, 7(1): 165–191.

# CHAPTER TWO

# The Great Proletarian Cultural Revolution (1966–1976) as an experience of contingency

*Liying Wang*

Reflecting on the horrors of world history and especially the catastrophes of the twentieth century, Reemtsma (2001) takes issue with Hegel's philosophy of history:

> The second half of the twentieth century has bankrupted Hegel's hope for History. It is exactly at that moment, the philosopher said, when we regard "History as the slaughter-bench on which the happiness of peoples, the wisdom of states, and the virtue of individuals has been sacrificed" that we must believe "these enormous sacrifices" to be serving an ultimate goal. The philosophy of history, that great attempt of European modernity to see itself as on the right road out of a world of violence into a future relatively or entirely free of it, was shaken by the First World War and refuted by Auschwitz. It is dead. We should not, we cannot even, lament its passing. (p. 172, translated for this edition)

With this pronouncement, Reemtsma challenges the teleological idea of history. The disillusionment of historical philosophy, stemming not least from the catastrophic experiences of the twentieth century, brings to the fore the awareness and experience of contingency. Among the century's terrible events, the "Great Proletarian Cultural Revolution" in China (1966–1976) must take its place. It is both an example of the many Chinese troubles of the period and their climax. The reach of the Cultural Revolution, impacting on almost all social classes throughout the country, was vast, its course prolonged and bewildering. For most participants, perpetrators as well as victims, the direction of the campaign was chaotic and confusing, because of contradictory instructions from on high; in this, the Cultural Revolution differs from other comparable events.

The shock of the Cultural Revolution lingers deep in individual psyches, as it does in Chinese society as a whole, and the trauma has not yet been dealt with. Its effects on the development of the nation are lingering. Without the Cultural Revolution, the reform policy that followed in the 1980s would have been unthinkable. The Communist Party also frequently points to this past convulsion to justify its rejection of democracy. As a political and social phenomenon, the Revolution needs explanation today on many levels. Publications and expressions concerning it that deviate from the Party line bring censorship, if not persecution. Both individual and collective memories are imprinted by the experience of chaos, catastrophe, arbitrariness, powerlessness, and meaningless suffering. I shall describe this experience of a world gone off the rails, of the collapse of known stabilities, under the rubric of the experience of contingency.

I should like to begin surveying the meanings of the word "contingency" and tracing how it has been defined in Western theories. Then, I will turn to the concept of fate in Chinese philosophy and its affinity to the contingency idea. A consideration of the Cultural Revolution experience will flow from these reflections.

### Contingency and fate: the concept and experience of contingency

I shall not attempt a full recapitulation of the development of the concept of contingency from antiquity to the present. For our purposes, a short sketch of its career in the history of ideas will suffice.

In philosophy, contingency is a concept of modality and designates that which is neither necessary nor impossible. What is contingent could exist in another form, or not at all. The concept is characterised by a double concession: the thing at hand is not necessary, need not exist, yet it is also not impossible (Holzinger, 2007, p. 26). Admittedly, this analytic framing of the concept does not say much about the various concrete manifestations of the contingent. What we call "contingent" has varied historically and according to perspective. The content of the concept has not remained static through European history. What we designate as contingent always depends on our experience.

Aristotle is the first to approach a definition of the concept. For him, contingency is manifest in that realm where human action has a role. Aristotelian contingency is the uncommon product of the encounter of previously unconnected chains of causality in a well-ordered cosmos functioning by stable laws. Granted, Aristotle never uses the word "contingency" in his works. The word "contingent" (*contingens*) is the Latin translation of the Aristotelian concepts of "being possible" and "accidence". According to Wetz (1998a, pp. 28–29), Kant is probably the first to equate the concept of contingency with the expression "chance", with "chance" being a translation of "accidence".

In the Christian metaphysical tradition, contingency conveys the idea that the whole world is the creation of a freely acting god who could also have not bothered to bring it into being. Being dependent on the will of God, the whole world is contingent; it need not ever have existed. Nevertheless, the world is not lawless. It is organised purposefully; its development is guided by divine providence. These theological conceptions give way in early modern times to rationalistic reflections about the contingency of the world. Schelling, for instance, distinguishes between the essential being and the concrete existence of the world, with the essence flowing from pure divine reason. He contrasts the essence, which must exist, with the individual or concrete, which is contingent. An entity that exists at a particular place and time in the world is accidental, or contingent, yet its essential being is a necessary thing. Schelling says that absolute reason is capable of determining the essential being of all things, in order that a reasonable order should arise; it is not able to bring all potential entities into concrete existence. Schopenhauer then replaces absolute reason with the blind, unreasoning Will as the ultimate cause of existence, thus opening the way to the modern concept of total contingency of everything there is (Renz, 1996, p. 62; Wetz, 1998b, pp. 88–92).

The consciousness of contingency in the modern era flows from the view that no essential higher order can be detected in the world.

The whole structure of things is the accidental product of nature, experienced as impenetrable chaos, arbitrariness, and fragility. Neither divine providence nor absolute reason is at work. The world is a quirk of nature or a series of coincidences. Even the human species is the result of natural processes without direction or plan (Wetz, 1998b, pp. 92–95). Whereas, for Aristotle, contingency concerns actions or events in an orderly cosmos, and in Christian theology describes the divine creative act, contingency in the modern era extends to the whole realm of human actions. Contingency for the moderns is universal. Industrialisation and the radical expansion of geographical horizons have rapidly complicated the field for human action. This mounting complexity overtaxes human reason even more. People lose the grasp of their world, the reference points for their lives. Science and technology disenchant the world and displace theological and metaphysical interpretations of it, while adding substantially to the complexity of society (Holzinger, 2007, pp. 46–51). The modern consciousness of contingency has found negative expression in general insecurity, in the collapse of worldviews and the sense of an objective world, and in the civilisational identity crisis after the First World War. On the other hand, it expresses itself positively in the human will to self-determination (Joas, 2004, pp. 395–396; Makropoulos, 1998, p. 25).

Human beings have always faced existential uncertainty. Accident, illness, the unexpected death of intimates, earthquake—all arrive as shocking catastrophes. Beyond that, economic and sociocultural conditions in any society bring their own hazards, which an individual experiences as violent visitations. Not only the individual, but also a whole social group, or even a whole society can be thrown into crisis by unpredictable vicissitudes. For modern people, such events are the very face of universal contingency, the absence of transcendence and meaning. People of earlier times, exposed no less to contingency, believed in a higher sense of the world, however hard this might be for human beings to grasp. They thought that what appears contingent reflects that higher order and can be entrusted to it (Holzinger, 2007, pp. 45–46). In all pre-modern societies, we see attempts to soften the arbitrariness of untoward events through religious or metaphysical explanations, making such "blows of fate" bearable. The ethnologist Müller (1992) shows how primitive societies reacted to exceptional, seemingly accidental events with religious rites and interpretations.

In dealing with contingency in modern times, we note a difference between discretionary contingency and fatal contingency. Discretionary circumstances in our lives are those that can be affected by our own actions, while fatal contingency comes to us without our participation and cannot be affected by what we do. This distinction is reflected in the subtly differing words "risk" and "danger". Risk is the kind of threat that one takes on with knowledge and which one could avoid by not performing certain actions. Danger is felt to be something environmental that one's actions cannot much control. Whether some accidental thing belongs to the category of risk or of danger is a matter of interpretation and the coping skills of the affected person. Many things that were seen a few generations ago as pure strokes of fate are now regarded as the result of conscious decisions. Modern societies differ importantly from pre-modern ones in their attitude towards contingency (Hahn, 1998, pp. 49–54). The modern consciousness of contingency is characterised not only by despair of guiding principles and by insecurity in the face of ungraspable complexity, but also by the will to overcome contingency, as in the control of nature, in social-technical formations, and in certain value systems (Joas, 2004, pp. 397–399). Yet, of course, modern people cannot get rid of fatal contingency. Again and again come those unaccountable "blows of fate" that we cannot predict or prevent, dramatically reminding us how little command we have over our existence. This confrontation with absolute contingency often sends people on a search for god; now, as in earlier centuries, religion serves as a strategy for overcoming contingency. Religion offers interpretations for painful reversals and provides support for people struck down by blind fate (Lübbe, 1998, pp. 40–47). When religious interpretations seem invalid and can no longer offer confidence to victims, there are other, if weaker, aids: the support of other people, repression, laughing and weeping, and acceptance, either stoic or insouciant.

## The concept of fate in Chinese thought

There has been a scholarly field called "Violence in China" for twenty years. The extensive annotated bibliography by Haar (S. J.) shows us that violent events like natural catastrophes, war, political chaos, and the arbitrariness of unjust rulers pervade Chinese history. Society and politics have been no more harmonious here than in the West. It is remarkable, though, that—as it now appears—Chinese philosophy lacks an equivalent to the concept of contingency; neither does a coherent concept of fate appear among its basic themes. Although the absence of the contingency concept in this tradition is not readily accounted for, several studies suggest an explanation. Theoretical reflections on contingency and the experience of contingency are connected with religious and metaphysical conceptions. Chinese philosophy, in its basic character, attaches much less importance to metaphysics than does Western philosophy (Forke, 1927, pp. 37–66; Fung, 1948, Chapter One; Geldsetzer & Hong, 1998, Chapters One and Two; Qian, 1997, part 2). In order to explore Chinese concepts concerning unaccountable vicissitudes, then, we must take an indirect path and look at the related idea of fate.

Like the concept of contingency, the notion of fate is bound up with the idea of god or a metaphysical entity, but fate, unlike contingency, is generally seen as a predetermination by higher powers of the course of an individual life or of history. Here, I shall limit myself to compiling the various stances described in the available studies.

## The concept of fate in folk religion

In the Xia era (ca. twenty-first to sixteenth century BCE) and the Shang period (ca. sixteenth–eleventh century BCE), primitive religions were based on the worship of natural objects, nature deities, and ancestral spirits (Mou & Zhang, 1997, pp. 78–79; Wang, 1991, pp. 96–127). Through the cycle of the seasons, these gods and spirits provide people with food and clothing, but also deliver catastrophe and death. Human fate and wellbeing depend on these entities. The border between the human realm and the world occupied by gods and spirits is experienced as fluid. Human beings can communicate with divinities by consulting oracles, making sacrifices, and performing magic. Divination predicts natural phenomena important for survival; advice concerning human actions is secured from gods and spirits. Rites and sacrifices serve to pacify these powers and to secure their favour and assistance (Bauer, 1989, pp. 23–29; Mou & Zhang, 1997, pp. 83–113; Poo, 2005, pp. 112–113). These early efforts to influence human fate with the help of supernatural powers survive in the contemporary practice of soothsaying. Various forms of divination and almanacs, books of advice for daily living apparently based on divination, are still accepted as guides by people of the middle and lower classes and even by some intellectuals. Divination literature is an important component of China's written heritage (Wang, 1991, p. 101).

### The concept of fate in the religion of heaven

"Shangdi", the highest divinity of the Shang era, is adopted by the Western Zhou Dynasty (eleventh century to 770 BCE) and renamed "Tian", heaven, though both labels continue to be used. While Tian/Shangdi still has some anthropomorphic traits, this supreme god of the early Zhou has become more abstract and more ethically based (Fu, 1952, p. 81; Mou & Zhang, 1997, pp. 116–22; Roetz, 1984, p. 118; Wang, 1991, p. 131). Heaven's rule over nature, human life, and politics is not arbitrary, but is guided by a moral calculus. It supports good people and punishes bad ones. Natural catastrophes, personal sufferings, individual lives and deaths, political misfortunes, and the succession of dynasties are all connected with immoral ways of life or individual guilt. Such phenomena are perceived as the will of heaven. A person can secure the favour of heaven through just actions, through virtue. A happy destiny can be earned by virtuous conduct, a fact that does not render sacrifices and divination unnecessary (Fu, 1952, pp. 104–105; Mou & Zhang, 1997, pp. 122–132). Yet, one should not rely on the favour of heaven, but, rather, on one's own actions. This viewpoint is crystallised in the classics, such as "The Book of Documents" (Roetz, 1984, sections 10 and 13; Wang, 1991, pp. 127–132; Yue, 1992, pp. 90–96). The relationship between Heaven and humanity involves first of all society's rulers, their use of power, their legitimacy even (the Mandate of Heaven).

Heaven is also perceived in the early Chou as unpredictable and arbitrary, raising the problem of theodicy. The evident injustice of many events on earth creates a challenge for the believer. If heaven works its will in earthly life only, without promising a reckoning in another world, doubts about either its justice or its power must arise. Roetz (1984, sections 11 and 12) thinks that this internal tension plays a considerable role in the decay of the old heaven worship.

## The Universist concept of fate

The concept of correspondences between microcosms and macrocosm, the mutual influences between nature and man, is known in philosophy as Universism (Roetz, 1984, p. 2). In the Chunqiu era (770–476 BCE) the heaven religion gradually begins to decay; the concept of heaven is secularised or naturalised. The will of anthropomorphic heaven merges with the concrete rules of nature (Loewe, 1994, p. 170). The laws of nature are manifested in the yin–yang oscillation, together with the circulation of the five elements. This cosmological speculation applied also to the human realm. A sympathetic relationship is posited between natural events and human activity; historical events are interpreted as if by natural science and natural events in terms of human actions (Roetz, 1984, section 4; Wang, 1991, pp. 135–138). A good ruler must accommodate himself to the processes of heaven and act in accordance with the rhythm of the four seasons. Acting in harmony with the power of nature is the key to good fortune. Disruption of this harmony leads to misfortune and catastrophe (Puett, 2005, pp. 61–68). Concerned to act rightly, the ruler consults a kind of almanac, or an oracle-means of mediation between cosmos and Man (Loewe, 1994, Chapters Eight, Nine, Ten).

## The fatalistic concept of fate

In the Chunqiu period, another trend becomes evident alongside the Universist speculations: a growing consciousness of the separation of nature and society. This view becomes prominent in the Zhanguo period (475–221 BCE), when dualism of nature and man is more prominent in philosophy than heretofore. For the Daoists Zhuangzi (ca. 380–310 BCE and Liezi (ca. 440–370 BCE), nature is a counter-world absolutely independent of humanity and obeying its own immanent, permanent law. Man is no longer involved with nature, as for the Universists, in a constantly recreated complementary relationship. The stability and regularity of nature, also called the Tao, is neither specified nor quantified, however. All emphasis is placed on the non-anthropomorphic character of nature. The operation of the Tao is spontaneous, without goal, and creative of everything of the world. It is not will, but blind causation that brings about the transformations of things. Fate is that which the Tao, the course of nature, brings.

Human actions have no influence whatever on rise and fall, fortune and misfortune; all human actions themselves depend on fate and are not the results of self-determination. One should practise inactivity and respond to the movement of the Tao (Cai, 2005, pp. 191; Forke, 1964, pp. 296–297; Roetz, 1984, pp. 244–245; Yue, 1992, pp. 108–116).

In the Han period (206 BCE–220 CE), Wang Chong (27–97 CE) was a decided proponent of this fatalism. Wang Chong praises the passive ethic of the Daoists and denies that human activity can affect destiny. Fate is determined by three factors: by the celestial fluid, by the stellar fluid, and by favourable or unfavourable accidents. The celestial fluid determines physical constitution, health and sickness, and length of life. Social success, such as wealth, power, and reputation, depend on the stellar fluid. However, unpredictable accidents can modify the fate the two fluids ordain. So, fate, according to Wang Chong, is traceable to material factors, a conception that could be labelled a natural determinism. Given his emphasis on accidents, one can even see the seed of the idea of contingency in Wang Chong's materialistic concept. There has been much discussion of how the deterministic tendency and the contingent tendency in Wang Chong's system relate. Yue (1992, pp. 116–123) and Wang Xiaoyi (2001) maintain that these two elements are not contradictory. The fate of a given person is ultimately determined by natural factors; the accidental element results from the naturally determined fates of other persons, which impinge on the first person as unpredictable, accidental events. The influence of Wang Chong's concept of fate on Chinese mentality is very strong, as expressed in the narrative literature of the Song Dynasty (960–1279) and the Ming Dynasty (1368–1644). On the one hand, these stories relate chains of purely accidental events; on the other hand, they proclaim the whole seemingly random sequence to be predestined. No attempt is made to reconcile these levels. This suggests a fatalistic attitude to life: what happens to us is due to an unfathomable fate.

## The humanistic concept of fate

The thought that people are masters of their own fate also has its origins, tradition says, in the Chunqiu period, but comes to flower in the Zhanguo period, the most fruitful era in the history of Chinese philosophy. This fundamentally humanistic perspective occurs in the writings of Mozi (ca. 480–400 BCE) and Zunzi (ca. 310–230 BCE). In these philosophies, fate is demoted from a higher power to a consequence of human actions. For the humanistically minded, there is no predetermined destiny (Fu, 1952, pp. 143–146; Roetz, 1984, p. 218); determinism or fatalism is rejected. Such optimistic rationalism, holding anything to be doable, culminates in the claim that Man is the ultimate victor over nature; it constitutes one of the inspirations for Maoist voluntarism.

## The multi-factorial concept of fate

In between fatalism and the belief in human autonomy lies the view that fate is a collaboration of heaven and human actions. Heaven, whether religiously or ethically conceived, determines fate in principle; but human will is not denied and has its own influence on outcomes. This concept is advocated by Confucius (551–479 BCE) and Mengzi (372–289 BCE). They agree that Heaven rewards the good and punishes the bad. Yet, in reality, virtuous people often get into difficulties; they, too, suffer misfortune and death. In such cases, there is a mismatch between the proper actions of people and the will of heaven. The virtuous person, though, will not let his moral efforts be disturbed by this discrepancy, will, rather, accept without resentment whatever fate brings. Even if heaven's will is not always understandable, the person should obey his fate, striving to act ethically and doing nothing to draw further misfortune on himself through recklessness or ill deeds (Fu, 1952, p. 137; Puett, 2005, pp. 56–61; Yue, 1992, p. 104). The lingering influence of these Confucian ideas is evident in proverbs popular in China to this day, such as, *People think; heaven, or fate, decides.*

## The concept of fate as karma

The spread of Buddhism in China introduces a concept of fate influenced by the theory of karma, or compensation. For the Buddhists, metempsychosis through rebirth is a kind of fate. One's present situation in life is determined by acts committed in former lives. The relation between current and prior incarnations is a matter of cause and effect. Good deeds secure a better existence in the next life, evil deeds, a worse. This Buddhist concept proves very attractive in China, not least because it assigns the decisive role in reincarnation to ethical behaviour (Grimm, 1922, Chapter II; Yue, 1992, pp. 124–131). A compensatory understanding of fate is also seen in religious Daoism. The spirits between heaven and earth note everything that people do. They reward good and punish evil. Human beings must chalk up the curses and blessings of life to their own account (Bauer, 1990, pp. 465–471).

The conceptions of fate described here show that Chinese philosophy, despite the absence of the concept of contingency, has its own ways of dealing with the fact of contingency or unpredictable reversals.

## Contingency in the Cultural Revolution

In hindsight, it is clear how much the twentieth century added to the cumulative Chinese experience of contingency. A great push to modernise, accompanied by a deep crisis of cultural identity, characterises the century; long before the Cultural Revolution, this was expressed in the raging attack on Chinese cultural tradition by the "May 4 Movement" of 1919. Lin Yü-sheng (1979) labels the condemnation of Chinese tradition in the "May 4 Movement" as "iconoclastic". That generation of Chinese intellectuals regarded the political structure, the established system of cultural norms, and other facets of communal life as an organic whole—to be rejected as a whole. The revolution of 1911 destroyed not only the last dynasty, but also the entire traditional political order. In its aftermath, the inherited value system was called into question. A deeper source for this attack on tradition lay in a paradigm of cultural determinism going back to the Neo-Confucianism of the Song and Ming. This model treats worldviews and values as the basis of society and regards ideas as the driving force for political and economic change. The intellectuals of the "May 4 Movement" were convinced that the transformation of Chinese society must begin with a revolution in culture: the destruction of the old system of symbols, values, and worldviews was the precondition for modernisation. This radical attitude towards the past inevitably led to a crisis of cultural identity, and to confusion and disorientation. The complex history of the early twentieth century cannot, of course, be reduced to a story of alienation and the loss of bearings. Not all cultural elements lost validity at once. Many values and thought patterns survived the collapse of the political system and, consciously or unconsciously, imprinted even the intellectuals of the "May 4 Movement". In less educated social groups, Confucianism, Daoism, and Buddhism merged into "that amorphous mass", an ideology combining Confucian exhortations to loyalty, Daoist love of life, and Buddhist indifference to poverty: an illogical compound, perhaps, but a useful one, and a mind-set the rulers found ideal in the ruled (Bauer, 1989, p. 362). It should not be overlooked, either, that the iconoclasm of the "May 4 Movement" was an intellectual current only, not a programme enforced by state power (Chen, 2002, pp. 131–133).

The Communist victory in China brought social upheavals that deeply affected not only private lives, but also the consciousness of all Chinese. The state monopolised and transformed the intellectual land-scape. No idea, Chinese or Western, that departed from Marxism or Maoism was tolerated any longer. Maoism, a sinified version of Marx-ism, was an established ideology in China even before the founding of the People's Republic. In 1945, it was proclaimed the guiding ideol-ogy of the Revolution and thereafter determined the political process in the country concretely and directly (Schram, 1991, pp. 1–96). Mao's concept for the construction of the socialist society in China is mani-fested in his writings. In the dialectical relationship of theory and practice, of knowledge and action, Mao gives pride of place to prac-tice, action, and human initiative. Mao declares the new China to be a *tabula rasa*, a blank page on which to paint his fantastic pictures. He believes in the magical, omnipotent will of the person in action, who is even able to override certain laws of history (Bauer, 1989, pp. 545–548; Hoffman, 1978, p. 54; Tang, 1986, p. 116). Mao's conviction about the relativity of truth is also based on this dialectical dance of theory and practice. Practice reveals, confirms, and further develops the truth. The knowledge thus gained guides a new round of revolution-ary practice. Practice, theory, practice, theory: this cyclical form creates an endless, ascending spiral of increasing understanding (Chan, 2003, p. 112; Bauer, 1989, pp. 539–540). In reality, though, this perceived reci-procal relationship proved very problematic. Mao often changed his theoretical pronouncements to match current situations and political needs. Ideas he promulgated often contradicted each other, so that it was difficult to distinguish underlying principles from the tactics of the moment. Mao's understanding of dialectics is an important aspect of his system. Rather than as the negation of negation, Mao saw dialectics as an eternal contradiction, a tension existing *a priori* in all phenomena, which keeps the oppositions in the world in constant motion. This basic structure of things implies that the world is always in a state of upheaval. Thus did Mao justify the necessity of permanent revolution and permanent struggle. The political meaning of this Maoist dialectics was evident in the "successive expulsions of allies" in the course of the Communist revolution in China (Bauer, 1989, pp. 540–554; Chan, 2003, pp. 113–124; Hsia, 1971, pp. 20–31;). In his leadership of the revolution Mao moved away at the end of the 1950s from "democratic centralism', which had contemplated participation of the masses in politics under Party supervision. Increasingly dissatisfied with bureaucracy, Mao now emphasised the "mass line', which left no place for bourgeois parliamentarianism. The "masses" were for Mao an inexhaustible fund of human material that he could mobilise for specific purposes, bypassing bureaucratic institutions (Chan, 2003, p. 123; Schram, 1991, pp. 1–96).

Under an ideology like Maoism, an eruption of human arbitrariness was only to be expected. During the Great Leap Forward (1958–1960) and the Cultural Revolution (1966–1976), technical competence

*Photograph 4.* People swim in the Songhua River to honour the anniversary of Mao's publicity swim in the Yangtze, which marked his return to power and the outbreak of the Cultural Revolution (Harbin, 16 July 1967).

and material means were to be replaced by revolutionary enthusiasm and ideological purity. Devastating economic catastrophes resulted. Lifton (1968, p. 107) characterises Mao's self-destructive actions as a "psychistic" phenomenon: "an attempt to gain control over the external environment through inner or psychological manipulations, through behaviour determined by intrapsychic needs, cutting off all contact with the realities of the world that one wishes to influence" (translated for this edition). It is no accident that Chinese intellectuals assessing Mao's legacy after the Cultural Revolution saw his voluntarism as the cause of the catastrophes in political life from 1949 on (Chong, 2005). The continual changes of political course meant that an action mandated yesterday could be criminal today. Functionaries of lower and middle levels would have to promulgate a policy one day and denounce it the next. They would be criticised alternately as radical leftist or as conservative rightest deviationists. Even Mao's most loyal followers could not be sure of the safe path on this shifting ground. During the Cultural Revolution, Mao often praised "great chaos under heaven" as a precursor to "great order under heaven" (Hoffmann, 1978, p. 129; Tang, 1986, p. 84; White, 1989, p. 33). Mao's Mass Line accommodated a certain amount of spontaneity on the part of the population as a means of shattering established power relationships. The masses were called to rebellion; Party organisation and bureaucratic apparatus collapsed in tumult (Harding, 1991, pp. 142–189). In the ensuing general chaos, rival mass organisations fought against each other, all under the flag of Maoism. In the name of Chairman Mao, countless people were arbitrarily accused.

Various factors contributed to the Cultural Revolution, the "Great Chaos" Mao so praised. The bewildering complexity of the phenomenon defeats any simple explanatory model. Only a combination of perspectives can bring the events closer to us. The Cultural Revolution has been discussed under the rubrics of ideology, power struggle, social conflict, the psychological dispositions of the actors, Chinese cultural tradition, and the political culture of communism (Gänßbauer, 1996, II. 2. 3/II. 2. 4; White, 1989, pp. 24–42). Maoism provided the ideological justification for this demented campaign, but how was this ideology put into practice? How was this politically extreme situation, in which so many people were involved as perpetrators, victims, or both, brought about? These questions are important for the experience of those affected by the chaos—their experience of contingency.

Unfathomable official intentions, arbitrary accusations, unpredictable attacks from all possible quarters, unfocused feelings of hatred, explosive violence on a huge scale—all these, according to White (1989), flowed from three policies of the Communist government. First, in the 1950s, all the inhabitants of cities and countryside were categorised in particular classes. For urbanites, personal dossiers were set up. Class labels did not reflect the current economic status of the subjects, but, rather, the political caste system of the new China, with some groups privileged and others subject to discrimination. A person's dossier was all-important and often contained unfavourable contents that were secret and against which no protest could be lodged. The uncertainty and discrimination produced by class labels and personal files caused conflicts among different political groups; these were mirrored in the factional battles of the Cultural Revolution. The second governmental action was the placement of all urbanites in work units that supervised every realm of life. Individual workers were even more dependent on the good will of their superiors than they had been in the social hierarchy of the past. This relationship produced arrogance in some and resentment in others, which would be discharged in the Cultural Revolution in attacks against the former power holders. The third political mode, which White (1989) calls the "mass campaign", was another source of unpredictability and repressiveness. To achieve an economic or political goal as fast as possible at low administrative cost, the authorities regularly suspended existing law and regular procedure. To produce total mobilisation, an overpowering propaganda storm would be unleashed, cowing people through an organised explosion of accusations and resulting in apparent unanimity. These shortcuts were efficient for the government in the short term; their fatal long-run consequence was chaos. Indeed, the Cultural Revolution can be seen as chaos promoted and guided by the state (Shan, 2003).

With its long, multi-layered tradition and its gigantic, slowly responding population, China was no "blank page". Maoism held that the realisation of the ideal socialist society required the total destruction of the past. Many scholars, such as Lin (1979, pp. 157–160) and Tang (1986), see the Cultural Revolution as the continuation and culmination of twentieth century radical Chinese anti-traditionalism. Indoctrinated in Maoism, the "New Men" of the new China were cut off from all other spiritual resources and robbed of every tiny refuge in social life. Given these circumstances, it is interesting to consider how Chinese, both learned and uneducated, attempted to cope with such a catastrophe as the revolution.


## Between past and future

In 1981 the Communist Party issued the official and still authoritative verdict on the Cultural Revolution in its "Resolution on certain questions in the history of the Chinese Communist Party since 1949" (see the Resolution of 1981, pp. 175–191, as well as the contribution by Gentz, pp. 1–34). Mao supposedly bears the main responsibility for the Cultural Revolution, but remains, none the less, a great revolutionary and the well-loved leader of the Chinese people. In practice, all the crimes committed in the Cultural Revolution are laid at the door of the "Gang of Four", which supposedly had taken advantage of the elderly Mao. Shortly after passing the resolution, the Party declared the Cultural Revolution to belong to the historical past. The people should now look toward the future.

This Party resolution amounts to a collective repression. It has largely set the limits of academic research on the Cultural Revolution within China ever since. After its promulgation, existing critical works on the Cultural Revolution were withdrawn from circulation or had to be published in Hong Kong and Taiwan (Sausmikat, 2002, pp. 38–44). Literary treatment of the catastrophe began immediately after it ended. This Scar Literature articulated the mood of the time. In these accounts, terror is portrayed, revolutionary ideals are shown in use as cloaks for treachery and brutality, and the suffering and losses occasioned by the crimes of the Gang of Four and its supporters are bemoaned. At the same time, optimism is the order of the day. Justice prevails in the end, the miscreants are punished after the change of regime, and a hopeful future beckons. This happy ending gives meaning to terrible experiences (Bucher, 1986; Chen, 2004; Hu, 1991; Xu, 2000). The forum that this genre offered to people traumatised by the Cultural Revolution is not to be undervalued. At the same time, it must be admitted that the discourse of this genre, influenced as it is by the Party resolution, is a problematic lens through which to view the real events. Can perpetrator and victim be so clearly distinguished as Scar Literature would have it? Were evildoers really punished in the aftermath? Have victims received their due? Does the politically correct schema of Scar Literature do justice to individual experiences? These tricky questions have not been convincingly answered in China to this day. One has the impression that the various groups involved, each with its own collective memories of the Cultural Revolution, have yet to come to any basic consensus.

The Chinese author Feng Jicai (2003) has collected the narratives of many anonymous survivors of the Cultural Revolution. These authentic stories are grotesque, absurd, and, sometimes, reminiscent of the crueller tales of the Brothers Grimm: windows into a Kafkaesque world. It is striking that the victims relate their weird experiences as naked facts, reporting them naïvely, without astonishment or a thirst for explanation. Tormentors are often unnamed or referred to abstractly as "they", "one". It was not only the masses that experienced powerlessness and the loss of moorings. The famous Indologist Ji Xianlin (1998) tells in his memoirs how he was at the mercy of the violence of the Cultural Revolution, surviving only due to an unexpected irruption of Red Guards into his home. The Nobel prize winner Gao Xingjian (2004) speaks in his semi-autobiographical novel of the reign of chaos, of total disorientation. These victims were helpless in the face of the capricious events of the revolution. Overwhelmed, they felt as though in the grips of a mighty natural catastrophe. Numerous recollections found on the Internet tell the same story. The sociologist He (2003, p. 406), now living in exile, sees Chinese fatalism as a constant in the nation's history. The likening of social upheavals to natural processes is a familiar trope in Chinese literature, a naturalisation of social evils that is doubtless rooted in the Universist and fatalistic concept of fate.

Alongside fatalism, another concept has a long tradition in China: the idea that misfortune and catastrophe have to do with the incompetence and despotism of rulers, as well as with a general decline of morals (Diefenbach, 2004, pp. 59–61). As the Scar Literature of the 1980s shows, there is no lack of awareness of the Cultural Revolution as a human-caused disaster. Despotism and excessive force seemed limitless then. People were abused, manipulated by power seekers, and treated like experimental rabbits in an enormous laboratory. When the authority of a ruler or of a political institution in a totalitarian system is heightened beyond measure, the leaders have complete freedom of action and can behave as brutally and mercilessly as they like, while the subjects are robbed of any role as actors, degraded to mere objects, and left nothing but resignation. The history of the People's Republic of China makes clear how the apotheosis of Mao, or of the party/state, simultaneously (on the one hand) strengthens the voluntarism of the rulers, inclining them to despotism, and (on the other hand) fosters fatalistic tendencies in the ruled. Arbitrary misrule by the strong and fatalism on the part of the weak: these are complements in China. With regard to the Cultural Revolution, only the Gang of Four is singled out for moral criticism, while Mao remains untouchable; his spell may not be broken. Any investigation of causes rooted in the political system is taboo. General reflections on human nature and human propensity to violence are also absent. The internationally known artist Ai Weiwei (2009), considering current incidents in China and his own abuse by the police, laments that China's social system creates injustice and unhappiness, permits no corrective action, and, thus, makes it impossible to hope. The key misfortune here is not that something unjust or unpredictable takes place. The problem is, rather, that catastrophes, even if imposed by human beings, are accepted as fate. Every attempt to communicate with the authorities, to discuss matters with them, is instantly suppressed. Ai Weiwei's statement encapsulates the continuing reality and presence of the Cultural Revolution. It is an open question whether China is politically or socially equipped to prevent or overcome such catastrophes in the future.

Küpper (1998, p. 223), reflecting on Hans Blumenberg's late work *Höhlenausgänge* (1996 (English: "Exits from the Cave")), characterises the acceptance of and acquiescence in the contingency of existence as "the last possible response to the absolutism of reality". This final answer, however, is a purely philosophical solution and does not represent "the whole truth". Human beings cannot avoid grappling with the problem of contingency in their practical living. The modern era, as contrasted with all previous ones, offers a specific model for overcoming contingency, one that strives to integrate contingency into a higher complexity—which itself is again contingent. The will to overcome contingency is demonstrated in attempts both to change and to understand the world. Blumenberg (1996, p. 791) is fully aware of this double face of modernity. He describes philosophy as "the art of resignation", which makes no "life-practical offers"; at the same time, he speaks of "practice", which, regardless of any philosophical attitude of resignation, is integral to human life. The control of nature through technical progress is not enough to overcome the contingency of existence. If Chinese society is to prevent future social catastrophes like the Cultural Revolution, it must ask how the arbitrary actions of the powerful can be kept under some control. Topics such as democracy, the rule of law, and the institutionalisation of human rights cannot be evaded now in China. The avoidance of social catastrophes, never guaranteed, depends on the will to overcome contingency. The modernity of China can be gauged by its ability to generate this will.

## References

Ai, W. (2009). Haishi zai lushang [Still on the road]. www.bullogger. com/blogs/aiww/archives/317498.aspx. Accessed 24 September 2009.

Bauer, W. (1989). *China und die Hoffnung auf Glück: Paradiese, Utopien, Idealvorstellungen in der Geistesgeschichte Chinas.* Munich: dtv.

Bauer, W. (1990). *Das Antlitz Chinas: Die Autobiographische Selbstdarstellung in der Chinesischen Literatur von Ihren Anfängen bis Heute.* Munich: Carl Hanser.

Blumenberg, H. (1996). *Höhlenausgänge.* Frankfurt: Suhrkamp.

Bucher, I. (1986). *Chinesische Gegenwartsliteratur: Eine Perspektive Gesellschaftlichen Wandels der Achtziger Jahre.* Bochum: Studienverlag Brockmeyer.

Cai, Z.-Q. (2005). Multiple vistas of Ming and changing visions of life in the works of Tao Qian. In: C. Lupke (Ed.), *The Magnitude of Ming: Command, Allotment and Fate in Chinese Culture* (pp. 169–202). Honolulu: University of Hawai'i Press.

Chan, A. (2003). *Chinese Marxism.* London: Continuum.

Chen, K. (2004). Bashi niandai zhishi qunti de jueqi [The rise of Chinese intellectuals in the 1980s]. www.dajiyuan.com/gb/4/6/30/n582787. htm. Accessed 15 September 2009. Lecture to the Washington Forum, 13 June 2004.

Chen, S. (2002). *Zhongguo dangdai wenxue guanjianci shi jiang* [Treatises on Ten Key Concepts in Contemporary Chinese Literature]. Shanghai: Fudan University Press.

Chong, W. L. (2005). Hubris in Chinese thought: a theme in Post-Mao cultural criticism. In: C. Lupke (Ed.), *The Magnitude of Ming: Command, Allotment and Fate in Chinese Culture* (pp. 245–271). Honolulu: University of Hawai'i Press.

Diefenbach, T. (2004). *Kontexte der Gewalt in Moderner Chinesischer Literatur*. Wiesbaden: Harrassowitz.

Feng, J. (2003). *Yibai ge ren de shi nian* [Those Ten Years in the Life of 100 Ordinary People]. Changchun, China: Verlag für die gegenwärtige Literatur und Kunst.

Forke, A. (1927). *Die Gedankenwelt des Chinesischen Kulturkreises*. Munich: Oldenbourg.

Forke, A. (1964). *Geschichte der Alten Chinesischen Philosophie* (2nd edn). Hamburg: Gram, de Gruyter.

Fu, S. (1952). Xingming guxun bianzheng [Disputation and vindication of the ancient glosses on "nature" and "destiny']. In: *Fu mengzheng xiansheng ji zhongbian yi* [The Collected Works of Fu Mengzhen—Part 2]. Taipei: National Taiwan University Press.

Fung, Y.-L. (1948). *A Short History of Chinese Philosophy*. New York: Macmillan.

Gänßbauer, M. (1996). *Trauma der Vergangenheit. Die Rezeption der Kulturrevolution und der Schriftsteller Feng Jicai*. Dortmund: Projekt.

Gao, X. (2004). *Das Buch eines Einsamen Menschen*, N. Vittinghoff (Trans.). Frankfurt: Fischer.

Geldsetzer, L., & Hong, H.-D. (1998). *Grundlagen der chinesischen Philosophie*. Stuttgart: Reclam.

Grimm, G. (1922). *Die Lehre des Buddha: Die Religion der Vernunft*. Munich: Piper.

Haar, B. J. ter (S. J.). Violence in Chinese culture: bibliography. Revised 30 October 2008. Accessed 4 August 2009, http://website.leidenuniv.nl/~haarbjter/violence.htm.

Hahn, A. (1998). Risiko und Gefahr. In: G. von Graevenitz & O. Marquard (Eds.), *Kontingenz* (pp. 49–54). Munich: Fink.

Harding, H. (1991). The Chinese state in crisis. In: R. MacFarquhar & J. K. Fairbank (Eds.), *The Cambridge History of China (Volume 15): The People's Republic. Part II: Revolutions within the Chinese Revolution 1966–1982* (pp. 107–217). Cambridge: Cambridge University Press.

He, Q. (2003). Xiandaihua de xianjing [China's Descent into a Quagmire]. Sunnyvale, CA: Broad Press.

Hoffmann, R. (1978). *Kampf Zweier Linien: Zur Politischen Geschichte der Chinesischen Volksrepublik 1949–1977*. Stuttgart: Klett-Cotta.

Holzinger, M. (2007). *Kontingenz in der Gegenwartsgesellschaft: Dimensionen eines Leitbegriffs Moderner Sozialtheorie*. Bielefeld: transcript Verlag.

Hsia, A. (1971). *Die Chinesische Kulturrevolution: Zur Entwicklung der Widersprüche in der chinesischen Gesellschaft*. Neuwied u. Berlin: Hermann Luchterhand.

Hu, Q.-H. (1991). *Literatur nach der Katastrophe. Eine Vergleichende Studie über die Trümmerliteratur in Deutschland und die Wundenliteratur in der Volksrepublik China*. Frankfurt: Peter Lang.

Ji, X. (1998). *Niupeng zayi* [Memory fragments from a cowshed]. Beijing: Verlag der Zentralen Parteihochschule.

Joas, H. (2004). Morality in an age of contingency. *ActaSociologica, 47*: 392–399.

Küpper, J. (1998). Mittelalterliche kosmische Ordnung und rinascimentales Bewußtsein von Kontingenz. In: G. von Graevenitz & O. Marquard (Eds.), *Kontingenz* (pp. 173–223). Munich: Fink.

Lifton, R. J. (1968). *Revolutionary Immortality: Mao Tse Tung and the Chinese Cultural Revolution*. New York: Random House.

Lin, Y.-S. (1979). *The Crisis of Chinese Consciousness: Radical Antitraditionalism in the May Fourth Era*. Madison, WI: University of Wisconsin Press.

Loewe, M. (1994). *Divination, Mythology and Monarchy in Han China*. Cambridge: Cambridge University Press.

Lübbe, H. (1998). Kontingenzerfahrung und Kontingenzbewältigung. In: G. Von Graevenitz & O. Marquard (Eds.), *Kontingenz* (pp. 35–47). Munich: Fink.

Makropoulos, M. (1998). Kontingenz und Handlungsraum. In: G. von Graevenitz & O. Marquard (Eds.), *Kontingenz* (pp. 23–25). Munich: Fink.

Mou, Z., & Zhang, J. (1997). Zhongguo zongjiao tongshi [General history of the religions of China]. Beijing: Social Sciences Academic Press China.

Müller, K. E. (1992). Reguläre Anomalien im Schnittbereich zweier Welten. Zeitschrift für Parapsychologie und Grenzgebiete der Psychologie, no. 1/2 (1992).

Poo, M.-C. (2005). How to steer through life. In: C. Lupke (Ed.), *The Magnitude of Ming. Command, Allotment and Fate in Chinese Culture* (pp. 107–125). Honolulu: University of Hawai'i Press.

Puett, M. (2005). Following the commands of heaven. In: C. Lupke (Ed.), *The Magnitude of Ming. Command, Allotment and Fate in Chinese Culture* (pp. 49–69). Honolulu: University of Hawai'i Press.

Qian, M. (1997). Der Westen versteht den Osten nicht: Gedanken zur Geschichte und Kultur Chinas. Dortmund: Projekt-Verlag. Translated from the Chinese by Chen Chai-hsin and Diethelm Hofstra, with an introduction by Michael Friedrich.

Renz, G. (1996). Zufall und Kontingenz: Ihre Relevanz in philosophischkosmogonischen, evolutionären und schöpfungstheologischen Konzeptionen. Dissertation, University of Tübingen.

Roetz, H. (1984). Mensch und Natur im Alten China: Zum Subjekt-Objekt-Gegensatz in der Klassischen Philosophie, Zugleich eine Kritik des Klischees vom Chinesischen Universismus. Frankfurt: Peter Lang.

Sausmikat, N. (2002). *Kulturrevolution, Diskurs und Erinnerung. Eine Analyse Lebensgeschichtlicher Erzählungen von Chinesischen Frauen.* Frankfurt: Peter Lang.

Schram, S. R. (1991). Mao Tse-tung's thought from 1949 to 1976. In: R. MacFarquhar & J. K. Fairbank (Eds.), *The Cambridge History of China (Volume 15): The People's Republic. Part II: Revolutions within the Chinese Revolution 1966–1982* (pp. 1–104). Cambridge: Cambridge University Press.

Shan, Z. (2003). Wenhua da geming: shenquan zhengzhi xia de guojia zuicuo [The Cultural Revolution: Crimes of the State under theocratic rule]. Dangdai zhongguo yanjiu [Modern China Studies], 3/2003. www.chinayj.net. Accessed 12 May  2009.

Tang, T. (1986). *The Cultural Revolution and Post-Mao Reform: A Historical Perspective.* Chicago, IL: University of Chicago Press.

Wang, X. (2001). Wang Chong de minglixue tixi (Wang Chongs Theorie über das Schicksal). *Kongzi yanjiu (Confucius Studies),* 6: 47–53.

Wang, Y. (1991). Zhongguo zongjiaoshi (Geschichte der Religionen Chinas). Jinan: Verlag Qilu.

Wetz, F. J. (1998a). Die Begriffe "Zufall" und "Kontingenz'. In: G. von Graevenitz & O. Marquard (Eds.), *Kontingenz* (pp. 27–34). Munich: Fink.

Wetz, F. J. (1998b). Kontingenz der Welt—Ein Anachronismus? In: G. von Graevenitz & O. Marquard (Eds.), *Kontingenz* (pp. 81–106). Munich: Fink.

White, L. T. (1989). *Policies of Chaos: The Organizational Causes of Violence in China's Cultural Revolution.* Princeton, NJ: Princeton University Press.

Xu, Z. (2000). *Weile wangque de jiti jiyi—jiedu wushi pian wenge xiaoshuo* [For forgotten collective memory: interpretations of 50 narrative texts about the Cultural Revolution]. Beijing: SDX & Harvard-Yenching Academic Library.*

Yue, H. (1992). *Yizhi yu mingyun—zhongguo gudian xiaoshuo shijieguan zongshu* [Will and Fate—Worldviews in the Classic Epic Works of China]. Taipei: Da'an.

CHAPTER THREE

# Red terror: the experience of violence during the Cultural Revolution

*Rolf Haubl*

The span of years between the founding of the People's Republic of China in 1949 and the death of Mao Zedong in 1976 can be subdivided according to the campaigns proclaimed by the Communist Party and its "Great Steersman": 1950: land reform; 1951: "Suppression of Reactionaries"; 1952: The "Three Antis" and "Five Antis" campaigns; 1955: "Liquidation of Reactionaries"; 1957–1958: "The Anti-Rightist Movement"; 1959–1961: "Three Red Flags", "Highway to Socialist Construction", "Great Leap Forward", "Great Steel Production", foundation of communes; 1963: Campaign of socialist education; 1966–1976: "Great Proletarian Cultural Revolution".

Reviewing the series, it is striking how campaigns aimed at modernising the nation alternate with campaigns intended to identify and combat opponents of the promulgated course. The rhythm suggests an interpretation: every time the Party fails to deliver on its promise of bringing increasing prosperity to the masses, and especially to the peasants, it turns to persecuting men and women who are accused of boycotting the effort.

Perhaps the greatest setback in the modernisation effort comes with the "Great Leap Forward" and the accompanying "Great Steel Production" campaign. China's agrarian society is to be transformed

57

into an industrial one in the space of fifteen years, with steel output the key measure of progress. Mao ordains that a large part of the rural population be pulled out of the countryside and set to making steel. The chosen strategy, the establishment of six million primitive small smelters, does not bring the promised production increase. Worse, the corresponding neglect of agriculture leads to one of the greatest famines in human history (Becker, 1996, pp. 270–277).

These failures undermine trust in Mao by revealing his economic incompetence, and he moves to counter any further erosion of his claim to leadership. The Cultural Revolution, with its explosions of violence and its total war against "landowners" and "rightist devia-tionists", seems to be a bid to divert attention—a murderous distrac-tion that drives all China into a "psychotic state" (Sloterdijk, 2006, p. 267). Of the forty-five to sixty-five million deaths that can be credi-bly laid at Maoism's door, an estimated five to seven million take place in the first three years of the Cultural Revolution.

### Red Guard violence as youth violence

The Red Guards are the active agents of the revolution. Earlier schol-arship saw them purely as a state institution; newer research shows that they must be understood as a social movement, specifically as a youth movement. Members are mostly middle-school pupils and older students, with lesser numbers of younger pupils and still fewer teachers and workers taking part. The following description now seems accurate:

> The movement began among small groups of middle school pupils and spent some time in internal political debates before it received state support and political legitimisation; finally it became an ever widening, collective challenge to all forms of authority. (Yang, 2000, p. 387)

To put it another way, the movement begins spontaneously, and then is instrumented and guided by the state, until it casts off these chains and—from the state's perspective—slips out of control. Freed of all restraint, the Red Guards become ever more violent and also less predictable, changing the targets of their attacks from moment to moment.

The violence of the Red Guards must be understood in the light of the known psychosocial conflicts of adolescence. In China, as in the West, it seems safe to assume, this developmental phase is characterised by wide emotional swings (Erdheim, 2002). Especially on the narcissistic developmental line, the challenge is to fashion a realistic ego ideal, in which phantasies of heroism are moderated to a soberer desire to work on behalf of the Good, whatever the Good, against a particular sociocultural background, appears to be. This progress is not consolidated for quite a while. Adolescents are vulnerable to regressions, notably when the promise is held out that phantasies of grandeur do not, in fact, need moderating, but can be lived out without inhibition. Adolescents might feel hurt by, and vengeful towards, people who suggest that they will not ever reach the imagined heights. If narcissistic regression is accompanied by narcissistic rage against such representatives of the reality principle, the propensity for violence increases.

In China at the onset of the Cultural Revolution (and, to some extent, still today), a strict seniority principle prevails. Older people demand unlimited respect, which younger ones show by suppressing any impulse to criticise. Our thirty-seven-year-old interviewee, Mr Li (4B; see the contribution of Plänkers, pp. 83–120), has this to say about his relationship with his father:

"Whatever we're talking about, my father doesn't see us at all as on an equal footing. The father is the father; the son is the son. That's his way. That's his idea. . . . For instance, when we are arguing about something and he can't win, because his argument just isn't convincing, he will say: 'You have to do it this way, because I'm your father.' I don't get the feeling that he is right, that it actually needs to be done this way, only that I did it his way, giving in to his demand."

This duty to obey is a variant of filial piety, one of the cardinal virtues in Confucianism (Roetz, 2003, p. 96). If a father kills his son in response to persistent disobedience, he can count on a mild punishment or none at all. Lack of piety towards the father, on the other hand, is one of the worst crimes that a son can commit. Even if the father has broken the law, it is a violation of piety to turn him in. A son is expected to protect his father under any circumstances.

This duty of obedience, carried forward under Communism, binds parents to their progeny (and, analogically, teachers to their students) in a love–hate relationship. If the fear of adult authority weakens, the heretofore suppressed rebelliousness is released:

When Mao Zedong mobilises the Red Guards for his purposes, he is seventy-two years old, of an age with the grandparents of those he is summoning to "guard" him against threats from enemies of the revolution—enemies belonging to the parents' generation. He calls youth from all corners of China to Tiananmen Square in Beijing, the spot where he proclaimed the People's Republic in 1949. There, in a grandiose tableau, he takes their personal oath of allegiance. In mid-August 1966, a million Red Guards, dressed in the uniform of the People's Liberation Army, are in action. By the end of the year, they number more than ten million. Mao gives them free rein to proceed with the most extreme brutality against all enemies of the revolution, even those found within their own families. The youths feel honoured and also encouraged in their thirst for revenge. Here is a chance to stand the seniority principle on its head and to violate filial piety without fear of punishment. Being disobedient to the parental generation yet obedient towards Mao, they can find a psychic compromise that frees them from guilt feelings. For the Red Guards, powerlessness becomes power. Instead of fearing the authority of those who had raised and taught them, they can themselves afflict adults with anxiety and terror.

## Constructed class enmity

The Red Guards take their ideological orientation from social categories established decades before. The Communist Party distinguishes three components of the population: the "Red Class", made up of pupils and students as well as workers and smallholder peasants; the "Grey Class" consisting of formerly prosperous farmers, petit bourgeois, and intellectuals; and finally the "Black Class" of landowners, rich farmers, reactionaries, rightist deviationists, and common criminals. Such categorisation is already a form of psychological violence.

In the first place, there are no precise criteria for these classes, allowing assignment to them to be arbitrary. Second, class members are presumed to cling stubbornly to particular attitudes, carried over even from generation to generation. Since these mind-sets are

*Photograph 5.*   Yuan Fengxiang (left) and Deng Guoxing stand in the forced
shame position as they are sentenced to two years of hard labour.
Ashikhe municipality, Acheng District, 12 May 1965.

considered so difficult to change, an individual can be accused at any
moment of having faltered in the attempt to acquire the revolutionary
spirit and to have relapsed into an inbred counter-revolutionary
stance.

The assignment of the Red Guards is to combat members of the
"Grey" and, especially, the "Black" classes. Because the targeted
people are assumed to disguise their motives, they must be turned
over to the authorities.

The class label system involves positive and negative stigmatisation, resting on splitting: the "Red Class" can only maintain its
monopoly of good characteristics because the bad ones are assigned
to the "Grey" and "Black" classes. Thus, the "Red Class" needs its

class enemies and must prevent the "new man" propagated by Mao from actually coming into broad existence. Class identity sets the direction of violence. Men and women of the "Black" and "Grey" classes are inherently guilty. If no plausible miscreants are available, the immediate next step is the "invention of subjectively [arbitrarily] defined class enemies" (Perry, 2002, p. 122).

This regressive Red–Black thinking leaves no room for nuanced examination of reality, the speciality of free-thinking intellectuals. Therefore, this group is defamed in the Cultural Revolution as "stinking Number Nine" in the list of hostile social groups (He, 2006, p. 426). Such troublesome intellectuals are to be replaced by others who have pledged allegiance to The Little Red Book and supposedly think only the standardised thoughts that Mao allows.

### Revaluation of traditional values: teacher as enemy

The first wave of Red Guard violence was directed at teachers and other learned people. Schools and universities were closed and stayed shut for years, with great harm to the Chinese economy. Revolutionary anti-intellectualism privileges physically exhausting work, symbolised by the peasant, over mental work of any kind; the effort expended in learning, the essence of sublimation, is denigrated.

In describing her childhood, Wu (2009, p. 75) reports an episode that illuminates how the student–teacher relationship is upended at this time:

> I knew Chen Congde. He had often come to our home, to talk to Papa and to get extra tutoring. Papa had told us that he was of "good peasant" stock, but a little slow, which was why he had been entrusted to my father for additional help. We exchanged glances. What an astonishing contrast with the modest, respectful student I had known before. "I am Chairman of the Cultural-Revolutionary Committee," he screamed. "Where is the Arch villain Wu Ninkun hiding?" "We have him," someone called from a neighbouring room. Chen Congde hurried there. Two students had grabbed Papa by the arms and hair and yelled, "You're coming with us, spy!"

Instead of being grateful for the special treatment he had received, Chen Congde experiences it as an unbearable dependency. His career as a Red Guard gives him the chance to unburden himself of this feeling in a dramatic way. As a Guard he is allowed, even required, to do what he yearns for: to humiliate his teacher. Given the history of the two, the accusation of spying has a particular meaning: it is the teacher who has seen the particular weaknesses that Chen Congde wishes to conceal, and which undermine his self-image. This is reason enough for the former mentor to be punished. The exclamation "I am Chairman of the Cultural-Revolutionary Committee" is the verbalisation of a manic triumph that seeks to extinguish all actual experiences—including the disappointing realisation that simply belonging to the "Red Class" does not, as the Party promises, nullify or disguise personal lacks. A teacher who has been an unselfish mentor probably must be punished with special severity in order to override the inhibitions induced by gratitude. The prevalence of such ambivalent feelings is shown again in the recollection of the former Red Guard Yuan Gao. He describes how he felt when his favourite teacher was accused of wanting to bring back the times of the Kuomintang. "I tried to banish my sympathy for Li from my mind and focus on his crimes. . . . When I did this, I began to hate Teacher Li. And yet a part of me still liked him" (Gao, 1987, p. 51). Excessive force can be a means of killing off such sympathies. More than that, attacking and destroying those with whom one sympathises testifies to one's revolutionary fervour, shying away from no sacrifice that the Communist Party, perceived as infallible, demands.


## Anarchistic joy in destruction

In its second wave, "Red Guard" violence turns away from the teachers but is unleashed all the more on the guards' own families and on cultural treasures, many of which are destroyed. Red Guards storm private homes and lay waste to them in the search for anything supposedly reflecting "bourgeois taste". Our interviewee Ms He (6B) tells that her older sister was a Red Guard who "denounced" their father as a counter-revolutionary. This leads to a "house search", which fortunately goes smoothly:

> "The Guards came into our home. Our parents loved literature, and
> the fact that their collection included many volumes of Marx's

*Collected Works* wasn't enough to establish their revolutionary creden-
tials; a lot of literary books were confiscated. Also, since my mother
had grown up in a [well-off] family, we had a lot of clothes and other
things at home, and these were all confiscated. [Interviewer: Things
that were considered bourgeois?] Exactly. My father came from a
peasant family, but he was intelligent. He played the violin and piano,
he took photographs, he ice skated, he swam, and at home we still
have many . . . many earlier records, Cantonese music, which came to
be criticised as reactionary, and many other things, they all were
confiscated."

Such searches can be more, or less, violent. Often residents are beaten
because the Guards find something; often because, unexpectedly,
nothing turns up. Frequently, the searches turn into looting, with the
sole purpose of garnering artefacts that can be sold by the looters.

Ms He states that her older sister "didn't think that the consequences [of denouncing her father] would be so serious". We cannot
take this report at face value. Since Ms He has scarcely forgiven her
sister to this day, we can hardly assume that there was a timely apol-
ogy. Yet, her statement captures something of the reality of the early
days of the Red Guards. It seems that pupils and students are often
quite oblivious of the political reach of their activities. There is an
atmosphere of "happening" or holiday. Mao ordains that Red Guards
be given free transportation and lodging wherever they go in the
country.

The early Cultural Revolution, we can almost say, was like a mass
mobilisation of tourism, or a vast pilgrimage movement, dedicated to
spreading the word of Mao's "new man" to the farthest corners of the
nation. While the appetite for violence must not be trivialised, at the
beginning it seems more an exaggeration of aggressive youthful
energy than a systematic political force.


## Chaos

Mao Zedong inaugurates the third wave of violence when he institu-
tionalises the Rebel groups. These are made up of adults, not youths.
With their aid, he "purifies" the Communist Party of elements that
stand in his way. He also deploys these forces against Red Guards
who are not content to be tools of the state. Finally, the "Great

Steersman" sends even worker-soldiers and the army into battle against them. These measures cost the lives of countless members of the millions-strong Red Guards. In addition, about twelve million young people are sent down to the countryside (Bernstein, 1977), where they are supposed to learn from poor peasants, whose own accumulated resentments make for an uncertain reception. "Rustication", ostensibly a benefit, becomes, in effect, a punishment.

Near the end of the Red Guards' career, new revolutionary splinter groups are constantly forming (Pennington Heaslet, 1972), "distinguished by seniority, ideology, personality and support for different Party leaders and external organizations" (Israel, 1970, p. 246). These fight each other bitterly like "warlords" (p. 246), concerned exclusively for their particular interests. Under such circumstances, almost anyone can be a target of persecution. Mr Li, born in 1939 and an engineer at the government railway research institute, captures this atmosphere in his narrative.

Many of the people working at the Institute had studied in the USA. After the start of the Cultural Revolution they are accused of being "capitalist authorities". Mr Li and his department try to shelter them. Then he and his colleagues themselves fall under suspicion of belonging to a certain "counter-revolutionary group", the organisation of "May 16" (for this history, see Sausmikat, 2002, p. 103). "No such group ever existed," says Mr Li; it was an invention of the "central leadership".

The workforce is divided. "Two camps had gradually formed. And it wasn't at all clear who belonged to which side." A rumour is circulated that there is a "list of persons" who are counter-revolutionaries. This is meant to forestall denial. For "as soon as someone was said to be a May 16 element, he had to make a confession". Those who refuse are put under pressure, directly and through their families. Mr Li's wife, for example, is told that she may join the Communist Party, as she has long wished, if she "convinces" him to "acknowledge his guilt". When she declines, Mr Li, like "hundreds" of other suspects, is tortured: "They tortured a large number of people. They inflicted burns on their buttocks with lighted cigarettes." Because of his good background as a "poor peasant", he escapes the worst of the beatings; even so, "it was so unbearable to me that I thought of killing myself". His accusers keep him awake for several nights in succession, interrogating him constantly, a tactic that especially gets to him.

But the power relationships are changeable. Although Mr Li spends two years in a work camp, "later people on the other [the accusers'] side would also be arrested".

As it unfolds, the Cultural Revolution plunges China into an anomic state. The traditional cultural order collapses without the substitution of new rules to go by. Social disintegration spreads rapidly, accompanied by deep psychic uncertainty. Old inhibitions fall away. Social relationships are dominated by fear. Not knowing just who is in charge produces a paranoid readiness to turn to force (Haubl, 2005). A decision to come to terms with any given faction can turn out overnight to have been the wrong guess. Today's perpetrator becomes tomorrow's victim, a perpetrator again the day after that. This history of reversals makes it difficult to this day to confront the past, because it allows a whole generation to claim victim status.

## Shaming and self-criticism as forms of torture

Among forms of violence, the public humiliation of people suspected of being enemies of the revolution is pivotal. We encounter it again and again in narratives of the time.

Someone who has fallen under suspicion has to answer to the "revolutionary masses" in "struggle meetings" in public spaces or stadiums. Denunciations of "crimes" scream from thousands of throats, interrupted by choruses of "Long live the great Chairman, our leader Mao", while copies of Mao's "Bible", *The Little Red Book,* are held aloft. The accused is usually brought in with many others on a long rope, beaten, kicked, and spat upon. The entryway is plastered with wall newspapers in which he is insulted and accused of having "betrayed" the revolution. He has to wear a placard around his neck and a long pointed hat on his head, on which his crimes are written. His face is smeared with black ink. On arrival at the place of the show trial, he is placed on a pedestal. If not executed immediately by a shot to the neck, he must stand there for hours, perhaps on a chair, in order to be better exposed to view. He must keep his head bowed to show shame for his errors. The torture is intensified in the notorious "aeroplane position", described, for example, by Mr Zhao (6A) in his interview:

"My arms were gripped behind my back and forced upwards while my head was pressed downwards. They said as they did it: 'A thousand feet are walking on you, you will never get up again'. My arms were permanently injured; it's as if the muscles are crippled and I can't feel anything any more, my arms are like two sticks."

Postures of submission to the "revolutionary masses"—even this extremely painful one—may have to be maintained for a long time. No cries of pain are expected to escape from the victim. If they do, it is interpreted as intransigence, bringing further tortures.

Someone who is under suspicion might have to suffer through several such "struggle meetings", followed in many cases by exile to a labour camp in the countryside. These sentences are imposed without regard for family separations, which often last for years and are especially hard on children.

The forms of violence sketched here are no invention of the "Cultural Revolution". They go back to the 1920s, when "landowners [are] forced to parade in front of those they have earlier oppressed. Each landowner wears a big pointed hat with a description of his misdeeds written on it". During the Cultural Revolution "students often could not make hats fast enough, and used garbage bags instead" (Daiyun & Wakeman, 1985, p. 157).

Historically, of course, such spectacles have an even longer pedigree. Every culture knows means of torture that incorporate gestures of shaming. The notion of Chinese culture specifically as a "shame culture" is currently popular. This concept goes back to an investigation by Benedict (1946), who hypothesised, relying on the case of Japan, that shame was a prime motivation in Asian cultures, in contrast to occidental cultures more driven by guilt. From its inception, this distinction (Singer, 1971) had a tinge of cultural imperialism; it treated guilt-based cultures as intrinsically superior, shame-based ones as laggardly. There is no empirical evidence that individuals of the two groups really differ in their sensitivities to shame and guilt. Yet, other theories making parallel distinctions have arisen: thus the contrast between (Asian) collectivism and (western) individualism, and between a (western) preference for autonomic concepts of the self and an (Asian) tilt toward heteronomic self-concepts. Even if it were possible to describe China as a shame culture by nature, this would not suggest that Chinese citizens exposed to torture would deal with humiliation differently than would members of other cultures.

*Photograph 6.*   The staff of the *Heilongjiang Daily News* accuses Luo Zicheng,
the work group leader appointed by the provincial Party committee, of having
taken the capitalist road and opposed the mass movement. His crimes are
written on his paper hat. On the wall behind him are portraits of Mao (left),
Liu Shaoqi, Zhou Enlai, Zhu De, Chen Yun, Lin Biao, and Deng Xiaoping.
Harbin, 25 August 1966.

One of the nastiest expectations in "struggle meetings" is that the
victims will become their own accusers, condemning themselves for
the "crimes" others impute to them. They are even supposed to show
gratitude for the lessons they are learning, which will supposedly
show them the way to rejoining the "revolutionary masses".

The Communist Party has always regarded self-criticism (also
called self-correction) as a revolutionary virtue. The practice also has
a place in Party-endorsed child-raising practices. Thus, Ms Liu (5B),
who was ten years old and handicapped at the beginning of the

Cultural Revolution, relates with pride how her father had encouraged her to write self-criticisms: "Yes, my father read my self-criticism and laughed, and that was that." But this release disappears when self-criticism becomes an instrument of terror and a brainwashing technique (Lifton, 1961) that produces a demoralising double-bind: self-criticism can only convince when it is voluntary. But it can hardly be freely given if it has been extracted in "struggle meetings" or under mortal threat. Thus the torturer has the option to discount the self-criticism at any moment on the grounds that it was offered under duress, and to demand its repetition—this time more credibly. At the same time the victim is revealed as a coward who did not dare to stand up for his real opinion, which fact (another turn of the screw) discredits the opinion itself. Only the torturer decides when a self-criticism is to be believed—and he can reverse himself at any time.

Torturing authorities deny that they are arbitrary. Supposedly, there are norms of procedure that allow the victim some control of what happens to him. Perhaps the torturer must believe in the legitimacy of what he does in order not to be confronted with its actual sadism. For a picture of how to torture "in good conscience", we can turn to a scene described by the exiled Chinese author, Lui Zaifu, in one of his autobiographical essays about the Cultural Revolution:

> Some teachers from my school . . . were even hung from beams and beaten. They were supposed to admit to being dregs of the Kuomintang. Red Guards demanded: "Are you dregs of the Kuomintang?" If someone answered "No," that meant he was resisting, so the Guards proceeded by the rules of "severe treatment"—they hung him up and beat him. When he couldn't take the punishment any more and admitted "Yes", the "little generals" would take him down, following the rules for "gentle treatment". Again they would ask him: "Are you a Kuomintang agent?" If he went back to denying it, he was once more deemed a resister, hoisted up, and beaten. When he couldn't stand it and confessed again, "gentle treatment" resumed and he was let down again to stand on the floor. The cycle kept repeating. Only when the "little generals" of the Red Guard were too tired to haul on the ropes, and all the teachers had admitted that they were "dregs", would there be a short break. While catching their breath, the "little generals" would discuss the experience and unanimously agree that this "up and down" embodied the revolutionary norm and the revolutionary line of "now severe, now gentle"; and since all the enemies

had given in at last, the Guards could really be pleased with themselves. (Hoffmann, 2007, pp. 27–28)


### Loss of moral discrimination

Ms Liu (5B) remembers her experience of the Cultural Revolution as
a ten-year-old child. At the centre of her narrative lies a deep confusion. Her parents have always appeared to her as model Communists,
so she cannot understand how they can be attacked by the Red
Guards, who also present themselves as model Communists. Both
claims cannot be true.

Her first experience of how prone the Red Guards are to violence
comes when they force themselves into the house in search of her
father, who has hidden there:

> "The roof our house has little windows. Through the panes we saw
> dark shadows of people. We were so frightened and knew that [Red
> Guards] were there. They really came! A few young giants came in. I
> was little, to my eyes they were giants. I shook like an aspen tree. Now
> I know what that means in your body; I understand the metaphor
> perfectly. You shake so much that you can't control yourself at all.
> . . . I tried to get hold of myself. Don't tremble, don't tremble, not like
> that! I was so afraid and shook like an aspen tree. . . . Later they
> searched our house again. After that I didn't shake when they came. I
> was furious when I saw them. Why are they persecuting my father?"

She tries but fails to control herself. When her father is seized, she
guesses that the Red Guards are going to torture him, a terrible realisation that sweeps over her anew with every new bit of news about
him.

> "I heard such things all day. They said he had been beaten senseless
> and taken to hospital. I had pictures like that in my head. Many people
> came by because they sympathised with my father. The told my
> mother things about his condition, terrible things. I listened and
> suffered terribly."

When her father is released, he says nothing of his experiences. So,
she is still left with hearsay and her own imagination.

"He said he couldn't remember anything. But that can't be right, for he does somehow remember: often he came home from shopping and told me he'd seen someone walking down the street with a tremor. People who had been beaten by the Red Guards had trembling legs and could not walk normally."

To see the father she loves and admires in such a state oppresses her. But she is even more concerned with the doubts that presently arise. "I didn't know if my father was a good or bad person. Intuitively [I knew him as a good man], but politically [he might be a bad one]."

Her confusion increases as her father's persecution continues and she comes across wall newspapers denouncing him: "I brought water and tried to remove them." She herself comes under pressure to write a statement breaking with him. She tries, unsuccessfully:

"It was so hard to write something like that. The teacher read what I wrote and said, 'No, that won't do! You haven't really separated from him.' . . . I had no idea what I should write. Yet my reports on the study of *The Collected Works of Chairman Mao* were always models for the class."

At the same time, her mother also comes under attack and is urged to distance herself from her husband. Unwilling to do this, she has to write self-criticisms; these, however, are not found convincing and only lead to demands for more of the same. Thus, the mother finds herself in a psychic situation similar to her daughter's. She, too, is confused:

"'Am I a good or bad person?' . . . My mother asked me that. . . . Of course she was a good person. In my eyes she was a good person. But she was so confused and she didn't herself know any more whether she was a good or bad person. . . . Yes. You think you're a good person. But you have to keep writing self-criticisms and are accused of things again and again. Then you ask yourself if you are a good or bad person. She was completely confused then."

The same people who torment the parents are often friendly to the child. At one moment they "bully Mother", so that Ms Liu "almost [wanted] to cry but [was] afraid to"; in the next they are patting her on the head: "You're a good child." "I didn't know if they were nice people or evil ones." She learns that people have "two faces", a public one and a private one. "Everyone wants to be seen as a good person"; goodness, however, depends on context: "On campaign, that is in public, people behaved as radicals", because "revolutionary behaviour was a standard for it [being a good person]. The standard was holy. One should meet these demands" that required fighting against the enemies of the revolution. "But people had another [private] side, too. Occasionally they also showed me their pity." Thus seen, radicalism and the associated brutality become matters of a public performance, remaining external to the actors. They do not behave brutally because they are "evil", they must show themselves in this light in order to belong; perhaps also to avoid being persecuted themselves. This is the idea with which Ms Liu tries to comfort herself. At the end of this section of the narrative, she makes what seems like a bid to resolve her doubts by an act of will: "I think there are more good people than bad ones."

This article of faith might also serve to quieten her lasting self-doubt. She recalls an immense internal conflict. On the one hand, she had found "comfort in the thought that [her] father stuck to his guns" and did not abandon his beliefs, as others did, to avoid persecution. This makes her proud, but, on the other hand, she "felt [inexplicably] angry at him", which she found psychically "relieving". The longer her father resists the Red Guards' accusations that he is an "evil" man, the longer she must go on fearing for his life. And her doubts about him keep stirring. Could he not have admitted to the charges, satisfying a *pro forma* demand in order to shield his family, thus being a "good" person? But his resistance excites her sympathy, too. She asks herself: is he a "good" father? Is she a "bad" daughter for asking such questions? These questions persist to this day.

Ms Liu's narrative affords us a deeply impressive insight into the psychodynamics of her experience. If the physical torments are unbearable, the psychic tortures that accompany them are no less so. The gamut of torture methods is aimed at producing a deep disorientation, including in moral distinctions. Considering the experiences Ms Liu relates, we can well understand how "many people (lost) their sense of identity and began to believe that they were exactly the villains their torturers insisted they were" (Thurston, 1990, p. 164).

## Salvaging lost ideals

Only one of our interviewees reports resistance to the Red Guards. Mr Hong (7A) is a high-ranking cadre from the class of poor peasants, a Party member from the earliest days. He has dedicated his life to the Party that freed him from his family's deep poverty. He experienced the Red Guards as a band of "children a dozen years old" lacking in all respect: "They had no scruples, paid no attention to history, did not think of a person's status, whether he was an old cadre." So he challenged them when they forced themselves into his area of responsibility and attacked his peers: "They didn't treat the cadres like people. I picked up the microphone and made a speech harshly criticising the Red Guards. After that the target changed from the others to me."

The Red Guards accuse him of being a counter-revolutionary. He is taken to "struggle meetings" and tortured. "The charge was without any kind of proof, just that I had taken a stand against the 'Great Cultural Revolution'." He does not offer the self-criticism that is demanded. "I didn't give in, though, I didn't want to give in." On the contrary, he provokes the Guards. The harder they beat him, the more

*Photograph 7.*    After a public trial, seven men and one woman are executed by a firing squad at the cemetery of Huang Shan Amid. Northwest of Harbin, 5 April 1968.

he shows them up as dumb boys. They cannot prove why he should be a counter-revolutionary. "Look, the Guards were baffled by me, baffled." Being in the right, though, gives him no real satisfaction. He and especially his wife are tortured all the more. Looking back, Mr Hong says: "I wasn't afraid. No. If only I had been!" He is haunted by the fact that he did not protect his wife. "Oh, how mixed up things were then! Damn it! When I talk about that . . . When I think back . . . Really . . . Really . . . now, I think it was all ridiculous. But in reality I connect these things with my nervous ailment."

At the time of the interview, Mr Hong suffers from a clinically relevant depression, which he himself traces to the time of his persecution, but which he understands as a physical, not a psychic, complaint. This depression is not solely due to guilt feelings towards his wife. More profoundly destabilising to his sense of self is the collapse of his idealisation of the Party, with which he was identified. Mr Hong is the type of the decent revolutionary. He credits himself with being "not spoiled, not morally depraved". He has come into conflict with other cadres who exploited their positions for personal advantage; he has fought injustice in general. In the interview passage where he describes his first "struggle meeting", he emphasises his probity: "As I was led to the criticism meeting, someone called out to me that anybody could be accused, but not I: I was a real revolutionary." This self-image gives him the confidence with which he faces the Red Guards: "As long I have nothing on my conscience that is counterrevolutionary, I'm afraid of nobody."

What Mr Hong fails to consider is the fact that, before the Cultural Revolution, he himself had played the role of persecutor. On behalf of the Party, he travelled the countryside, "gathering evidence and fighting against rightist opportunism". He makes an unstated distinction between just and unjust use of force. For a long time, he refuses to believe that Mao Zedong could know about and sanction what the Red Guards are doing. "It was definitely some left extremist [and not Mao] who caused all that." After a while, though, he begins to have doubts:

> "Our party really wasn't what it had been before. Chairman Mao was also not what he had been before. He did make mistakes, didn't he? . . . But you could say such things only to yourself, in your heart. In public you didn't dare to express doubts about Chairman Mao."

He salvages what he can by positing a change in the Party and in its chairman; this permits him to retain the memory of an earlier time in which his own actions, too, were right. His final verdict epitomises his internal compromise: "Chairman Mao made only one mistake in his lifetime. But this mistake was terrible." This compromise, however, cannot protect him, like so many among the old cadres, from a depressive hollowing out of his life: "I had no big ideals any more."

## Self-inflicted violence: depression and suicide

We do not know how many people developed clinically relevant depression, psycho-traumatic burdens, or personality disorders in the course of the Cultural Revolution. As with the count of deaths, estimates are vague; yet the psychic casualties could outnumber the physical ones, amounting in the end to many millions. The diagnosis "depression" was not applied during the Cultural Revolution. Chinese psychiatry, though in touch with international discourse, went its own way. What in other countries would have been called depression, Chinese psychiatrists described as neurasthenia, a diagnosis applied to Mr Hong. The neurasthenia diagnosis is still largely favoured in China today (Kleinman, 1986)—probably because it casts psychic disturbances as socially more acceptable somatic ones. Depression, especially when it occurs on an epidemic scale, is a political annoyance to totalitarian systems: it undermines the expected public enthusiasm for the officially sanctioned road to utopia. Bad individual morale suggests bad social morale and points to social conditions that have made a self-respecting life impossible.

To be sure, depression is only one of various grounds for suicide. Protest against repression is another. The fact is that thousands of men and women killed themselves during the Cultural Revolution, many in order to escape the violence to which they were subjected. While killing oneself does not contradict Confucian ethics, it is deplored by the Communist Party. In all totalitarian systems, suicide, like depression, strikes the leadership as provocation. Where the authorities claim sole power over life and death, the suicide's choice to decide his own fate is an offensive assertion of freedom—even if official persecution has driven the victim to the fatal step.

Again and again in totalitarian systems we find the practice of "killing" the suicide a second time, or violating the body, thus wiping away the gesture of freedom and showing the authorities' power as absolute:

> One night Sun Maomo's oldest brother got up, went to the nearby pond, and waded out farther and farther, until he drowned. When the Red Guards found his body the next day, they insulted the deceased and threw his mortal remains to the wild dogs outside the city wall. (Wu, 2009, p. 114, translated for this edition)

## Endless terror

Who can count how many people killed themselves during the Cultural Revolution because their egos succumbed in an inner battle with a tyrannical ego ideal? It is beyond question that such tension exhausts psychic powers. Just as mass psychological considerations lead us to expect, a weak ego tries to defend its ideal as long as possible, even at the cost of distorting reality, blocking out the fact that this very defence further weakens the ego. By making himself a charismatic figure, Mao Zedong intends from the start to occupy this psychic position in the minds of his countrymen. As his own mortality looms, he promotes a cult of personality that is supposed to set him above all earthly criteria, including moral ones (Lifton, 1968).

Witness the sacralisation of his words as collected in *The Little Red Book*. To be sure, only a tiny fraction of this text is really his, a fact unknown to the public during the Cultural Revolution. A large proportion comes straight out of Chinese philosophical classics, formerly absolute textual authorities in China. Chinese culture loves citation. Quoted sayings and stories serve as maxims for the solution of concrete life problems. Mao claims his place in this tradition, demanding that his words be received and understood in the same way as the words of Confucian sages in traditional China (Mittler, 2009, p. 39). From this perspective, words are not the bearers of statements that might be true or false, but, rather, eternal, unfalsifiable truth in themselves. Can forty billion volumes of Mao's works printed and distributed be wrong (Barmé, 1996, p. 9)? The practical impact the words had as they were cited and chanted across the land has not been examined to date. It seems likely, though, that the specific content mattered less than the fact that masses of people were induced to speak with one voice.

It is a sacrilege to contradict, even in private, a leader thus deified. Since Mao embodies the ego ideal even of doubters, they come to question their own normality. Ms Song (5A), born in 1921, can describe the circumstances precisely:

> "The situation then was like this: you're a Party member. If a political campaign starts, you have to obey the Party and take part in everything. You have to conscientiously perform the assignment that comes down, right? Everyone wants to be in the front rank and on the left wing. Nobody wants to be neutral or to the right. You want to cut a good figure and show yourself to be as revolutionary as possible. People don't question the Central Committee, do they? If you have doubts about the Central Committee, you immediately wonder if you're normal. [Interviewer: You accuse yourself.] Yes. Often you thought that something about this movement wasn't right. But instantly you'd warn yourself against such thoughts: my mind-set is problematic. I must do a self-criticism, I have problems. It's not the Central Committee that has them. A movement launched by Chairman Mao is always right. I was very orthodox and leftist at that time. I couldn't . . . I believed in the Central Committee. I felt happy to have been born in China. All the other socialist countries had fallen into revisionism; only we had held to the correct line under the good leadership of Chairman Mao, we would never make mistakes. I obeyed Chairman Mao and the Party, did everything they said. I was happy doing that and did not have to worry about thinking." (Laughs.)

Given this psychic constellation, rage wells up when the identification is not rewarded. Thus, Ms Song, who understands herself to "really have fought for the revolution with hand and heart", cannot bear to be suspected of being a counter-revolutionary. After she is publicly accused and denigrated, no one will talk to her any more. Her silence in response draws additional criticism. When she cries, her tears are expressing not least the rage she would like to direct at her tormentors but does not, because they are, after all, acting in Mao's name. Therefore, she turns her anger on herself—and almost suffocates on it:

> "Yes, I often tried to stifle my tears. Once I just about suffocated. You just have to think that you can't survive another day, and you already

feel the anger building up in you, and a single fit of rage is enough to suffocate you. It could really have happened. . . . I felt as if I couldn't get any air. Even if you were dead, nobody would give a hang, I thought. I got so angry that my lungs could almost have burst. I could scarcely move. I could have died in that moment."

Others in similar situations have killed themselves. She knows this. She, too, thinks about suicide but does not make an attempt: "I couldn't have committed suicide under any circumstances, because that would be treachery to the Revolution." Her Party loyalty wins out. She adduces two further reasons for wanting to stay alive: for the sake of her children and because, as she tells herself, "no one will take the trouble to clear up [her] case" if she is gone.

She and her husband, a high-ranking cadre who was also perse-cuted, are rehabilitated in 1976, but this official act is not enough for her. To this day, she feels herself to have been treated with the deep-est injustice. She longs for restitution in the form of an unimpeachable confirmation of her self-image as a virtuous revolutionary. This is not to be had. Who can provide this confirmation, if the guardians of the revolution are themselves discredited? So, there is no one to whom her longing can be addressed: "Oh, I remember what Chen Yi says: 'Good is rewarded by good, Evil is punished by evil. If this does not happen, it means only that the time has not come.'"

If she could recover the happy *naïveté* of the time when she joined the Party, she might be able to forget the violence that has so deeply scarred her memory and her body. Since she herself was compara-tively little tortured, it is the cries of worse-tormented people, over-heard by her, that pursue her: "Just fear, I trembled inside, I had trouble breathing myself, and my heart couldn't stand it." The fear comes back to this day any time she hears a noise that reminds her of the sounds of beating. "I fear the noise of beating so much, that I can't get to sleep [for hours]. When I hear something, I get up and listen. I'm afraid." Flashbacks force us to recognise that past events cannot be made to disappear.

## "You are old, but we are young—Mao Tsetung!"

This is the motto of a "Red Guard", but not of the Chinese one: rather, of a German version (Koenen, 2002, p. 148). During the student move-ment, Mao Zedong becomes an icon of protest for certain political tendencies in Germany, a legitimisation of anti-authoritarian action. This reception of Maoism involves either total denial of the excesses in China, or their romanticisation (Gehrig, Mittler, & Wemheuer, 2008).

While such blind spots have largely been eliminated in the West in the intervening years, the present authorities in China have a difficult time allowing a realistic picture of Maoism to emerge. In its verdict of 1981, the Communist Party described the Cultural Revolution merely as an "error". Guilt is assigned to the "Gang of Four" in order to clear Mao himself of responsibility. From that point on, Party doctrine holds that the Cultural Revolution was 70% good and 30% bad. Under cover of this formula, the Party loosens the ban on public discussion of the violent time. With Scar Literature (Daiyun, 1986) a forum arises inside China in which traumatic experiences can be described and their effects explored. This conversation becomes a germ cell of the Democracy Movement of 1989. The demands of students for basic democratic rights go too far for the Party, however, and the movement is suppressed with military force—in order, it is said, to prevent China from sinking into the chaos of a second Cultural Revolution. So it is that the rather thorough suppression of the work of collective mourning leads to the unhealthy repetition and perpetuation of violence.

On the fortieth anniversary of the Cultural Revolution, a notable article by a contemporary appeared on the Internet. It characterises the excessive violence of the Red Guards as a concealed democratic impulse: "The special character of the Cultural Revolution lies in the fact that it is both a form of red terror affecting the whole people and also a limited form of political freedom for the people" (Hu, 2007, p. 4, translated for this edition).

The author whips himself up into a fantasy of revenge against today's rulers:

In Chinese history we see in every dynasty acts of rebellion against corrupt and venial officials, but when did it ever happen that the masses exposed and combated the bulk of officialdom? It happened exactly once—in the Cultural Revolution! . . . How much more careful they would be, all of today's government officials, heads of companies, village mayors, county directors and school principals, if they knew that in seven or eight years they will face another Cultural Revolution. . . . If officials and government cadres are locked in a cage every seven or eight years and exposed to the free, fearless criticism of

the people, that is not so very different from the election of representatives every four or five years in the West. This Chinese invention,
free criticism of officials generated from the bottom up, has definite
similarities with the free elections that were invented in the West. (Hu,
2007, pp. 10–11, translated for this edition)

In this concept of democracy, violence proceeds from the people,
literally.

> So long as there continues to be no real means for people to put offi-
> cialdom in its place, and so long as people continue to live under the
> rule of work units—just so long will the memory of the Cultural
> Revolution live; more than that, it will be something people long to see
> repeated. This nightmare for cadres and officials cannot be gotten rid
> of. . . . In this light the Cultural Revolution is definitely a destabilizing
> factor for the future development of Chinese society. (Hu, 2007,
> pp. 12–13, translated for this edition)

If this author correctly reads the psychic proclivities of his fellow
citizens, then modern China, with its steadily growing economic
power, is only a lacquered façade. Behind it lies the diffuse penchant
for violence of millions of people who, officially forbidden to remember their history, can form no realistic picture of themselves. At the
same time, Hu Jingbei embodies a pre-democratic Chinese tradition
that visualises the balancing of social interests as something only
accomplished by force, outside the realm of regulated social agreement.

## References

Barmé, G. (1996). *Shades of Mao: The Posthumous Cult of the Great Leader*.
New York: M. E. Sharpe.

Becker, J. (1996). *Hungry Ghosts: China's Secret Famine*. New York: Free
Press.

Benedict, R. (1946). The *Chrysanthemum and the Sword: Patterns of Japanese
Culture*. New York: Houghton Mifflin, 2006.

Bernstein, T. P. (1977). *Up to the Mountains and Down to the Villages: The
Transfer of Youth from Urban to Rural China*. New Haven, CT: Yale
University Press.

Daiyun, Y. (1986). *Als Hundert Blumen Blühen Sollten.* Berne: dtv.

Daiyun, Y., & Wakeman, C. (1985). *To the Storm. The Odyssey of a Revolutionary Chinese Woman.* Berkeley, CA. University of California Press.

Erdheim, M. (2002). Ethnopsychoanalytische Aspekte der Adoleszenz und Omnipotenz. *Psychotherapie im Dialog, 3:* 324–330.

Gao, Y. (1987). *Born Red: A Chronicle of Cultural Revolution.* Stanford, CA: Stanford University Press.

Gehrig, S., Mittler, B., & Wemheuer, F. (Eds.) (2008). *Kulturrevolution als Vorbild? Maoismen im Deutschsprachigen Raum.* Frankfurt: Peter Lang.

Haubl, R. (2005). Vertrauen in Misstrauen: Über paranoide Gruppenprozesse. *Jahrbuch für Gruppenanalyse, 11:* 77–95.

He, Q. (2006). *China in der Modernisierungsfalle.* Hamburg: Hamburger Edition.

Hoffmann, C. V. (2007). Liu Zaifu: essays über die "Kulturevolution". Unpublished Master's thesis in Sinology, University of Freiburg im Breisgau.

Hu, J. (2007). Die Kulturrevolution und die historischen Zyklen in China—zum 40. Jahrestag der Kulturrevolution, T. Zimmer (Trans.). *China-Report, 45:* 1–15.

Israel, J. (1970). The Red Guard phenomenon: precedents and prospects. *Youth & Society, 1:* 245–260.

Kleinman, A. (1986). *Social Origins of Distress and Disease: Neurasthenia and Depression in China.* New Haven, CT: Yale University Press.

Koenen, G. (2002). *Das Rote Jahrzehnt. Unsere Kleine Deutsche Kulturrevolution 1967–1977.* Frankfurt: Fischer.

Lifton, R. J. (1961). *Thought Reform and the Psychology of Totalism: A Study of "Brainwashing" in China.* New York: Norton.

Lifton, R. J. (1968). *Revolutionary Immortality: Mao Tse Tung and the Chinese Cultural Revolution.* New York: Random House.

Mittler, B. (2009). Von verrückten alten Männern, die Berge versetzen wollten. Die Überzeugungskraft der Worte Maos. *Heidelberger Jahrbücher, 52:* 37–60.

Pennington Heaslet, J. (1972). The Red Guards: instruments of destruction in the Culture Revolution. *Asian Survey, 12*(12): 1032–1047.

Perry, E. J. (2002). Moving the masses: emotion work in the Chinese revolution. *Mobilization, 7*(2): 111–128.

Resolution on certain questions in the history of our Party since the founding of the People's Republic of China. www.marxists.org/subject/china/documents/cpc/history/01.htm. Accessed 22 May 2013.

Roetz, H. (2003). Konfuzianismus. In: B. Staiger, S. Friedrich, & H. W. Schütte (Eds.), *Das große China-Lexikon* (pp. 385–390). Darmstadt: Primus.

Singer, M. B. (1971). Shame-cultures and guilt-cultures. In: G. Piers, M. B. Singer (Eds.), *Shame and Guilt* (pp. 59–110). New York: Norton.

Sloterdijk, P. (2006). *Zorn und Zeit*. Frankfurt: Suhrkamp.

Thurston, A. F. (1990). Urban violence during the cultural revolution: Who is to blame? In: J. N. Lipman & S. Harrell (Eds.), *Violence in China: Essays in Culture and Counterculture* (pp. 149–174). New York: State of New York Press.

Wu, E. (2009). *Feder im Sturm: Meine Kindheit in China*. Munich: Knaur.

Yang, G. (2000). The liminal effects of social movements: Red Guards and the transformation of identity. *Sociological Forum, 15*(3): 379–406.

# CHAPTER FOUR

# The Cultural Revolution in the mirror of the soul: a research project of the Sigmund Freud Institute[1]

*Tomas Plänkers*

Our China Project was conceived in the continuing education seminars in psychotherapy for Chinese psychiatrists and psychologists, initiated by Alf Gerlach in Shanghai. The case reports discussed with our Chinese colleagues aroused our interest in the psychological meaning of the dramatic social upheaval brought about by the "Great Cultural Revolution". As German psychoanalysts, we naturally saw parallels with our own history and the now extensive scientific literature on the psychic implications of the Nazi era and in particular of the Holocaust. Investigations such as those of Laub and Auerhahn (1993), Kestenberg (1989, 1993, 1995), Jucovy (1995), Bergmann (1996; Bergmann, Jucovy, & Kestenberg, 1995), Faimberg (1987, 2009), Herzog (1995), Eckstaedt (1989, 1997), and Grubrich-Simitis (1979, 1984)—to name just a few—show clearly that the traumatic psychic structures of one generation affect the next. Thus, it interests us to see whether these findings can be replicated with regard to witnesses of the Chinese Cultural Revolution and their children and whether there are cultural variables that affect the psychic working out of traumatic experiences or which need to be taken into account in interpreting these experiences. For this reason, we structured our investigation as a combination of psychoanalytic, sinological, and social-scientific lines of investigation.

Psychoanalytically, we explored the individual processing of experiences from the Cultural Revolution. Through studying interviews, we sought to establish how traumatic experiences are further dealt with psychically and if or how these aspects express themselves in the participants and in the succeeding generation. Sinologically, the focus is on the extent to which the individual's ways of coping with the past are determined collectively by political discourse: for example, through prescriptive role models of socialistic child-rearing campaigns (see the contribution of Gentz). Furthermore, in social-psychological terms we are interested in the investigation of forms or violence inflicted and suffered (see the contribution of Haubl, pp. 57–82).

To get a better idea of the difficulties to be expected in carrying out the planned interviews and the methodological considerations that would apply, we agreed with our Chinese colleagues to conduct a series of trial interviews, which were carried out in 2003 and 2004. The transcripts were translated and discussed in our project group in Frankfurt; the results of our conversations were communicated to our colleagues in China. In addition, I travelled to China a number of times and met with the project group there. Even this early, it struck us that the Chinese interviewers did their work with a certain restraint: they let themselves be satisfied relatively easily with descriptions of superficial details, avoided probing too deeply on certain points, or abruptly changed the subject when painful memories were brought up. In some cases, the whole topic of the infantile history of the interviewee, so important from the analytic point of view, was simply omitted. We surmised that, alongside a lack of professionalism in interview conduct, there was another factor to blame: that the interviewers themselves belonged to the "second generation". Some of the interview contents were painful to them also, arousing conflicts and spontaneously inducing psychic resistance. This hypothesis was confirmed later. We also asked ourselves what it might mean to the interviewers that the interviews were to be read by westerners. Could there be a tendency to understate painful aspects of one's own history in a presentation for foreign eyes: to soften, to conceal, to play down?

To aid our interviewers in the organisation and conduct of the interviews, we developed a set of guidelines concerning formal and content aspects. The following subjects were to be covered in every interview, allowing a comparative view of how different interviewees dealt with specific topics:

- Biography:
  Experiences in early childhood
  Parents' child-rearing style
  Family origin
  Meaningful events (separations, losses, illnesses, changes of residence, etc.)
  Education and career development
  Choice of partner
  Own family
  Significant relationships
  Psychic symptoms, especially traumatic experiences
- The Cultural Revolution:
  Memories of the Cultural Revolution (as perpetrator and/or victim)
  Personal experiences, especially traumatic ones
  Processing of these experiences
  Opinion of the Revolution, then and now
- Close of the interview:
  How did you find this conversation?

These content guidelines were designed to generate life-history interviews that would include certain standard points, while leaving room for spontaneous narration and sudden inspirations. We saw that a semi-structured format would invite the interviewees to tell their stories at length. Only thus could we get reports extensive enough to permit recognition of structural characteristics, unconscious motives, conflicts, and psychic contents being defended against. This research design is very different from one based on questionnaire data or on interviews that proceed through a series of scripted questions. The insight into psychodynamic structures that this procedure allows comes, of course, at the cost of statistical representativeness. The small count of our interviews is a far cry from the large numbers required for statistical analysis. The choice between these alternatives was, however, not a difficult one. Extensive interviews would allow us psychodynamic, social-psychological, and sinological insights that could be of real use in formulating research questions of general interest. Our approach reflects the high value now placed on life narratives in qualitative psychotherapeutic research (cf. Luif, Thoma, & Boothe, 2006).

Our research method, directed as it was at the surfacing of significant contents, of course required a form of explication going beyond the statistical. It was our goal to take full advantage of the expertise of psychoanalysts in a transparent and verifiable manner. The psychoanalytic reading of a text is orientated to latent meanings that manifest themselves not only in its symbolic contents, but also in its compositional structure and in the countertransferences it generates in the reader. The experience gained by analysts in interaction with their own patients provides an important background. Therapy can, in fact, be seen as a particular form of textual interpretation within the therapist–patient relationship, directed at grasping the layers of emotion, experience, conflict, and defence involved in latent relationship structures.

To guide the formation of analytic assessments, we drafted two evaluative questionnaires: one for the first generation containing thirty-eight questions, and one for the second generation comprising thirty-one. Then we gathered a group of five psychoanalysts, persons deeply acquainted with the land and culture of China, some of whom had taught in the country for years. Each read the interviews without consultation and filled out the appropriate questionnaire. Then the five met for a so-called consensus rating to establish the overlaps and differences in their evaluations. In order to assure the necessary integration of the individual contributions, this meeting was moderated by myself. Regarding the points of disagreement (naturally the most interesting), the group worked towards consensus by laying out their individual views. A consensual assessment of each interview was arrived at and captured in a questionnaire. When necessary, we also referenced statements from the individual questionnaires. It was interesting to see how much common ground there was among our five experts and how easily differences in assessment were resolved once the bases for each opinion had been thoroughly discussed. Although this method of evaluation was both intensive and time-consuming, we were very pleased with the results. We gained a wealth of psychoanalytic assessments for each interview, the generation of which could be verified and retraced.

In the evaluation of the interviews, we did not, of course, imagine that we were dealing with objective representations of lives: rather, with stories, formed very subjectively, in which certain elements are passed over in silence, briefly mentioned, or painted in broad strokes only. Interested in getting at traumatic experiences, we recognised that the descriptions in the interviews, made many years after the events, reflected years of processing and psychic defence work. Psycho-traumatic impacts were to be uncovered rather than to be found on the surface of the texts. One interesting factor was the order in which interviewees spoke of events. Some speakers followed chronology, while others manifested a certain confusion as to time.

This psychoanalytic assessment was supplemented by analyses from viewpoints of narrative analysis and social science, as shown in the contributions of Gentz and Haubl to this book.

We carried out fourteen semi-structured interviews, seven with members of the first generation and seven with second-generation informants. Six from each group were carried forward for evaluation; one pair did not meet our content requirements. Approximately half of the interview partners in each age group were very motivated to take part in the conversations; they hoped that the interview process would help them deal with their internal conflicts. The participation of the other half seemed initially to be due more to courtesy.

### Some general findings

Basic information about the interviewees from the first and second generations is given in Tables 1 and 2.

### How do the interviewees tell their stories?

The interviewees reveal their lives in different ways. In interpreting them, it is important not to treat them as quasi-objective presentations of events, but as subjective looks backward, undertaken, in many cases, from a post-trauma state of mind.

In general, the interviewees of both age groups were very co-operative, trusting, and friendly to their interviewers. Interviewers could sense that their partners—even those who had initially agreed to take part out of complaisance—were implicitly seeking help with impressions they had not yet come to terms with. In every case, the interviewees presented themselves as they see themselves—that is, there was no distancing in the sense of imagining how matters might

Table 1. Basic data for interviewees of the first generation

| | Mr Zhang 1A | Mr Wang Sr 3A | Mr Li Sr 4A | Ms Song 5A | Mr Zhao 6A | Mr Hong 7A |
|---|---|---|---|---|---|---|
| Age at interview | 66 | 76 | 67 | 86 | 87 | 83 |
| Birth year | 1940 | 1920 | 1939 | 1918 | 1921 | 1924 |
| Siblings: S (sister) B (brother) | S −2, −12 B +10 | S +7 +7, +5, +4 | S −15 B −2, −7, −9, −11, −20 | B −3 | 2 S −3 B +6, +4, +2 −2, −4 | S +10, +7, −7 B +5 |
| Former profession | Internist | Policeman | Railway construction engineer | University librarian | Army political officer | Cadre with rank of section chief |
| Present profession | Retired | Retired | Railway construction engineer | Retired official | Retired | Retired cadre |
| Married? | Yes | Yes, 2nd marriage | Yes, separated 1987–2001 | Yes, 1939–1993 | Yes | Yes, 2nd marriage |
| Children | 1 daughter 1 son | 2 daughters 1 son | 2 sons | 5 daughters 2 sons | 3 daughters | 4 daughters |
| Living arrangement | Lives with son Married | Married | Married | Married | Married | Married |

*Table 2.* Basic data for interviewees of the second generation.

| | Ms Yi 1B | Mr Wang Jr 3B | Mr Li Jr 4B | Ms Liu 5B | Ms He 6B | Ms Fan 7B |
|---|---|---|---|---|---|---|
| Intergenerational relationship | Father–daughter | Father–son | Father–son | Mother–daughter | Father–daughter | Father–daughter |
| Age at interview | 35 | 37 | 34 | 53 | 54 | 50 |
| Birth year | 1971 | 1969 | 1972 | 1954 | 1953 | 1957 |
| Siblings: S (sister) B (brother) | B −1 | S +13, +9 | B +2 | S ++7, +5, +4, +3 2 half-brothers | S +1, −3 | S −3, −6 B +7 |
| Professional training | Studied medicine and psychology | Trained as TV photographer-journalist | University graduate at 20 studied marketing in Russia | | Studied medicine and psychology | |
| Present profession | Doctor | Photographer | Works in administration of a railway research institute | Counsellor to handicapped persons | Psychological adviser and therapist | University professor, lawyer |
| Married? | Yes | No | Yes | Yes | Yes | Yes |
| Living arrangement | Own home | Space in parental home | Space in parental home | Space in parental home | Space in parental home | Own home |

appear to someone else. Apparently, the subjects have great difficulty stepping back from their own experiences, their own judgements. Especially for the first-generation people, who are, after all, elderly, it was sometimes punishing to come into contact with their old hurts. Yet, all the interviewees seemed to feel the urge to unburden themselves by sharing personal experiences with an interested listener—a novel opportunity: for, in every case, this conversation was the first on this subject after years of concealment or self-protective silence.

In three of the first-generation interviews, the predominant narrative style is fragmentary and relies heavily on clichés. No coherent story emerges. Our expert panel understands this to be the expression of a post-trauma state. Our analysts also noticed a change over the course of the interviews, however. At the beginning of the process, when the interviewer is perceived as a threat, descriptive, fragmentary storytelling is the rule, seldom rising to a reflective level. Later, narratives gain in coherence and anecdotes are more developed: signs, perhaps, that an urge towards harmony is beginning to prevail.

## About the interviewers

Our Chinese interviewers were very motivated as they embarked on these conversations. However, it soon became clear that, training sessions notwithstanding, the organisation and conduct of the interviews gave them trouble. In the interpretation stage, at the latest, it was evident that their confrontation with the interviewees' experiences had caused reactions in the interviewers that interfered with the task. The interviewers alternate between moments of empathy and (frequent) unempathic reactions, sometimes making suggestive interventions. It is striking how rarely they go into object relations, and how seldom they probe further at emotionally meaningful moments. A question-and-answer mode predominates. Sometimes, the interviewer changes the subject at exactly the point where psychic suffering is evident and a receptive interview style would be indicated. All this applies to interviews with both generations. Apparently, the interview training conducted beforehand was overridden by the defensive needs of the interviewers. Perhaps we are also dealing with a symptom of early traumatisation, in that lingering concretely on superficial details serves as a substitute for going progressively deeper.

On the other hand, we have asked ourselves whether a cultural, rather than a personal, factor might be at work: whether a weakly developed subjectivity, specifically Chinese, is here evident, a collectively shared avoidance of "private feelings" in communication. In that case, what we interpret as an expression of traumatisation might be merely a cultural habit, a kind of collective numbing.

The yield of a psychoanalytically orientated research interview is the product of both partners. It depends largely on the interviewer whether doors can be opened to psychic contents that have been defensively shut away, or whether the conversation triggers his or her own need to defend against latent traumatic experiences (cf. Henningsen, 2009). Our four interviewers are pretty much in the same boat, biographically and historically, as their partners. As members of the second generation, they are themselves affected, directly or indirectly, by the Cultural Revolution. Furthermore, they share the experience of child-rearing practices widespread in China, including the "handing over" of the child to its grandparents, more or less abruptly and often for long periods.

Our project included a group conversation with the interviewers about their own life experiences. Divers traumatisations were revealed. Interviewer 1, a woman, was suddenly taken from her mother at the age of three, when the parent was sent to work in the countryside. On several occasions, she spent as long as six months in a live-in kindergarten. Her father suffered from depression and attempted suicide several times. When he was publicly accused in the Cultural Revolution, he did, in fact, kill himself. The interviewer was twelve years old then and reacted in conflicted ways: on the one hand, she was terribly sad, on the other, she was furious at her father for abandoning the family. At the same time, she felt guilty because she could not prevent the suicide. At the ages of thirteen and seventeen, she saw classmates beating their teachers. She thinks she survived the Cultural Revolution owing to the social support of peers and other family members. Interviewer 2 says he is still much burdened by unresolved early separation experiences. As a one-year-old child, he was left alone, locked in the home, for long periods while his mother went to work. He feels this experience is the source of his current tendency to depression. Even today, for example, he can hardly bear to be alone in a hotel room.

Similarly, with Interviewer 3: the four-year-old was sent to his grandmother, suddenly and without warning, and stayed there for four years. Interviewer 4, by contrast, is the only one to report positive experiences of the Cultural Revolution period: she grew up in a residential quarter reserved for government officials. Her father was a mid-level bureaucrat who remained neutral during the Revolution. In this period, she felt sheltered by the large group of officials' children. It was a good time, with no school and much play. She experienced no threat to her family or to those she knew.

If the traumatic experiences recounted by the interviewees reactivate similarly painful memories in the interviewers, it is not surprising that the defensive needs of one group are answered by defensive reactions in the other. Both partners participate in the unfolding of a conversation that contains elements both of revelation and of concealment. This is something we know from the training and supervision of analytic psychotherapists: that the therapist conversing with his patient can go no deeper than his own defence needs allow him to. As with every therapeutic technique, our interview method is constrained by the therapist's level of attainment in working through personal fears and conflicts. In spite of these problems, highly interesting interviews were obtained. The evaluating panel believes that the material does allow a good understanding of the psychodynamics of the interviewees.

## What sort of families do the interviewees come from?

Their relationships to their nearest family members were complicated in that many of them did not grow up in their families of origin. Of six people, two grew up with grandparents, one in a foster family. Remarkably, it appears that only one, Mr Zhang (1A) was actually raised in a family that left him untraumatised and allowed him a steady development of relationships and attachments. Four of the interviewees (3A, 5A, 6A, 7A) were found to be subject to early separation traumas or to existential fears produced by radical poverty.

When the talk in the interviews turns to early relationships, whether to parents or grandparents, we usually hear of a depressive attachment to the mother or grandmother (3A, 4A, 5A, 6A). Not so with fathers: among all the interviewees, the representation of the father is either lacking or negative. Either the father is barely mentioned, or hate and disdain predominate. The early mother relationship seems to dominate in all cases.

In contrast to the second generation group, all but one of the older interviewees come from families with many (three to seven) children, Strikingly, however, relationships with siblings do not emerge as narrative elements. Whatever is said on the subject takes the form of concrete details: for example, the need to support the family of a brother (6A) who had hung himself in the course of the Cultural Revolution, or that siblings obey and look up to the informant (4A). Only Mr Hong (7A) gives expression to guilt feelings, because he feels responsible for the early death of siblings.

This relative silence about siblings might be attributed, we surmise, to the advanced age of the interviewees, or to early traumatic experiences that do not permit a family narrative to emerge.

## *What are the central experiences of the first generation during the Cultural Revolution?*

When our interview subjects speak of the Revolution, they tend to present themselves as victims: they lay out the acts of violence they have suffered and their consequences. It is far more difficult, apparently, to discuss any role as inflictor of violence; feelings of shame and guilt seem to intervene. Only Ms Song (5A) acknowledges having done something to someone else: she searched through personal files for so-called "impure elements" and denounced those she found. In two other interviews, a perpetrator role is vaguely indicated. It is really to be expected that the interviewees had experienced both roles. In the ten years of the Cultural Revolution, perpetrators and victims frequently changed places as rival factions rose and fell, each persecuting, then being persecuted. Many people were also forced to take part in public accusation meetings.

Germans reporting their experience of the Nazi era, it has been noted, also exhibit this selective memory, to be interpreted a psychic defence process. Personal participation in destructive–narcissistic actions, as in the participation in a totalitarian movement, produces what the Mitscherlichs (1967) have called an "inability to mourn" (see also Bender, 2006). In these remarks, we merely suggest a possible interpretation. We do not seek to diminish the personal authenticity of the very real sufferings presented in our interviews. Psychic defence is not the same thing as untruth: rather, it is partial truth.

The sheer quantity of violence reported as suffered or witnessed by our small number of interviewees is impressive. On the one hand, they describe force inflicted on others. For instance, Mr Zhang (1A) tells of one of his professors who, having denounced "Soviet imperialism", was publicly branded as a right deviationist. Another professor had dared to say that a word of Mao's was only a word, departing from Lin Biao's dictum that every word of Mao's was worth 10,000. For this "crime" he was driven through the streets in a public parade, fitted out with a dunce's cap, dustpan, and broom, and he had to accuse himself: "I am Zhang Yong, an active counter-revolutionary!" After this, he jumped to his death from the fourth floor of a building. Another university employee, accused of having an "incorrect lifestyle", was publicly humiliated by being forced to wear around his neck a chain made of red ping-pong balls.

The interviewees were witnesses to suicide (1A, 4A, 5A), torture (4A, 7A), and arrest (5A). They also had to experience people of their own social milieux—people to whom they were close and from whom they had never expected such conduct (such as students)—turning suddenly violent.

More space, naturally enough, is devoted to descriptions of violence suffered by the informants themselves. We will hear at greater length from three of them.

Mr Wang Senior (3A, compare also p. 144) describes an attack of Red Guards on his home, after he had been denounced as a "landowner": "They beat me all night long and destroyed everything in the room." In addition, he was publicly humiliated: "The next day the Street Committee called a public accusation meeting. The words "landowner" and "arch villain" were written on a big sign." He was tortured: "The shirt I was wearing stuck to my cuts with the blood. They tore the shirt off, got salt from the kitchen and sprinkled it on the wounds." Then he was locked in a "little dark room". In spite of his job as a policeman, he was later sent to the country for re-education. He could not take his children with him.

Ms Song (5A) describes how, after the beginning of the Cultural Revolution, her husband was arrested and then jailed and tortured for years. Then the attention turned to her: "I was persecuted because of him." She was "the stinking woman of a traitor!". Wall newspapers were put up about her. She was arrested, sent to the country (1966–1972), forced to write self-criticisms, and exposed to petty harassment (being required, for example, to turn in her criticisms at night). She experienced many humiliations and accusations, violence, homelessness (dissolution of the family: seven family members sent to six different locations), minimal living quarters (destruction of intimate space), social isolation (none of her former comrades would speak to her), hunger, and the deaths of two children. She saw the destruction of lives (the many suicides) and health.

Mr Zhao (6A) was initially mocked in wall newspapers and by public display, being led through the streets in a dunce's cap, accompanied by the beating of gongs. Then he spent three and a half years in isolation in the "doghouse", a small kennel at a laboratory without light and with little air. Later, he spent four more years in a re-education camp. Family visits were not allowed. There were marathon interrogations during which he was supposed to make "confessions". His wife petitioned on his behalf, but was given the run-around. He was badly beaten and forced to assume unnatural, painful postures. He had to write down sayings of Mao hundreds of times over. He was taken to the top of a building and urged to commit suicide. After the isolation period, he did hard physical work for years in the name of "re-education" in a cadre school in the country. His father died "of shock" when Mr Zhao was denounced as a counter-revolutionary. After witnessing his humiliation, one of his brothers hanged himself.

The interviewees of the first generation are united by a broad range of outrages endured. They had to suffer the violation of the private sphere (for instance, destruction of household goods, 3A) and of family togetherness (3A, 5A). Their careers were damaged (1A). They were persecuted (5A, 6A, 7A), publicly accused and humiliated (1A, 5A, 6A, 7A), insulted (1A, 6A), socially isolated (5A), jailed (5A, 6A), and tortured (6A). In the name of retraining, they underwent traumatising practices of "brainwashing" (3A), rustication (5A), the writing of self-criticisms, re-education camps, and marathon interrogations under torture. These practices were not new. The Communists began using them shortly after their victory in 1949. Lifton (1961) impressively described "brainwashing" and its results. Prolonged physical violence combined with constant interrogation and ideological instruction aim at the creation of a traumatic state in which the victim is ready to take anything in, to believe and assent to whatever his tormentors want to infuse him with. The scientific label "menticide" expresses the goal of the process far better: the partial or entire destruction of the personality.

Yet, these types of physical and psychic torture are only extreme forms of the permanent ideological barrage to which the population was subjected during the Cultural Revolution. An example known outside China through Bertolucci's film *The Last Emperor* is the case of Pu Yi, last of his dynasty, who underwent "re-education" meant to change him from monarch to simple comrade. It is striking that only the extreme forms of brainwashing are mentioned in our interviews, not the constant, daily forms, expressed in the ideological uniformity of the media, schools, and universities, the bombardment of whole neighbourhoods with radio broadcasts, the wall newspapers, the criticism meetings, and the courses devoted to *The Little Red Book*.

In addition to violence aimed at a reformation of thought, our interviewees experienced plenty of violence that seemed to be inflicted for its own sake. 3A's tormentors, for instance, beat him with leather straps, rubbed salt in his wounds, urinated in his children's food, and destroyed his household effects. 4A reports night-long interrogations, sleep deprivation, and blows. 6A was interrogated under torture, beaten so badly that his legs were permanently crippled, and smeared with sewage; cigarettes were stubbed out on his skin; his head was kicked and knocked against the wall; he was forced to strip naked and driven toward suicide. Interviewees suffered the death of family members (5A, 6A) and forced labour in camps (4A, 6A).

## What are the psychic effects of these experiences?

It is hardly surprising that the all of interviewees of the first generation suffer severe and chronic effects from what they have been through. This is especially the case when we consider that some of the interviewees entered the period with a heavy load of prior psychic traumatisations. Five of the six cases show traumatic experiences as children, either through early separation from the primary objects (3A, 5A) or through extreme poverty (4A, 6A, 7A) of a sort reported even today in the Chinese countryside. Children are sometimes left to their own devices in the search for food. One informant tells us that his family possessed only one pair of pants, reserved for whoever had

*Photograph 8.*   Governor Li Fanwu, accused of looking too much like Mao, has his hair brutally cut and pulled out by over-eager young Red Guards in the Red Garden Square. Harbin, 12 September 1966.

to go out: "We shared our quarters with pigs, cattle, and donkeys. Often the whole family had only one blanket and only one pair of trousers. Only the person who was going out got the trousers" (6A). In many regions of China, these conditions culminated in politically motivated cannibalism: "Eating class enemies had become recognised as a revolutionary act" (Zheng, 1993, according to Schwarcz, 1996, p. 4). The Chinese dissident Ma Jian reports from villages in the southern province of Guangxi, close to the Vietnamese border:

> I had to think of the pupils ... who slaughtered their teacher during the Cultural Revolution. In order to show their gratitude to the Party, they cooked the pieces of his body in a washbasin and ate them for supper. They found they liked fresh organ meat, and before killing their next victim, they cut a hole in his ribcage and kicked him in the back, so that his liver jumped out into their hands. The villages here consumed an average of three hundred class enemies. (Ma, 2009, pp. 305–306)

In the case of Mr Zhang (1A), the traumatic experiences occurred to his parents, so that he grew up in a family climate marked by fear.

Almost all interviewees report prior traumatisations and, thus, a heightened susceptibility to the traumas of the Cultural Revolution. Their capability of processing, of mentalizing, the serious experiences they report was severely limited even before 1976:

> Missing out an early attachment experience (as for the Romanian orphans) creates a long term vulnerability from which the child may never recover—the capacity for mentalisation is never fully established, leaving the child vulnerable to later trauma . . . (O'Connor et al., 2003, Rutter & O'Connor, 2004; quoted in Fonagy, 2008b, p. 7)

This limitation is shown also by the manner in which memories from the Cultural Revolution are brought up in the interviews. The reports tend to be purely descriptive; only seldom do we see reflection or the taking of a position on what was undergone.

The effects of traumatisation anticipated under the rather superficial rubric of post traumatic stress disorder (PTSD) appear: five of our interviewees show symptoms of PTSD. These are primarily: thoughts and memories that well up unwilled (3A, 4A, 5A, 6A, 7A), symptoms of overstimulation (3A, 5A, 6A, 7A), and avoidance behaviours (4A, 5A, 6A, 7A). The self-esteem levels of five of the six subjects were assessed as bad or fragile by our experts. Only Ms Song (5A) is found to have good self-esteem.

The victims suffer from the sudden appearance of images from the past, as expressed, for example, in Interview 3A:

> "When I remember it, I feel pain, nothing but pain. The memory of this time is unbearable. Often I don't even dare to think about it. . . . The place where I live now, for instance. When I see the courtyard, enter the building or see the objects, then I remember it. When it snows in winter, then I remember: it's snowing now. On the day that I was exiled, it was also snowing. A big truck, the bundle of sheets, a board, two wooden benches, lots of snow. When it snows, I remember back then. When I arrived, I was white as a snowman and terribly cold. Certain feelings are connected to certain scenes."

Or, in Interview 5A,

> "I was afraid of the sound of people being beaten . . . Since then I can't listen any more, when people are beaten. . . . Every time I tremble inside. I can't stand hearing beatings, or crying or screaming."

And, in Interview 6A,

> "In the Cultural Revolution—I won't tell you details—I was locked
> into a doghouse for three and a half years. Then I was sent to a cadre
> school for re-education by hard labour, three years locked up. These
> were my best years, when I could have done good work for the Party.
> After the Cultural Revolution, everything collapsed in my heart."

In the aftermath, the speaker withdrew socially and developed a sort
of emotional numbness.

I would like at this point to discuss a specific form of traumatic
punishment that seems characteristic of Asian cultures and was practised incessantly during the Cultural Revolution: public shaming, the
deliberately induced "loss of face". This was achieved through humiliations such as the wearing of dunces' caps and "confession" of errors
at public meetings. Here, the victims had to remain for long periods
in the so-called "aeroplane posture", a forced kowtow to the "revolutionary masses" that is extraordinarily painful. In Interview 6A, this
form of public stigmatisation is described thus:

> "My arms were gripped behind my back and forced upwards while
> my head was pressed downwards. They said as they did it: 'A thou-
> sand feet are walking on you, you will never get up again.' My arms
> were permanently injured; it's as if the muscles are crippled and I can't
> feel anything any more, my arms are like two sticks. It was hard for
> me. . . . Then the Rebel put his foot on the chair, he had a whip in his
> hand, he interrogated me. They grabbed me by the arms, ran their
> fingernails into my flesh, it bled."

In a culture where shame plays such a central role, this kind of
humiliation has an existentially traumatising effect parallel to that of
physical torture; it plunges the victim into a social void.

This must be understood against the background of the Confucian
tradition still dominant in China. Confucius (ca 551–479 BCE) created
a new image of human character: no longer determined by nature and
the spirits of ancestors, but by moral attitudes. Confucius introduced
something like "humanism" or "enlightenment" into Chinese thought
(Bauer, 2001, pp. 57–59), but at the price of an enormous strengthening of the superego. The emphasis was placed on the individual's
place in the hierarchy, on the honouring of rituals, on family ties.

Confucius saw shame as a central regulating affect for society. Even more than by laws, the state is sustained by

> a generally accepted consciousness of what is proper and what prevents people from violating social norms: namely shame and the fear of disgrace. Shame is a great political force. In a society based on good faith and honesty, it hinders people from breaking the boundaries of custom. Whoever does so nevertheless is subject to shame, through which he loses respect, 'face', and is excluded from society. (Wickert, 2002, p. 46)

Alongside shame, the attitude of respect or reverence is especially important. In this culture, centred on the place of the individual within the group, it is the violation of social linkages that is most likely to draw the punishment of shaming.

Recent psychoanalytic reflections on the concept of shame emphasise exactly this intersubjective dimension (cf. Bohleber, 2008; Schüttauf, 2008). Shame calls into question the core of narcissistic balance, self-respect, and is connected with the unconscious, infantile phantasy of losing the loving attention of the mother. Since the mother is *the* primary object, the loss of her devotion amounts on an unconscious level to an existential rejection. Before language develops, the eye, the gaze, is the central organ linking child with mother; therefore, it plays a central role in shame. The shamed one cannot bear to be seen. The Asian metaphor "face" has to do with this relationship through looking or regard: whether one can recognise oneself in the gaze of another, feel oneself appreciated there, and return appreciation in the same manner. Much more than guilt, which, of course, also damages self-respect, shame attacks the basis of self-esteem. Shame impinges psychically on the relationship to the primary object and socially on the relationships that carry our sense of ourselves.

Even today in China, a professor is significantly higher up the ladder of prestige than in Western cultures. To lead such a person through the streets in a humiliating masquerade, exposing him to ridicule, was intended to produce a fatal loss of "face" and make him incapable of facing others. Public shaming is a show aimed at producing social death, the ejection from society—not infrequently answered, in the China of the Cultural Revolution, by the victim's physical suicide.

*Photograph 9.*    On the steps of the North Plaza Hotel in Harbin, a venue for
Red Guard criticism meetings and mass demonstrations, a group of Rebels
forces the leader of a rival faction to kneel and subject himself to criticism
(Harbin, 17 January 1967).

"Just as the outward show of shaming culminates in exposure, the
internal process culminates in the sudden recognition that one has
been destroyed in the eyes of others" (Schüttauf, 2008, p. 845). The public accusations were supposedly unmaskings, revealing that a previously esteemed member of society has been secretly acting as its enemy
and now belongs to the "stinking number nine". This was how intellectuals were branded during the Cultural Revolution: as the ninth
category in a list of enemies, following "landowners, rich peasants,
counter-revolutionaries, evil powers, right-wingers, traitors, spies, and
powerful people taking the capitalist way" (He, 2006, p. 426).

The parallels to the preliminaries to the destruction of Jewry in the
Nazi era are evident. Here, too, it was supposedly a matter of exposing "enemies of the German folk community", bringing about their
public humiliation and making them ridiculous—a prelude to the
industrial-scale destruction to come. This historical comparison also
illuminates what is distinctive in Chinese culture. A much more thorough uniformity of thought and action was achieved in the China of
the Cultural Revolution than in Nazi Germany (cf. Lifton, 1961, 1968).
Since individuals valued and defined themselves much more in terms
of the surrounding society, they were much more wounded, at the

basic level of self-acceptance, by social rejection. Thus, public humiliation often resulted in suicide, as it did not in Germany.

To return to our research result, looking back on the Cultural Revolution, most of the interviewees feel a mixture of depression and rage. Their verdict on the period is thoroughly negative. Mr Zhang expresses this vividly. Reacting to the Party's official assessment that the Cultural Revolutionaries' actions were 70% right and 30% wrong, he demands, "What does this mean, 70% or 80%? I don't believe it, it's 100% wrong." Of the interviewees of the first generation, three regard the revolution as "rule by the primitive masses", as a "chaotic, terroristic, and anarchic happening", as a catastrophe provoked by power struggles at the top. Two spoke rather neutrally of an error; only one interviewee spoke in a distanced manner of "an episode in the great river of the revolution". It is not surprising that their relationship to the political authorities of the country was also negatively influenced. Most express something between disappointment in, and rejection of, the current powers-that-be. Instead, they emphasise their own principles (3A) and independent thinking (5A).

These results correspond with the assessment by Goldman (1986), who posited that the Cultural Revolution would make Chinese people more sceptical of their political leaders and harder to sway. This might apply to those who experienced the revolution themselves, but what about the following generations? Our interviews with the second generation show that the negative attitude toward the political authorities is no longer dominant. The majority conforms, though two informants (5B, 6B) emphasise their very critical relationship to the leadership.

The East Asia specialist Sausmikat (2002) cites Zuo Jing, who said, "We, the generation that was born in the 1970s, are not interested in history, prefer to know nothing about it, and concern ourselves with other things". She believes that the state, or particular strong social groups, have so overdosed the population with history, in a politicised and ideologised form, that something like an allergy has set in: people simply want nothing more to do with history, with memory even.

## Some characteristics of the second generation

Most of our informants (four) get their information about the Cultural Revolution from family members, the remaining two from other sources. Four of the interviewees give the impression of having actively sought information about the revolution; two are passively accepting. Half of them think they know quite a bit about their parents' experiences, the other half report little knowledge (1B, 3B, 4B). Four of six assess the effects of the Cultural Revolution on their own family as serious, two as minor (1B, 4B). Like the first generation, they more or less agree in their negative verdict on the revolution and its catastrophic consequences for the population. Only Mr Wang Junior attempts to make a distinction between the ideals of the Cultural Revolution and the manner in which they were implemented.

## On the psychodynamics of the second generation and of intergenerational transfer

What does the material gathered tell us about whether, and in what ways, the traumatic experiences of the first generation have affected the second? The kind of transmission we are concerned with here is less the conscious sharing of knowledge than an unconscious process: what Faimberg (1987, 2009) labels "telescoping". First, we asked the interviewees how they consciously assess the ramifications of their parents' Cultural-Revolutionary experiences for themselves. Four of the group speak of lasting impact, while two assess the effects as slight or non-existent (1B, 7B). Then, we examine childhood experiences as described to draw indirect conclusions regarding intergenerational transfer.

Five of the six interviewees portray their parents' child-rearing as very demanding, strict, and achievement-orientated (1B, 3B, 4B, 5B, 6B). Ms Yi says about her father, "His pedagogical principle was—beat them! Beating is the way to produce children full of filial piety."

Just three of the interviewees find positive elements (warmth, love, stimulation) in their parents' behaviour towards them. Five report a negative mother relationship in the sense of cool distance, disappointment, or hatred. This often forms one pole in a split between mother and grandmother, with the latter experienced as a positive alternative. In three cases, however, the father is the alternative love object.

Significantly for the question of intergenerational transfer, three of the six interviewees report infantile (separation) traumas (3B, 5B, 7B), and those interviewees who experienced the Cultural Revolution as children report traumatic loss experiences related to it (5B, 6B, 7B). Experiences are traumatic to the degree that they overtax children's capacities to understand and integrate. At the time of the interviews, we could confirm a post traumatic stress disorder diagnosis, in the sense of the *ICD-10*, in only two of the interviewees, while one more, Ms He (6B), showed a post-trauma personality disturbance. All three, however, exhibit excessive arousal symptoms. Generally, we assess the psychic health of the second-generation interviewees as between good and moderate, thus plainly better than that of the first generation.

Transgenerational transmission is more clearly evident in the psychodynamics of the interviewees of both generations. Here, we can definitely conclude that the second generation is significantly handicapped in its ability to experience and to relate: an effect of trauma reinflicted by the parents, as well as of unconscious processes of identification.

\* \* \*

Mr Zhang (1A), born in 1940 and sixty-six years old at the time of the interview, describes his family of origin as "an intellectual family", imbued with Confucian values:

> ". . . practically everything was Confucian. We were told again and again how to behave toward others: that you should do good, that you should not get into fist-fights with people outside the family, that you should learn to make concessions so as not to come into conflict with others."

Apparently, there were formative experiences of loss. An uncle died fighting in the civil war, a pivotal and terrifying moment in his parents' lives. "My father and mother didn't want to see any films about war." At the age of twenty-five, Mr Zhang, the oldest of three children, lost a brother who was ten years his junior. Mr Zhang was apparently a good student, popular with his teachers. At the beginning of the Cultural Revolution, he was attending a medical college and lived in the associated central hospital. Soon, he was confronted with the public denigration of docents and professors, with endless meetings and compulsory lectures. Teachers were branded as "rightist deviationists" and driven to "suicide". This made him very anxious and afraid of "getting sucked in". Although he was forced by his fellow students to join them in "revolutionary actions", he emphasises that he had no part in "shenanigans", that he had carried out no radical acts. He describes his stance during the Cultural Revolution as "neutral": "After that I became one of the neutrals, I didn't get involved in such things." He stuck to this attitude throughout his time in school: "So I basically experienced these things, but I practically never took part in them." The sudden intrusion of the revolution into his life back then was apparently so shocking that even now he cannot grieve about it. He says simply, "The Cultural Revolution ought not to have happened." In retrospect, though, Mr Zhang regards his conduct during the period as "cowardly". He says that this cowardice was based on a great timidity that he acquired from his parents. "Anyway, my father and my mother were very cowardly." He connects the sleep difficulties and hair loss that afflicted him at the time to suppressed anger.

At the time of the interview, Mr Zhang has an extraordinarily clear opinion about the events of the Cultural Revolution and about Mao Zedong: "I find that the Cultural Revolution ought not to have happened. It is Mao's greatest mistake. It brought a terrible catastrophe to the nation. It was a fatal error."

He sees little hope in the current political situation, either. "Today everything is being liberalised, we've gone from one extreme to the other." At the time of the interview, he is a timidly conforming, conflict-avoiding person whose underlying mood is subdepressive–resigned. He has a marked inhibition of aggression, wants to avoid violence in every form, and shows a strong need to orientate himself by norms of reasonable behaviour. He is still identified with the Confucian training imparted by his parents.

Through identification with his father, he developed a stern super-ego and a high ego ideal. He lives, so to speak, more in his superego and ego ideal than in his ego, and shows an over-valuation of Confucian achievement goals. His inhibition of aggression has also handicapped him in his career. This could reflect unconscious guilt feelings from the violence he witnessed in the Cultural Revolution. He makes self-accusations on several other fronts, too: he was stupid, did not try hard enough, made bad choices.

His two children were born in 1971 (daughter) and 1972 (son).

*   *   *

Ms Yi, Mr Zhang's daughter (1B), is thirty-five at the date of the interview. She centres the conversation on her problematic relationship with her father. Ms Yi says she "did not grow up as a happy child". The main cause of this is her relationship to her father, who escaped his expected fate as a farmer through his medical studies, but did not "entirely reach his goal". In compensation, he pressed his daughter to study extraordinarily hard: "He loads his wishes on to his children. I am the oldest and have a younger brother. He projects all his wishes on to me"; "His pedagogical principle was—beat them! Beating produces children full of filial piety." This made Ms Yi frightened and nervous: "I was really afraid of the beatings"; "I was very nervous"; "Yes, very frightened. After all a child is afraid of being hit." In her second year of school, she began falling back, whereupon her father had her repeat the grade:

> "I repeated the second grade and felt disgraced. I found myself with kids the age of my younger brother . . . I lost face by staying back. After that I worked very hard and became good again in school."

A little later, she passed the entrance exam for the Chinese medical university: "My father was very proud of me." During the following nine years, at ages 15–24, she lived at university and visited the family only at weekends. At first, though, distance did little to lessen her father's supervision. Again and again, Ms Yi emphasises the burden imposed by his demands.

Yet, in spite of her fear of him, behind the psychic and also physical pressure he applied, she also posits a positive concern: "Later I understood that study was my only escape from being a village farmer."

Ms Yi speaks little about her mother. "The influence of my mother is—well, much less than my father's." Her farmer grandmother, though, is more present in the interview. This is the only person from whom she experienced a loving, caring attitude:

> "I think my grandma influenced me more than my mother. . . . I was always with her, from when I was very little . . . I was still nursing when my mother became pregnant again. She couldn't take care of me any more and shoved me off on my grandma."

At the same time, the grandmother represents the life from which she is trying to distance herself. The child's behaviour towards her grandmother probably expresses the resulting tension: "I didn't return her kindness enough." She still feels strong guilt feelings on this account. When the conversation turns to her grandmother, she is overcome by her emotions and weeps. She describes the relative as "kind, timid, and cautious", as "not strict", and "not very demanding or picky". The grandmother's death when Ms Yi was nineteen deprived her of the opportunity to atone for the guilt she felt towards the older woman.

In the unfamiliar new environment of the university, Ms Yi later developed an eating disorder. In hindsight, she guesses that an "inferiority complex" lay behind it: "At the university I found myself surrounded by many excellent students and suddenly was no longer at the top." In an attempt to approach her ideal image of a girl— "tender and cuddly as a little bird"—she fasted during the day, but succumbed at night to hunger attacks. The result was the opposite of her intent. "I wasn't just tall, but fat, too. I felt bad and withdrew." By this time, the pressure from her father was lessening, yet the pressure she applied to herself only grew: "My fear of father subsided, because he wasn't around. But I was more worried about my appearance." Her relationship to food normalised itself only years later, after her marriage.

In her choice of husband, Ms Yi took the advice of her father and decided on a man who did not fit her "ideal image of the other sex". They have a son together, but disagree about matters of gender roles and child-rearing.

Through contacts, Ms Yi found a job, and she began her study of psychology, which continues, and which she says helped her to become more self-reflective. The relationship with her father seems to have stabilised:

"My judgement of him is like today's judgement of Chairman Mao. Did he do great service? Yes, great service. Did he make mistakes? Yes, he also made mistakes. He did not make these mistakes with evil purpose. His capabilities were limited. He was a prisoner of his time. As one person, he could only do so much."

Her relationship to her husband has changed, too: "I feel the quietness in me"; "I have become aware that I want this or that thing from him, want to change him according to my idea. That isn't right."

On the one hand, she thinks that the Cultural Revolution did not leave "too much of a mark" on her family. She also thinks that "these influences were not passed on to me". Based on "the verdicts of others" and "books and films", she accepts that the Cultural Revolution was "surely a bad time in our history"; yet, her personal impressions do not confirm this.

Ms Yi seems psychically identified with the image of the strict, intropressive father. She adopted the severe superego that he modelled for her. She also strikes her daughter, for example, and is every bit as focused on achievement as her father was. At the same time, we diagnose a disturbance of her female identity. In both generations, we understand the drive to achieve as a defence against emotional realisation of one's own weaknesses, fears, traumatic life experiences, and fears.

*   *   *

Mr Wang (3A; see the contribution of Markert, pp. 143–162) was born in 1920 and was aged seventy-six at the time of the interview. As a small child, he appears to have suffered a separation trauma: the two-month-old infant was given to his grandparents. He felt loved and favoured by his grandmother and developed an idealised, symbiotic relationship to her. Her death—when the subject was only twenty-three—was a "terrible blow": "I jumped into the grave and wanted to follow my grandmother." He fell into a deep depression. This lightened when he married at age twenty-five and had two daughters. His wife, however, died in 1964, throwing him back into despair. The next turn of the screw was the Cultural Revolution. The Red Guards destroyed his house, beat and tormented him; he was arrested (three weeks) and later exiled (four years). He was subjected to every cruelty and humiliation. In addition, his wife's death of breast cancer when he was thirty-four plunged him anew into depression. He was forced to remarry, partly to secure care for his children, but then his new wife refused to take on this role. A divorce was not allowed and he suffered severe guilt feelings towards the children. The relationship to his second wife remained bad. Externally, he is doing better, but he is sick, hardly capable of movement, and would like to die. At the time of the interview, Mr Wang presents as cumulatively traumatised with symptoms of post traumatic stress disorder.

Mr Wang Junior (3B, cf. the contribution of Markert, pp 143–162), born 1969, is aged thirty-nine at the date of the interview. He is the son of the second marriage of Mr Wang Senior, a relationship he paints as quarrelsome. In his first year of life, he had a liver infection; in his fourth, he suffered feelings of loneliness and bit his nails. In early childhood, he developed the stutter that plagues him to this day. Up to the age of three, he was left alone, locked in at home; he grew up rather isolated from the exterior world. The parents thought that the neighbourhood children would "spoil him and be bad influences on him". His childhood was also marked by poverty, blows, strictness, speechlessness, and the constant quarrelling of his parents, who ignored his needs and him as an individual. He developed a close, highly ambivalent bond with his mother. Mr Wang compares the household atmosphere and his parents' child-rearing style with "brainwashing". "Things were hammered into you" and "drummed into you". At the date of the interview, he shows himself to be crippled in the development of his autonomy; he lacks the feeling that he can shape his life independently. He tends to tamp down his feelings, to withdraw from society, and to keep his distance from the other sex. We wonder how strong his homophilic tendencies might be. To social contact, he prefers withdrawal into daydreams and phantasy worlds. He is a film fan. He seems incapable of forming bonds. He seems able to stand relationships with other people only at a distance. Otherwise, they overtax him quickly; he experiences them as pressure and pulls back—while at the same time longing for "spiritual comfort". He feels his life as empty (he thinks only about what he *does not* want); he is unhappy and touchy (has fits of rage). Structurally, he appears sub-depressive.

Like his cumulatively traumatised father, the younger Wang experienced an early separation trauma, in this case through being frequently left alone, locked in, up to his third year of life. His marked psychic withdrawal and the narcissism linked to it reflect a failure of linkage in childhood. The traumatised father was apparently incapable of finding the positive maternal object in his second wife. The pattern repeats with the son. To this extent, the son's narcissistic pathology also reflects a defensive posture toward unbearable traumatic experiences.

\*   \*   \*

Mr Li Senior (4A) was born in 1939 and is sixty-seven at the date of our interview. He grew up in deep poverty and had early experience of war (with Japan), civil war, massive deprivation, cold, and hunger. Three of his eight siblings died shortly after birth. He grew up with his maternal grandparents, and apparently was often left to his own devices. His mother had to beg, which filled him with shame. In 1961, when he was twenty-one, his father and maternal grandmother died of starvation. Probably this left him with guilt feelings: "If my maternal grandparents had had a son, maybe they wouldn't have starved to death." In the Cultural Revolution he was accused of links to the "Organisation of 16 May", arrested, placed in a labour camp, and tortured. The images of these terrible events persecute him; he does not want to talk about them any more. Cumulatively traumatised, he shows a defence against these experiences in the form of an emotional numbness. Yet, the suffering that Mr Li experienced specifically in connection with the Cultural Revolution seems to pale in comparison with his long-standing existential and familial stress.

* * *

Mr Li Junior (4B) was born in 1972 and was thirty-four years old at the time of the interview. He is the second son of Mr Li Senior. As a small child, he apparently experienced little emotional resonance or empathy from his traumatised parents. His mother was to him a fear-inducing object, a source of blows; he developed a massive, unconscious hatred for her, which he controls through marked reaction formations, through willed indifference and exaggerated dutifulness. He seems emotionally closed. As a boy, he was rather feeble and often humiliated. He found an alternative object to his mother not in his distant father, but with his paternal grandparents, especially his grandmother, who was his one sure source of love and security. To her, he developed a tight and positive bond. He experienced his father as absent, disinterested in him. "When my mother beat me, he did nothing." The father was, however, also authoritarian; he could not bear contradiction. His shouting and attacks of rage were "terrible", a "horror". An earthquake caused the boy to be separated from his parents in his second and third year and sent to live with his grandmother and his brother (two and a half years older). This move probably magnified his inner distance from his parents. At the time of the interview, he seems rather fatalistic, gets little satisfaction from his work, and regards his marriage as a loveless matter of duty. He experiences his wife, unconsciously, as like his mother: strict, aggressive, unloving.

His father's emotional numbness, authoritarianism, and choleric disposition, results of the older man's accumulated traumas, certainly contributed to the want of empathy the son felt at home. The negative relationship experiences of his childhood, combined with his parents' divorce, replay themselves in his own marriage, which disappoints him as much as his father's did him. Here, also, we see a definite relationship incapacity as the consequence of earlier negative relationship experiences, which are, in turn, the product of the father's traumatised state.

\*    \*    \*

Ms Song (5A), eighty-six years old at the time of our interview, was born in 1918. She suffered an early separation trauma at the age of three, when her mother died and she was moved to a foster family that she experienced as exceptionally strict, rigid, and unempathetic. She coped with the experienced coldness and the beatings by fleeing to an alternative interior world: she read a great deal and so managed an "escape to the secret place". At the age of seventeen, she realised this secret escape in concrete terms, leaving the family to join the Communists. Here, she found an idealised alternative world and an idealised husband, nine years her elder. She believed she had found a world full of harmony, a place where nothing was lacking. The Party became for her the essence of the good object, to be defended against any perceptions that might undermine it. She worked selflessly for others, thus showing devotion to the projected needy part of herself. Further traumas were the deaths of two of her seven children, the first of whom died of hunger in 1941. She wards off the emotional impact of the violence she has experienced, as well as of her persecution and isolation during the Cultural Revolution, by believing these things to be necessary sacrifices for the Party's sake. She maintains an impassivity that presumably dates to her childhood. Other things she tells us about—her severe early panic attacks, her thoughts of suicide, and her current ultra-sensitivity to scenes of violence—give us a glimpse of what lies behind this defensive formation.

\*    \*    \*

Ms Liu, born to Ms Song in 1954 and fifty-three years old at the time of the interview, is the only other person mentioned often in her mother's interview. As an infant, she fell ill with polio; later, a congenital heart disease became evident. She was handicapped as a result and even today needs crutches to walk. Illness brought a series of traumatising treatments; for instance, she once spent a year in hospital. On the other hand, her condition brought her much more parental attention than her siblings received: she was, in fact, spoiled.

This experience gives her the feeling of being a special person, with a strong sense of self-esteem. Even before starting school, she had mastered the writing of fifty Chinese characters. Independence became a primary goal for her. At nine years old, she already had to take care of herself, and from the age of twelve she lived alone. Since her mother was absent and not very empathetic, the relationship with her father became primary. Spending more time at home than the mother, who went off to work, he took great care of his daughter, played with her, and taught her to read and write. Ms Liu appears to be very identified with her father.

During the Cultural Revolution, she had to see these idealised parents, especially her beloved father, accused, arrested, and tortured. The image of her father after torture is still terrible, unbearable for her; the memory of his blackened legs, for example, is traumatic. These experiences gave rise to traumatic fears of loss.

Yet, Ms Liu developed a good ability to sublimate. She is helpful and sympathetic. Even as a child she was good at imaginative play and storytelling, and is well able to keep herself occupied when alone.

During the Cultural Revolution, her relationship to her mother was characterised by role-reversal, or parentification. They were sent together to a school for cadres. The mother, more traumatised, used the daughter as a container, "dustbin", or "tape", a place to offload the trauma of the situation in order to endure it. By a process of identification, Ms Liu developed great empathy for the sufferings of others, in whom she meets a projected component of herself. At the time of the interview, she works as a counsellor to the handicapped. She stabilises herself by helping others.

\* \* \*

Mr Zhao (6A), born 1921, is eighty-seven years old at the time of the interview. He comes from an extremely poor family with little education. He and his seven siblings were mostly left on their own. In his first sixteen years, his family offered him little sense of security ("No one was there for me"; "There was no way out"). He has always felt deep sympathy for poor and disadvantaged people. At seventeen, he joined the army, one year later the Communist Party. There, he learnt Communist theory, which he built into his ego ideal as promising a friendly and—above all—just world. The Party became a substitute family.

His life is punctuated by experiences of terrible violence and shows an accumulation of traumatic experiences. His early childhood was marked by extreme poverty, lack of emotional support, and absence of physical and emotional security. There are, none the less, signs of a deep connection with, or longing for, his mother. This mother, illiterate, is said to be "kindly". Whenever possible, she shared her limited means with others; Mr Zhao identifies with his mother in this regard. When he comes to tell how his mother, years later, fell to her knees to beg that he be spared from a beating, he almost sobs.

Mr Zhao also underwent trauma as a prisoner of the Japanese, where he experienced mistreatment and forced labour and witnessed extreme cruelty. He was in mortal danger at times and also thought of suicide.

Escaping from the Japanese, he next became victim of his own Communist Party, which suspected him of being a spy. Once more, and long before the Cultural Revolution, he was the object of persecution, hours-long interrogations, and discrimination.

It was the Cultural Revolution, though, that brought his most severe traumatisation. He was stigmatised as a spy, right deviationist, and counter-revolutionary; for two years he was locked into a "dog-house"; he spent another four years in a forced labour camp. He underwent torture and humiliations. Although he toyed with the idea of suicide, he ruled this out as an implicit admission of guilt: "You'd be lucky if you could just die!" He derived support from his wife and children, who accompanied him to the re-education camp. "These were my best years, when I could have done good work for the Party." "After the Cultural Revolution, everything collapsed in my heart." He never recovered from the shock of being tormented by members of the very Party to which he had devoted all his powers and which gave meaning to his life.

His self-image is determined by a tyrannical ideal of the "good Communist", which still forbids him to compromise, even when such refusal harms him. He has constantly had to try to bring his personal experience of violence into accord with his idealised picture of Communism. This effort has almost driven him crazy, especially since he is constantly suppressing his hatred.

Through suppression, extenuation, denial, and explaining away, he attempts to maintain his Communist ideals. For example, he deploys philosophical ideas in an attempt to cut the ground out from under his resentment, saying, for instance, that "the Cultural Revolution was just a necessary episode in a revolutionary process". He is trying to forgive, or, at least, to hold his vengeful impulses at arm's length.

At eighty-seven, Mr Zhao is a broken man who is clinging with his last strength to his ego ideal, all the while being buffeted by Parkinson's disease and by a deep, suicidal depression with sleep disturbance (excessive arousal syndrome). Further symptoms of the latter are irritability, affectual intolerance, and inability to concentrate. He suffers from unbidden memories and thoughts of traumatic experiences and tries to avoid the reactivation of such experiences. Completely discouraged, he experiences his life as senseless and actually would just as soon arrive at its end.

*  *  *

Ms He (6B) is the second of three daughters (the others one year older and three years younger, respectively) of Mr Zhao. She was born in 1953 and is fifty-four years old at the time of the interview. She grew up with a very traumatised father (see above) and with a mother who was absent, very busy professionally, and unable to meet the needs of her child. As a consequence, she developed a great emotional distance from her mother. She says "there was a lack of emotions at home". At the age of three, she was sent away to a live-in kindergarten, which produced anxiety and insecurity. Like her father, then, she suffered an infantile separation trauma. These early separation and abandonment experiences made her an insecurely attached child.

When Ms He was about ten years old, the Cultural Revolution erupted into her life. "Through the Cultural Revolution", she says, "the life of the family was fundamentally changed"; "Yes, destroyed." The family's protection disappeared. She experienced her father's humiliations and felt great fear, despair, and powerlessness. She read a lot and created a fantasy world for herself, "because the real world had shown itself to make no sense at all—because it was impossible to identify with it." Thus, she remained alone with her hatred and her fear. She feels the consequences even now as anxiety, uncertainty, and hostility towards people in general. She developed a withdrawn character dominated by these emotions. Her uncertain attachment in her adult object relationships mirrors that of her father.

*  *  *

Mr Hong (7A) was born in 1924 and is eighty-three at the time of our interview. He is the fourth of five children (a brother five years older, sisters ten and seven years older, and the last sister seven years younger). The family was very poor. They lived in a cave, and, as a child, Mr Hong had to forage for his own survival. Along with hunger and lack of clothing, he emphasises the poverty of words, explanations, and education. Because he feared being blamed and shamed, he could speak to no one about his traumatic experiences. For instance, a sister died when the family cow pushed her off a cliff. It would have been his job to lead this cow to pasture, and he had refused. Now he thinks that his desire to keep on playing was what cost his sister her life. At about eight years old, he fell into a well and nearly drowned. He denies having been terrified, but since then he has had symptoms that can be understood as somaticised fear. His father was "a bad character" who often beat him pitilessly; once the boy pleaded, "Just finish it and beat me to death!" His mother was emotionally closer to him. When he wailed with pain, she rocked him in her arms, but she could not intervene. At fourteen, he enlisted in the army.

Leaving home proved rather calming. With his mother's death shortly after his entry into the service he lost his last positive emotional connection to his biological family. Now his family was the Communist Party and the army. During the war against Japan and in the ensuing civil war, Mr Hong must have experienced terrible things, which, however, are hardly touched on the interview ("fought a lot of battles"). The Cultural Revolution brought more abuses. He was physically attacked and knocked down by the Red Guards; his wife was mishandled. The overall impression, though, is that the traumatisations Mr Hong suffered before the revolution affected him significantly more than those that happened during it.

He developed a contraphobic way of handling the fear-inducing situations that mark his entire life. His rebellion against his father continues as a permanent rebellion against military, political, and professional authorities, and he enacts this revolt without considering the negative consequences for him. Because he felt himself pursued by early guilt, he could not stand having guilt assigned to him. He saw himself always as in the right and engineered tests of strength, sometimes in an arrogant spirit and sometimes as a matter of survival, in which he by no means always prevailed.

His life fell apart when his wife died and he had to care for three children. "My wife's death was a catastrophe for me"; "the sky fell down." Here, again, he presumably feels haunted by guilt, for his wife's illness began shortly after the end of the Cultural Revolution, from which she suffered longer than he did, though he tried to protect and to hide her.

The relationship to his second wife lessened his acute depression without eliminating what he calls his "depression syndrome". As he ages, it becomes even stronger; it is difficult to distinguish the components of depression and beginning dementia. Mr Hong has cancer (concerning which he is inadequately informed) but is fighting more than that. He feels sick: forgetful, confused, dizzy, lacking appetite or interests. Stomach pains, headaches, and insomnia reach far back into his childhood. He feels so guilty that he questions whether he has a right to live. His exhaustion is also an expression of guilt feelings that he is less and less able to control. His "depression syndrome" centres on these feelings, in combination with unprocessed traumatic experiences.

*    *    *

Ms Fan (7B), fifty-three years old at the time of the interview, is the second of Mr Hong's four children (a brother seven years older, sisters eighteen months and six years younger). Her elder brother was premature and died; she was a "replacement child". When she was a year and a half old, her first sister was born. Because both parents worked, the two were raised by substitutes, Ms Fan by her grandmother and an aunt. Presumably, she suffered traumatically from the separation from her parents; the children's resistance against being sent away to a five-day sleep-over kindergarten speaks of this. "Who wanted to go to kindergarten? Nobody. A car picked us up on Monday, brought us back on Saturday." There are probably several different kindergartens. As a result, she possesses no secure connection to her parents. Her mother cast Ms Fan as the model for her younger sister, so that Ms Fan felt favoured. When she was fifteen, her mother fell ill with cancer. Ms Fan sees this as a reaction to the death of her father in an aeroplane crash as well as to attacks undergone in the Cultural Revolution. For the three years of her mother's fatal illness, Ms Fan cared for her and occupied the maternal position in the family; presumably, she was chronically overtaxed; her own interests took a back seat. At the same time, she functioned somewhat as her father's wife, grew very close to him, but was disappointed by him in her oedipal love.

Ms Fan witnessed the persecution of her parents in the Cultural Revolution from close up: the mother was badly humiliated; the father, who took a stand against the Red Guards, was beaten; the household was looted. Ms Fan experienced these events as a traumatic de-idealisation of her parents, even though it was her father's courage that prevented worse things from happening.

Ms Fan unconsciously re-enacts the separation experiences of her childhood, in the active position, by leaving her still-young daughter with a grandmother while she works in a faraway job. She travels to Hong Kong, returning to visit her family at long intervals. "We really didn't pay a lot of attention to our child, but she seemed to be growing up fine."

\* \* \*

This concludes a brief summary of our interviews under the aspect of transgenerational transmission of traumatic experiences. Certain methodological difficulties (compare the contribution of Plänkers, pp. 83–120) impede a quick answer to the question of whether and how psychotraumata of the first generation intrude into the psychic structure of the second (telescoping, after Faimberg, 1987, 2009), take on a particular object status in that structure (transposition, after Kestenberg, 1989, 1993, 1995), or cause the formation of a mentalization gap (Laub & Auerhahn, 1993). A definitive answer to the question would entail a considerably more detailed and nuanced psycho-diagnostics of all family members than we could realise in our investigation. We are limited in our conclusions owing to having interviewed only one first-generation parent in each family, to having seen each interviewee just once or twice, and to the professional limitations of the interviewers.

Nevertheless, our expert reviewers found that the available material concerning the first generation was helpful in creating psychodynamic understanding. However, it was less so for the second generation, where the review found adequacy in only half the cases.

Despite these limitations, our examination of parental function in the first generation, and our psychodynamic assessment showing parallels in the two generations, do yield strong evidence for unconsciously powerful identifications that have led to the repetition of traumatising behaviour—accompanied by defensive stances that block the emotional or intellectual appreciation of these consequences.

## Note

1.    Supported by the Foundation for Psychosomatic Disorders.

## References

Bauer, W. (2001). *Geschichte der Chinesischen Philosophie: Konfuzianismus, Daoismus, Buddhismus*. Munich: C. H. Beck.

Bender, T. C. (2006). "Die Unfähigkeit zu Trauern"—ein Verdrängtes Fragment Psychoanalytischer Sozialpsychologie. Unpublished lecture, Freiburg im Breisgau, Germany, 30 June 2006.

Bergmann, M. S. (1996). Fünf Stadien in der Entwicklung der Psychoanalytischen Trauma-Konzeption. *Mittelweg, 36*(5): 2, 12–22.

Bergmann, M. S., Jucovy, M. E., & Kestenberg, J. S. (Eds.) (1995). *Kinder der Opfer, Kinder der Täter: Psychoanalyse und Holocaust*. Frankfurt: Fischer.

Bohleber, W. (2008). Zur Psychoanalyse von Schamerfahrungen. *Psyche— Zeitschrift für Psychoanalyse, 62*: 831–839.

Eckstaedt, A. (1989). *Nationalsozialismus in der "Zweiten Generation': Psychoanalysen von Hörigkeitsverhältnissen*. Frankfurt: Suhrkamp.

Eckstaedt, A. (1997). Traumatische Folgen des Nationalsozialismus in der 2. und 3. Generation—Eine Spurensuche. Unpublished lecture.

Faimberg, H. (1987). Die Ineinanderrückung (Teleskoping) der Generationen: Zur Genealogie Gewisser Identifizierungen. *Jahrbuch der Psychoanalyse, 20*: 114–142.

Faimberg, H. (2009). *Teleskoping. Die intergenerationelle Weitergabe Narzisstischer Bindungen*. Frankfurt: Brandes & Apsel.

Fonagy, P. (2008b). Bindung, Trauma und Psychoanalyse: Wo Psychoanalyse auf Neurowissenschaft trifft. Unpublished lecture at Joseph Sandler Research Conference, Frankfurt.

Goldman, M. (1986). Religion in Post-Mao China. *Annals of the American Academy of Political and Social Science, 1*: 145–156.

Grubrich-Simitis, I. (1979). Extremtraumatisierung als kumulatives Trauma: Psychoanalytische Studien über seelische Nachwirkungen der Konzentrationslagerhaft bei Überlebenden und ihren Kindern *Psyche—Zeitschrift für Psychoanalyse, 33*: 991–1023.

Grubrich-Simitis, I. (1984). Vom Konkretismus zur Metaphorik: Gedanken zur psychoanalytischen Arbeit mit Nachkommen der Holocaust-Generation—anlässlich einer Neuerscheinung. *Psyche—Zeitschrift für Psychoanalyse, 38*: 1–28.

He, Q. (2006). *China in der Modernisierungsfalle*. Hamburg: Hamburger Edition.

Henningsen, F. (2009). Psychisches Trauma und posttraumatische Belastungsstörung (PTBS): Übertragung und Gegenübertragung bei Diagnostik und Therapie. Unpublished lecture at Saxony Institute for Psychoanalysis and Psychotherapy, 30 January 2009.

Herzog, J. (1995). Welt jenseits von Metaphern: Überlegungen zur Transmission des Traumas. In: M. S. Bergmann, M. E. Jucovy, & J. S. Kestenberg (Eds.), *Kinder der Opfer, Kinder der Täter: Psychoanalyse und Holocaust* (127–146). Frankfurt: Fischer.

Kestenberg, J. S. (1989). Neue Gedanken zur Transposition: Klinische, therapeutische und entwicklungsbedingte Betrachtungen. *Jahrbuch der Psychoanalyse, 24*: 163–189.

Kestenberg, J. S. (1993). Spätfolgen bei verfolgten Kindern. *Psyche—Zeitschrift für Psychoanalyse, 8*: 730–742.

Kestenberg, J. S. (1995). Überlebende Eltern und ihre Kinder. In: M. S. Bergmann, M. E. Jucovy, & J. S. Kestenberg (Eds.). *Kinder der Opfer, Kinder der Täter: Psychoanalyse und Holocaust* (pp. 103–126). Frankfurt: Fischer.

Laub, D. (1998). Empty circle, children of survivors and limits of reconstruction. *Journal of the American Psychoanalytic Association 46*: 507–530.

Laub, D., & Auerhahn, N. C. (1989). Failed empathy, central theme in survivors' holocaust experience. *Psychoanalytic Psychology, 6*: 377–400.

Laub, D., & Auerhahn, N. C. (1991). Zentrale Erfahrungen des Überlebenden: Die Versagung von Mitmenschlichkeit. In: H: Stoffels (Ed.), *Schicksale der Verfolgten. Psychische und somatische Auswirkungen von Terrorherrschaft* (pp. 254–276). Berlin: Springer.

Laub, D., & Auerhahn, N. C. (1993). Knowing, not knowing: massive psychic trauma, traumatic memory. *International Journal of Psychoanalysis, 74*: 287–302.

Laub, D., & Podell, D. (1995). Art and trauma. *International Journal of Psychoanalysis, 76*: 991–1006.

Lifton, R. J. (1961). *Thought Reform and the Psychology of Totalism: A Study of "Brainwashing" in China*. New York: Norton.

Lifton, R. J. (1968). *Revolutionary Immortality: Mao Tse Tung and the Chinese Cultural Revolution*. New York: Random House.

Luif, V., Thoma, G., & Boothe, B. (Eds.) (2006). *Beschreiben, Erschließen, Erläutern. Psychotherapieforschung als qualitative Wissenschaft*. Lengerich: Papst Science.

Ma, J. (2009). *Red Dust. Drei Jahre Unterwegs Durch China*. Munich: Schirmer-Graf.

Mitscherlich, M., & Mitscherlich, A. (1967). *Die Unfähigkeit zu Trauern*. Munich: Piper.

Sausmikat, N. (2002). *Kulturrevolution, Diskurs und Erinnerung. Eine Analyse Lebensgeschichtlicher Erzählungen von Chinesischen Frauen*. Frankfurt: Peter Lang.

Schüttauf, K. (2008). Die zwei Gesichter der Scham. *Psyche—Zeitschrift für Psychoanalyse, 62*: 840–865.

Schwarcz, V. (1996). The burden of memory: the Cultural Revolution and the Holocaust. *China Information, 11*(1): 1–13.

Wickert, E. (2002). Wir Tugendländler—Die biederen Deutschen haben plötzlich die Korruption im Haus: Ein Vergleich mit den ethischen Vorstellungen Chinas. *Frankfurter Allgemeine Zeitung*, 27 April, p. 46.

# CHAPTER FIVE

# Psychic trauma between the poles of the individual and society in China

*Tomas Plänkers*

The world we live in is only superficially civilised and only partially accessible to our control. This fact underlies our modern sense of life and contributes greatly, as Sigmund Freud noted as early as 1930, to our chronic uneasiness and anxiety. In spite of all international institutions and diplomatic efforts, war, famine, poverty, and social catastrophe seem unavoidable. Many people perceive that our ordered life is insecure and is subject to dangers that can emanate, in our time, from any corner of the globe. Despite a hundred years of psychoanalytic teaching, the analogously perilous condition of our psychic world is not so universally grasped. Freud's early (1923b) model of the personality suggested the image of an iceberg: just as most of the berg's mass is below waterline, the unconscious—the unsocialised part of the mind—is more extensive than the conscious. According to Freud's initial theory, neurosis arises when traumas stored in the unconscious break through into consciousness. This first trauma theory posited an injury initially inflicted from outside that becomes troublesome later in life when it is given a secondary meaning (deferred action). It was only later (1920g, p. 35) that Freud made room for the thought of an essentially endogenous trauma, in which psychically unintegrated drive impulses produce an overstimulation. According to this more fundamental perspective, our conscious mental structures, built up through socialisation, are constantly endangered by incursions from our unconscious drives. The "Great Wall of China", built to protect a civilised empire from peoples regarded as uncivilised barbarians, is a kind of metaphor in stone for this psychic situation. Like the physical wall, the attempt on the individual level to "civilise" human instincts has limited success. The process of their psychic integration only goes so far; it is a constant of human existence to be in danger of traumatisation from the eruption of the barbaric within us.

We distinguish this "normal" danger of endogenous trauma from specific, exogenous traumata; yet the outside stresses derive their impact from the way they affect the interior trauma landscape. So, we cannot simplistically contrast inner conflict and outer trauma; rather we must grasp their complicated interplay (cf. Bell, 1998; Britton, 2005; Plänkers, 2008a).

Another kind of interchange, that between culture and psyche, demands our attention. Take, for example, the Oedipus complex, which psychoanalysis holds to be universal: it assumes different forms in China than in Western Europe (cf. the contribution of Markert, pp. 143–162). In interpreting a traumatisation, we could be applying psychoanalytic concepts based on theories developed in Europe to persons at home in another cultural context. A basic tension arises between the observer's ways of perceiving and understanding, from which he might not be able to escape, and those of the observed. While this conflict might admit no easy solution, it is not, in fact, so different from what the analyst encounters every day; every patient confronts us with a strange "ethnicity", an unfamiliar inner world. In every psychoanalysis, we try methodically to reach understanding of what is alien. Yet, if the difficulties met in the encounter with a Chinese person are not really different in kind, matters of culture and language do make them substantially greater.

In order to make a decent start at understanding and assessment, we need to arm ourselves with additional knowledge about Chinese history and culture, and about the principles that guide socialisation in China. Let me mention a few aspects that need to be taken into account. In the traditions of Buddhism, Daoism, and Confucianism, the bearing or acceptance of suffering has a central role. This is even symbolised in the Chinese word *ren*, pronounced *shen*, and written as a character composed of the symbol for knife above the symbol for heart. Objects featuring this character are widely sold and seen in many homes. One interpretation of this sign is that one should leave the knife embedded in your heart: if you pull it out, you will die. While other readings are possible, the association of "heart" and "suffering" is key. It embodies the concept of "enduring, bearing, tolerating" in order to become a good member of society. To endure suffering patiently, not to become too excited about it, not to become indignant or to fight against it: these are part of the concept of psychic maturity in China. One accepts the hardships of life, such as natural events. The Cultural Revolution, too, can be understood as "fate", with the character of an "act of god": something bad, something regrettable, but just not avoidable, that must be put up with. In anthropological terms we can speak of "the experience of contingency" (cf. the contribution of Wang, pp. 35–56), something in the cards that cannot be influenced and must simply be endured.

Another cultural angle of vision is important for our investigation of intergenerational transfer: the Confucian ideal of filial piety. This explicitly demands a far-reaching identification of son with father, rejecting outright the idea of the child's individuation.

Making due allowance for cultural characteristics, there are certain natural limits to what the mind can "digest", to use a more colloquial image for the containment function: what can be absorbed without injury to psychic functioning. The Chinese do not fail to sense these limits. In China, too, a violent breach of them produces trauma. In China as in Europe, the conditions under which trauma occurs and the effects it produces must be investigated on an individual basis, honouring the individual biography as a structured history of meaning. Unquestionably, the concept of psychic trauma in all its aspects is psychopathologically relevant for the Chinese. A painstaking, individually orientated diagnostic process is just as necessary in China as in the Western world, for the aetiology and symptomatology of trauma are extremely variable.

\* \* \*

The witnesses and victims of the Cultural Revolution that we interviewed have experienced physical and psychic injuries of the most varied type and degree, ranging from isolated events with rather minor consequences to "extreme" traumatisations. The concept of extreme traumatisation arose in the course of Holocaust research and designates the cumulative effect of separate experiences, each traumatising by itself, devastating in combination (cf. Grubrich-Simitis, 1979; Rosenbaum & Varvin, 2007; Varvin, 2001, 2003b). We could establish extreme traumatisation in, for example, the interviews with Mr Wang Senior (3A), Mr Li Senior (4A), and Mr Zhao (6A).

The marks these men bear affected their later lives and, notably, also their parenting, in a complex and multi-layered manner not adequately captured by the merely phenomenological classification "post traumatic stress disorder". The popular psychological understanding of trauma, reflected in some sinological discussions, also

*Photograph 10.*    Files, securities, and savings books found in household searches are burned at a meeting organised by the Red Guards. Harbin, 19 September 1966.

does not do justice to the psychic damage uncovered in our interviews. Limiting the idea of trauma to major and fateful experiences, it has led writers to debate, for example, whether the Cultural Revolution qualifies as a traumatic event at all (Pye, 1986), whether the trauma concept applies in the Chinese context, and to what degree we can speak of collective, as well as of individual, trauma.

Our psychoanalytic understanding of psychic trauma, by contrast, is based on the medical model. In medicine, trauma is understood simply as an injury or wound resulting from the application of force from outside. This concept contains two elements: the intrusion from outside, and the internal consequences. From this simple basis, psychoanalysts have developed complex concepts of trauma, emphasising now one aspect and now the other, and employing various models of psychic function. The existence of psychic illness or wounds to the ego has been recognised in our field for a long time. In the past thirty years, however, understanding has deepened due to investigations of the effects of the Holocaust and of war experiences on the subjects and on successor generations. Research has been multi-faceted and publications abundant.

In psychoanalysis today, we distinguish two fundamentally different models of trauma (Bohleber, 2000, 2006; Plänkers, 2003). Freud developed what we call a drive-economic model: he viewed the traumatic injury of the ego as a penetration of the protective shield against stimuli by a psychic excitement too strong to integrate (Freud, 1920g). Initially, he was thinking of outer events and their traumatic effect, as in his seduction theory; later he supplemented this approach by acknowledging that inner processes can also overwhelm the ego. Because the trauma overpowers established forms of defence, the subject is helplessly exposed both to outer threats and to inner fears. Breaking through defences, the traumatic experience simultaneously gives new strength to early phantasies, impulses, and fears that have been defended against. The assault activates traumata from earlier life that, piled one on another, have amounted to cumulative trauma (Keilson, 1979; Khan, 1977). The so-called object-relations models of traumatisation, developed later, focus on massive impairment of internal and external object relationships. The traumatic experience lastingly disturbs trust in what we call the good object and its protective function, and activates very early fears, impulses, and phantasies. Two possible results are paranoid perception of the objects and lasting depression. The traumatic experience is translated into a specific form of inner object relationships in which the so-called bad inner objects dominate. Our increasing understanding of the genetic and structural vulnerability of the ego has also brought a deeper grasp of family and social circumstances that can traumatise. In addition, the object-relations models of trauma focus on the loss of the ego functions that provide support, that is, containment. The concept "containment" goes back to the psychoanalyst Wilfred Bion, who connected the strength and stability of the ego with its capability to build meaningful structures out of sense impressions that are not at first understood. Containment is Bion's term for the process of digesting raw input and making meaningful patterns of it. In Freud, it is excessive drive potentials, unconscious conflicts as well as sudden, strong intrusions from the outside world, that can overwhelm the ego with stimuli; in Bion, by contrast, the overtaxed and unsuccessful containment function is the focus. More recent concepts that build on Bion's idea of containment are "symbolisation", "psychisation", and "mentalization". The common underlying thought is that the impossibility of sensibly integrating emotional and cognitive experiences leads to a partial or total collapse of ego structures. Thus, the patient's personality structure, his unconscious to conscious psychodynamics, is lastingly and often chronically affected, with impacts on behaviour and bodily constitution. This is a more comprehensive view of psychic traumatisation than the one implicit in the category "post traumatic stress disorder", which is described simply as a list of symptoms:

> [PTSD] arises as a delayed and/or protracted response to a stressful event or situation (either short- or long-lasting) of an exceptionally threatening or catastrophic nature, which is likely to cause pervasive distress in almost anyone (e.g. natural or man-made disaster, combat, serious accident, witnessing the violent death of others, or being the victim of torture, terrorism, rape, or other crime) (*ICD-10*, F43.1).

Psychically traumatised people can display symptoms immediately following the event(s) or after a delay, even of years (late-onset post traumatic stress disorder). One or more of the following systems are often reported:

- recurrent, involuntary, oppressive thoughts and memories of the trauma (mental pictures, nightmares, flashbacks);

- memory gaps (partial amnesia);
- symptoms of overstimulation (sleep disturbance, jumpiness, irritability, affective intolerance, difficulty concentrating);
- avoidance behaviour (avoidance of trauma-linked stimuli);
- emotional numbness (general withdrawal, loss of interest, inner indifference).

This listing of symptom clusters reflects the phenomenological approach to the classification of psychic illness taken in the *International Classification of Diseases* (*ICD*). This system has drawn criticism from various quarters. For example, Varvin (2003a) has pointed out that traumatic experiences constitute dramatic incursions into relationship life, so important for psychic functioning, and that they affect relationships on both inner and outer levels, including those to significant others, to the group or society, and to the complex system of culture. Trauma impacts both inner and outer reality, both the individual and the surrounding group and society, both body and soul. The concept is necessarily many layered. This complexity is not mirrored in the notion of PTSD, focused as it is on the single sufferer. It should also be noted that the trauma model based on object relations concerns not only the results of a traumatisation but also its inception—in the framework of some external relationship—and its connection to inner object relationships.

In their textbook on psycho-traumatology, Fischer and Riedesser (2009, pp. 149–159) distinguish six aspects of trauma: (1) intensity; (2) frequency and duration of the events (3) manner in which the subject is harmed; (4) causation; (5) relationship between victim and perpetrator; (6) psychology of the clinical situation. It is particularly traumatising when a personal relationship between perpetrator and victim has been violated, which "shakes the [victim's] basic trust in the dependability of social relationships in general" (p. 152). Such was the case for those among our interview partners for whom the Communist Party had been a substitute family: for example, Mr Li Senior (4A) and Mr Zhao (6A): they were "persecuted, humiliated, tortured, arrested, and threatened with death" by their "family members". These relationship traumas are mirrored in the psyche, where there is no longer a network of good inner objects with the values they embody (cf. the contribution of Haubl, pp. 57–82): thus, a reintegration or containment cannot occur.

The massive shock occasioned by a violation of a person's understanding of self and world is echoed internally by damage to those structures that generate understanding. Ba Jin (1904–2005), who, in 1980, became Chairman of the Chinese authors' group PEN and was a moral authority for the time after the Cultural Revolution, portrays this process vividly in an autobiographical passage:

> Beginning in September 1966, under threat from "the directorate of the rebels" (or the directorate of the whip), I changed the way I used my brain. If everyone roared "Down with Ba Jin!" I raised my right hand and joined in the chorus. Thinking now about my conduct back then, I can't understand it. But it wasn't that I was lying; I was expressing an honest wish to be crushed by the others, so that I could make a new beginning, become a new person. (Ba Jin, 1981, cited in Saechtig, 2005, p. 36, translated for this edition)

This transformation of his very essence in identification with an external force was, at the time, a life-saving measure; yet, in retrospect, it seems as though a foreign body had inexplicably invaded him. His own thinking and understanding were suspended. Ba Jin sees the effects of this and other traumatic invasions of self in constantly recurring images of the cruelties he suffered and in nightmares that point to an unending inner battle with unprocessed intrusions:

> My goal is inner quiet. Only when everything that I want to say has been said, only when all the dirt and filth piled up in me has been cleared away, only when I can explain and get a grasp of what happened to us in those ten years—only then will I be able to find my peace. (Ba Jin, 1985, p. 15, translated for this edition)

This swathe of destruction in inner and outer worlds is conceptualised as the assumption of dissociative states (Davies & Frawley, 1994); as a "hole in the psychic landscape" (Grubrich-Simitis, 1984; Hopper, 1991; Kinston & Cohen, 1986); and as the assumption of an absent or destroyed mentalization (Fonagy, 2008b; Laub, 1998; Laub & Auerhahn, 1991; Laub & Podell, 1995). The concept of dissociation, going back to Janet (1889), identifies the collapse of the unity of conscious processes as a result of a traumatisation too massive to be overcome. Thereafter the term was widened to cover a range of concepts describing the collapse of the unity of the personality and the continuity of perception of self and other, and employing terms like "fractionating", "fragmentation" or "horizontal and vertical dissociation" (cf. Brenneis, 1998; Brenner, 2001; Davies, 1996; Fischer & Riedesser, 2009; Gullestad, 2005; Thiel, 1997). The whole or partial failure of psychic processing of traumatic experiences is expressed in the metaphor of a psychic "hole" used by Kinston and Cohen (1986, 1987) to designate the damage to "emotional understanding and the growth of psychic structures" in the victims. Laub and Auerhahn (1989, p. 391) use the similar image of a "black hole" in the psychic structures of Holocaust survivors. The idea of a hole reminds that damage is not total: areas of mature psychic functioning exist in these persons alongside zones of deep regression. These dead zones result from the destruction of inner relationship structures by the concentration camp experience, permitting no empathic connection of subject and object and, thus, no empathic self-awareness. The authors emphasise the peculiar nature of trauma resulting from a collective attack on the lives of the victims, as on Jews in the Nazi era. Of course, the attempted elimination of the Jews is not to be equated with the attack on arbitrarily defined "class enemies" during the Cultural Revolution; yet, the collective nature of the attacks make them parallel in traumatic effect, striking a heavy blow at the victims' perception of self and objects.

Currently there is particular interest in viewing trauma from the angle of distorted mentalization (Fonagy, 2008a; cf. Bohleber, 2000, pp. 821–825). Mentalization is understood in the context of attachment theory as the ability to grasp the thoughts and emotions of others (Fonagy, 2008b). The loss of this ability through traumatic experience is accompanied by the phenomenon of psychic equivalence, in which internal mental conditions are equated with external ones. One thinks one knows everything, so there is no reason to consider, to question. Fonagy connects this and other conditions with an activation of the attachment system, that is, the search for emotional closeness. Attachment traumas, in which the person who is turned to for love and support is the same person who traumatises, are particularly serious. Thinking, which can serve as a buffer between feeling and action, is rendered rudimentary or impossible, and impulses towards action dominate. There are other frameworks than attachment theory, of course. Trauma consequences have been characterised as the impossibility of forming metaphors or thinking symbolically (Grubrich-Simitis, 1984). Alternatively, the harm may be expressed in spatial terms, as damage to the three-dimensional psychic space (Klüwer, 2005; Plänkers, 2008b; Weiß, 1998) that constitutes the inner representation of oedipal relationships. In a healthy mind, a momentary collapse into two dimensions can always be countered by the introduction of a third point of view, restoring perspective. A traumatic experience destroys three-dimensional space, producing a direct regression and, thus, preventing a mature form of containment. Winnicott (1974) spoke of the fear of breakdown. In the individual, this means the fear of losing the structuring work of the ego, its containment, so that the psychic maturation process regresses to the primary condition of primitive agony. The loss of the ability to think, to reflect, was very evident in our interviewees, visible in the absence of reflective distance and also, to some degree, in the fragmentary concretistic narrative style, scarcely allowing the emergence of a real story (cf. the contribution of Plänkers, pp. 83–120). There are interesting parallel results from neurobiological research: suggestions that heavy and lasting stress damages neurons in the hippocampus, in turn impeding the development of consistent narratives (Bremner, 2001, cited by Beutel, 2009). The achievement pressure that children of the second generation complain of (1B, 3B, 4B, 5B, 6B) is a further indication of disturbed containment function, for progress in Chinese schools and universities is still gauged principally by memorisation, not by critical thinking ability.

Our understanding of the psychic consequences of traumatisation has been significantly expanded in recent years by the yields of neurobiological research pointing to the somatic effects of traumatic experiences. Animal experiments show

> . . . that young animals exposed to excessive periods of separation show changes in neurobiological regulatory mechanisms . . . Life events produce alterations in the neurotransmitter system, in the production of endogenous opiates, and in the neuroendocrine system [surveyed in van der Kolk, 1987, pp. 31–62]. . . . The neuroendocrine changes that have taken place promote cyclical mood swings, such as we see in circular depression (Fischer & Riedesser, 2009, p. 198).

Investigations of human memory function also show that memory is not merely information storage in the cortex, but, rather, involves the whole sensory and motor system. Describing this phenomenon, Leuzinger-Bohleber, Henningsen, and Pfeiffer (2008) employ the

English word "embodiment". Traumatisation of the psyche leaves its marks in the body as well. Psychotherapists are often impressed by the bodily dramatisations their patients produce. "Sensomotoric coordinations are a 'royal road' to understanding traumatizations, including very early ones, for the body does not forget anything" (Leuzinger-Bohleber, Henningsen, & Pfeiffer, 2008, p. 159). This phenomenon made a strong appearance in the interview with Mr Wang (3A), who foamed at the mouth as he began to talk about the loss of his adored grandmother in his childhood.

The consequences of trauma are, indeed, varied, and it must be noted that by no means everyone who has been through trauma displays post-trauma disturbance. The individual's earlier experiences, or, rather, the psychic precipitates of those experiences, might make the difference. If the shape of the present traumatic experience lines up with an analogous psychic structure, realising an unconscious object-relations phantasy, then the probability of developing long-term traumatic symptoms is greater than if the challenge finds no such internal echo. Even in the latter case, it matters whether there are good object relationships to provide support and help in the processing of the traumatic experience. In the best case, symptoms produced by a trauma can fade out in a few weeks or months. Here, we speak of individual and social resilience factors.

This short and by no means exhaustive survey of some trauma models reveals points of congruence. Despite all conceptual differences, the theories converge at the level of psychic processes involving the relation of self and objects. It is not just recurring memories that torment the victims. They suffer also, and crucially, from damage to their ability to perceive themselves and others, to empathise and to understand—damage, in many cases, massive, inflicted by prolonged and collectively organised traumatisation. To grasp what is going on requires going beyond a psychoanalysis orientated around the psychology of drives and turning to object relations theory. The exogenously produced traumatisation only becomes real trauma when it activates psychic dispositions that have destructive effects on ego functions (Plänkers, 2008a). This is why we find such differences in psychic consequences among victims who have experienced comparable external traumatisations. Because the trauma overpowers established forms of defence, the victim is left helplessly open both to outer threats and to inner fears that have been held in check. Besides overwhelming the defence system, the violation also seems to verify early phantasies, fears, and impulses that have been defended against. Particularly, it activates traumas that have occurred earlier in life, producing a cumulative and sequential traumatisation (Keilson, 1979; Khan, 1977). Our interviewees reached adulthood considerably burdened by childhood traumas, which were activated when they took part in the Cultural Revolution, whether as perpetrators, witnesses, or victims (see the contribution of Plänkers, pp. 83–120).

## Transmission

In close connection with object relations theory, another perspective has developed, one focusing on the social dimension of trauma as it affects the parent–child relationship. Although this investigational direction has generated its own concepts, it is based on the developmental psychology recognised by psychoanalysis. While most of these studies concern the traumatic effects of the Holocaust on the first and second generation, they also provide an important conceptual background for study of the Cultural Revolution in China. We know that children absorb less from their parents' conscious, explicitly verbalised messages than they do from the forms the parent–child relationship assumes, as expressed in countless behaviours, day by day. Severely traumatised parents often communicate a lack of security, empathy, patience, and understanding. The parents are stuck, so to speak, in their traumatic past and have trouble dealing with their children in a way that is empathetic and orientated toward the new life situation of the child (cf., for instance, Bergmann, Jucovy, & Kestenberg, 1995; Bohleber, 2000, 2006; Eckstaedt, 1986, 1989, 1997; Gerlach & Haag, 2000; Grubrich-Simitis, 1984; Haag, 2006; Haag & Zhao, 2004; Leuzinger-Bohleber, 1989, 1990, 2003; Leuzinger-Bohleber & Zwiebel, 2003).

Through their daily attitudes and actions, parents share more with their children than they think they do. Herzog (1982, p. 104) points to the finding, repeated so often in family therapy, that children react to events of which, in their parents' opinion, they should be ignorant. Herzog speaks of the parents' ability (or lack thereof) "to create a safe place in the adult relationship of two adults" (p. 106) in which the traumatic experiences brought into the relationship by either partner or both can be contained. Herzog hypothesises:

The more constricted the shared safe space between the spouses, the less the opportunity for healing and containment within the relationship and the more the child (or children) of survivors is asked to serve as a special kind of self-object whose job is to share, undo, ameliorate, and restitute. (p. 106)

In this formulation, Herzog was thinking of Holocaust survivors, but the fundamental thought is applicable to the familial situations in China after the Cultural Revolution. Parents with extreme traumatisations that limit their empathy, their ability to symbolise and to understand, can hardly create this "safe place" within a marriage. The key question is whether parents are capable of seeing the development of their children as something new and unique, or whether they rely on the children to help them maintain their own fragile psychic balance. Of course, most cases fall somewhere between these two poles: all children are seen by parents as part of their own story. The question is how and to what extent this view excludes treating children as psychically separate beings in their own right.

One currently popular model of trauma transmission between generations is the one that Faimberg (1987, 2009) dubbed "telescoping", a metaphor expressive of the transgression of generational boundaries. By subtle processes of intrusion and projective identification, the traumatic story of the first generation intrudes psychically into the following generation or generations. As a result, the generations are not really psychically separate; in important areas, they interpenetrate (telescoping). In the most extreme form, the following generation is defined by an identity that is not its own.

Kestenberg (1989, 1993, 1995) conceptualises this central fact, the lack of psychic separation between the generations, as "transposition". She concentrates on the unconscious assignment of roles that can occur in the families of severely traumatised parents: for instance, when children take over the parts of lost family members of the parents' generation, or take on fears and phantasies of one parent or both. Children are called on to compensate for the loss of people important to the parents. The expression "transposition" is borrowed from music: the conversion of a piece into another key.

Similarly, Kogan (1990, 1995, 1998, 2002) discusses parents with inadequate containment function and child traumatisation through (1) the exploitation of the child for the repetition of the parent's trauma; (2) inadequate empathy; (3) traumatisation in phantasy; (4) loss of self. Each of these concepts, of course, captures only certain aspects of disturbed family situations, but they have in common the idea of a missing psychic separation between parents and child.

## Society

The disturbed, traumatically damaged containing function within a family can be recapitulated on the level of large groups, even whole societies. In Germany after the Second World War, it was decades before the consequences of the Nazi era for victims and perpetrators became a subject of public discussion. Translating the concept of three-dimensional psychic space into the social level, we can ask whether a society, in carrying out its public communicative functions, creates and promotes this three-dimensionality, or not (Plänkers, 2001, 2006). Bion assumed that groups serve as containers for individuals, but can fail in this function just as a mother can fail with her child. The relationship between individual and group can provide a nurturing containment, or its opposite. Just as a borderline patient fears the perceptions of a third person as catastrophic, a society or group might find the possibility of three-dimensional relativisation threatening to its makeup. Can we not deem a whole society to be traumatised, if it fears that the removal of official repression would lead to a catastrophic disruption of social relationships?

On the other hand, a society that is capable of producing this three-dimensional space for discussion is demonstrating some psychic maturity. Granting the traumatised citizen permission to tell his individual story in the context of the whole society's story tends to heal the rift that the traumatic experience has made in individual mentalization (Bohleber, 2000, pp. 823–825).

To see how out of the question this healing is in today's China, consider the silence that reigned in 2006, the fortieth anniversary of the beginning of the Cultural Revolution, the thirtieth anniversary of its end. This history received no official notice anywhere in the country. Granted, a cultural difference must be taken into account here: what in our Western eyes appears scandalous seems natural in the Far East, where the greater good ranks higher than acknowledgement of personal suffering. Here, the Western striving for enlightenment comes into friction with the Eastern longing for harmony—a tension that pervades every attempt to communicate psychoanalytic theory, therapy, and diagnostic methodology, including the present effort at psychoanalytic social research on the psychic consequences of the Cultural Revolution.

The literature reflects another relevant debate: whether we are entitled to speak of collective, cultural, or public memory. Is there really memory beyond the individual level? The historians Noa Gedi and Yigal Elam (2004, quoted in Pillemer, 2004) are not alone in rejecting talk of collective memory; they accord this concept only a metaphorical, not a genuinely explanatory, value. While this position seems correct in principle, the fact that the idea of collective memory is repeatedly raised points to an unmet need. Whether or not a public storehouse of memory might exist, the question remains: is a society ready to make room for, and allow, public discussion of diverse views of its own history?

After the terror attack on the World Trade Center in New York, the concept of "national trauma" was much discussed. The central idea is that "the ramifications of a great national trauma . . . are not restricted to the people directly affected . . ." (Silver et al., 2002, quoted in Brunner, 2004, p. 7, translated for this edition). American and Israeli studies yielded the surprising result that the count of immediate victims is not predictive of the extent of symptoms of post traumatic stress syndrome. "People who were direct victims of terror appear by no means to develop PTSD symptoms to a greater degree than their fellow citizens who saw the victims on television" (Silver et al., 2002, quoted in Brunner, 2004, p. 8). We speak now of "onlooker trauma" and note that electronic media, too, can be channels for traumatisation. "Today one can be farther away from the actual events in space and time and still count as a victim of the trauma" (Silver et al., 2002, quoted in Brunner, 2004, p. 9).

I think that these considerations are applicable to the China of the Cultural Revolution, even though the electronic media played a smaller role then than now. Many Chinese, even if they were not direct victims of the violent excesses, were, voluntarily or involuntarily, witnesses of these deeds. The concept of onlooker trauma confirms the finding of psychoanalytic perception theory that all information is received partly in the light of inner psychic reality. To witness physical violence often excites and strengthens unconscious components of the self that are destructive, massively undermining the stability and function of the ego.

Through passive traumatisation of witnesses, through transmission between family members, and through lack of containment on a national level, Chinese society suffers a secondary traumatisation (Zimering, Munroe, & Gulliver, 2003). Like an infection, the individual trauma continues to spread unconsciously through the network of social relationships, within and between the generations.

Considering the long series of social catastrophes that marks the twentieth-century history of China, the thought that this people might be collectively traumatised is no far reach. "It is a very traumatised realm" (Wurmser, 2010[1990], p. 110); "In a general view one can speak of a cumulative traumatisation of the Chinese people, characterised by a long-lasting anomie" (Haag & Zhao, 2004, p. 353). To me, however, the diagnosis of collective traumatisation seems not very helpful, since it leaves the territory of empirically anchored diagnostics and quickly takes on the character of a moral judgement. On the other hand, it cannot be denied that a severely pathological large-group phenomenon of such long duration must leave some traces in the population as a whole.

Our first-generation interviewees, in some cases very old now, are plainly deeply marked by the catastrophic events of the Cultural Revolution. "Never again!" they say. The second generation, while recognising the Cultural Revolution as an awful fact of Chinese history, do not regard a recurrence as a present danger. In addition, they are not inclined to think much about, or to engage critically with, present social circumstances. If Chinese society does not remember, then Freud's dictum (1914g, p. 150) applies: ". . . the patient does not *remember* anything of what he has forgotten and repressed, but *acts* it out". Present modes of action in China are unmistakably imprinted by the bustle of blistering economic growth. It seems much more important to take one's place in this process of original accumulation, as Marx called it, than to confront history. China is a long way from such a moment as arrived in Germany on 12 February 2009, when parliament had its first discussion of the problems of soldiers returning from war zones. For Germans, this official political recognition of psychic trauma marks the end of one stage on a long journey of social and scientific confrontation with the phenomenon, beginning with the Holocaust and continuing with the Vietnam War and the wars in

Africa and the Near East. It also symbolises a moment of social containment. In China, such a moment is still a distant dream. When will the acknowledgement that Ba Jin called for—in the form of a "Museum of the Cultural Revolution"—be made?

> It is not the job of some particular person to erect a museum of the Cultural Revolution. Each of us is responsible for communicating the painful lessons of these ten years to coming generations. "Don't let history repeat itself!" must be more than an empty cliché. The best way to allow each person to see clearly, to really get the impression of the thing, is to create a Cultural Revolution Museum in which solid, realistic objects and movingly accurate scenes will make it clear just what happened on Chinese soil twenty years ago. Let everyone retrace the whole course of events and think what he did during those ten years. Let the masks drop. Let your conscience speak. Show your real face and repay debts, small and large, from yesterday. If no room is left for egoistic motives, we will not be overwhelmed and stumble into the trap; we will trust ourselves to speak the truth and not casually credit rumours. Only when we have let the reality of the Cultural Revolution sink into us can we prevent history from repeating itself, and guard against a new eruption of a Cultural Revolution. The erection of a Cultural Revolution Museum is vital. Only he who does not forget "the past" will be master of "the future" (Ba Jin, 2005, p. 41, translated for this edition).

This call to action has brought no results in China to date. A "museum" of the Cultural Revolution" is only to be found on the Internet, at http://museums.cnd.org/CR/english/firsthand.htm (cf. the contribution of Gentz, pp. 1–34).

## References

Ba Jin (1985). *Gedanken unter der Zeit*. Cologne: Eugen Diederichs.
Ba Jin (2005). Gedanke 145. In: Jiang zhen hua de shu. Chengdu: Sichuan Renmin Chubanshe, A. Saechtig (Trans.). *Mut: Forum für Kultur, Politik und Geschichte, 449*: 38–41.
Bell, D. (1998). External injury and the internal world. In: C. Garland (Ed.), *Understanding Trauma: A Psychoanalytic Approach* (pp. 167–180). London: Karnac.

Bergmann, M. S., Jucovy, M. E., & Kestenberg, J. S. (Eds). (1995). *Kinder der Opfer, Kinder der Täter: Psychoanalyse und Holocaust*. Frankfurt: Fischer.

Beutel, M. E. (2009). Vom Nutzen der bisherigen neurobiologischen Forschung für die Praxis der Psychotherapie. *Psychotherapeutenjournal*, 4: 386.

Bohleber, W. (2000). Die Entwicklung der Traumatheorie in der Psychoanalyse. *Psyche—Zeitschrift für Psychoanalyse*, 54: 797–839.

Bohleber, W. (2006). Zusammenfassung des Hauptvortrags und Weiterer Vorträge zum Trauma. *IPA-Newsletter*, 1.

Brenneis, B. C. (1998). Gedächtnissysteme und der psychoanalytische Abruf von Trauma-Erinnerungen. *Psyche—Zeitschrift für Psychoanalyse*, 9–10: 801–823.

Brenner, I. (2001). *Dissociation of Trauma: Theory, Phenomenology and Technique*. Madison, CT: International Universities Press.

Britton, R. (2005). Endogenous trauma and psycho-phobia. Paper given at the IPA Congress in Rio de Janeiro, July 2005.

Brunner, J. (2004). Politik der Traumatisierung: Zur Geschichte des verletzbaren Individuums. *Westend. Neue Zeitschrift für Sozialforschung*, 1: 7–24.

Davies, J. M. (1996). Dissociation, repression and reality testing in the countertransference: the controversy over memory and false memory in the psychoanalytic treatment of adult survivors of childhood sexual abuse. *Psychoanaytic Dialogues*, 6: 189–218.

Davies, J. M., & Frawley, M. G. (1994). *Treating the Adult Survivor of Childhood Sexual Abuse: A Psychoanalytic Perspective*. New York: Basic Books.

Eckstaedt, A. (1986). Two complementary cases of identification involving "Third Reich" fathers. *International Journal of Psychoanalysis*, 67: 317–327.

Eckstaedt, A. (1989). *Nationalsozialismus in der 'Zweiten Generation': Psychoanalysen von Hörigkeitsverhältnissen*. Frankfurt: Suhrkamp.

Eckstaedt, A. (1997). Traumatische Folgen des Nationalsozialismus in der 2 und 3. Generation—Eine Spurensuche. Unpublished lecture.

Faimberg, H. (1987). Die Ineinanderrückung (Teleskoping) der Generationen: Zur Genealogie Gewisser Identifizierungen. *Jahrbuch der Psychoanalyse*, 20: 114–142.

Faimberg, H. (2009). *Teleskoping. Die intergenerationelle Weitergabe Narzisstischer Bindungen*. Frankfurt: Brandes & Apsel.

Fischer, G., & Riedesser, P. (2009). *Lehrbuch der Psychotraumatologie*. Munich: Reinhardt.

Fonagy, P. (2008a). Psychoanalyse und Bindungstrauma unter neuro-biologischen Aspekten. In: M. Leuzinger-Bohleber, G. Roth, & A. Buchheim (Eds.), *Psychoanalyse, Neurobiologie, Trauma* (pp. 132–148). Stuttgart: Schattauer.

Fonagy, P. (2008b). Bindung, Trauma und Psychoanalyse: Wo Psychoanalyse auf Neurowissenschaft trifft. Unpublished lecture at Joseph Sandler Research Conference, Frankfurt.

Freud, S. (1914g). Remembering, repeating, and working-through. *S.E., 12*: 145–156. London: Hogarth.

Freud, S. (1920g). *Beyond the Pleasure Principle. S.E., 18*: 7–64. London: Hogarth.

Freud, S. (1923b). *The Ego and the Id. S.E., 19*: 3–66. London: Hogarth.

Freud, S. (1930a). *Civilization and Its Discontents. S.E., 21*: 59–145. London: Hogarth.

Gerlach, A., & Haag, A. (2000). Trennungstraumata in der Chinesischen Kulturrevolution. In: A. Gerlach (Ed.), *Die Tigerkuh: Ethnopsycho-analytische Erkundungen* (pp. 123–141). Gießen: Psychosozial.

Grubrich-Simitis, I. (1984). Vom Konkretismus zur Metaphorik: Gedanken zur psychoanalytischen Arbeit mit Nachkommen der Holocaust-Generation—anlässlich einer Neuerscheinung. *Psyche—Zeitschrift für Psychoanalyse, 38*: 1–28.

Gullestad, S. I. (2005). Who is who in dissociation? A plea for psychodynamics in a time of trauma. *International Journal of Psychoanalysis, 86*: 639–656.

Haag, A. (2006). Die Seelenkulturrevolution. *Frankfurter Allgemeine Zeitung*, 27 April, p. 36.

Haag, A., & Zhao, M. (2004). Kollektive Traumatisierung—Chinesische Schicksale im 20. Jahrhundert. *Psyche—Zeitschrift für Psychoanalyse, 58*(4): 352–366.

Herzog, J. (1982). World beyond metaphor: thoughts on the transmission of trauma. In: M. S. Bergmann & M. E. Jucovy (Eds.), *Generations of the Holocaust* (pp. 103–119.). New York: Basic Books.

Hopper, E. (1991). Encapsulation as a defence against the fear of annihilation. *International Journal of Psychoanalysis, 72*: 607–624.

Janet, P. (1889). *L'automatisme psychologique: Essai de la psychologie experimental sur les formes inférieures de l'activité humaine*. Paris: Félix Alcan.

Keilson, H. (1979). *Sequentielle Traumatisierung bei Kindern*. Stuttgart: Enke.

Kestenberg, J. S. (1989). Neue Gedanken zur Transposition: Klinische, therapeutische und entwicklungsbedingte Betrachtungen. *Jahrbuch der Psychoanalyse, 24*: 163–189.

Kestenberg, J. S. (1993). Spätfolgen bei verfolgten Kindern. *Psyche—Zeitschrift für Psychoanalyse, 8*: 730–742.

Kestenberg, J. S. (1995). Überlebende Eltern und ihre Kinder. In: M. S. Bergmann, M. E. Jucovy, & J. S. Kestenberg (Eds.). *Kinder der Opfer, Kinder der Täter: Psychoanalyse und Holocaust* (pp. 103–126). Frankfurt: Fischer.

Khan, M. M. R. (1977). Das kumulative Trauma. In: M. M. R. Khan (Ed.), *Selbsterfahrung in der Therapie* (pp. 50–70). Munich: Kindler.

Kinston, W., & Cohen, J. (1986). Primal repression: clinical and theoretical aspects. *International Journal of Psychoanalysis, 67*: 337–355.

Kinston, W., & Cohen, J. (1987). Urverdrängung und Andere Seelische Zustände: Der Bereich der Psychostatik. In: H. Luft & G. Maass (Eds.), *Psychoanalyse des Konflikts—Konflikte der Psychoanalyse* (pp. 41–82). Work meeting of the German Psychoanalytic Association, Wiesbaden, 18–21 November.

Klüwer, R. (2005). M. C. Escher—Spielen mit Bildern und Gedanken: Psychoanalytische Assoziationen zu Einem Dreidimensionalen Modell der Inneren Realität. In: *Jahrbuch der Psychanalyse* (pp. 50, 191–221). Stuttgart: frommann-holzboog.

Kogan, I. (1995). Love and the heritage of the past. *International Journal of Psychoanalysis, 76*: 805–824.

Kogan, I. (2002). "Enactment" in the lives and treatment of Holocaust survivors' offspring. *Psychoanalytic Quarterly, 71*: 251–272.

Laub, D. (1998). Empty circle, children of survivors and limits of reconstruction. *Journal of the American Psychoanalytic Association 46*: 507–530.

Laub, D., & Auerhahn, N. C. (1989). Failed empathy, central theme in survivors' holocaust experience. *Psychoanalytic Psychology, 6*: 377–400.

Laub, D., & Auerhahn, N. C. (1991). Zentrale Erfahrungen des Überlebenden: Die Versagung von Mitmenschlichkeit. In: H: Stoffels (Ed.), *Schicksale der Verfolgten. Psychische und somatische Auswirkungen von Terrorherrschaft* (pp. 254–276). Berlin: Springer.

Laub, D., & Podell, D. (1995). Art and trauma. *International Journal of Psychoanalysis, 76*: 991–1006.

Leuzinger-Bohleber, M. (1989). "Ich will leben und meine Katze auch': Psychoanalytische Anmerkungen zu Überlebensstrategien in der "Katastrophe'. *Psychosozial, 36*(11): 62–81.

Leuzinger-Bohleber, M. (1990). Veränderung kognitiver Prozesse in Psychoanalysen: Versuch einer empirischen Annäherung an den psychoanalytischen Prozeß. In: *Empirische Forschung in der Psychoanalyse* (pp. 27–73). Symposium, 4 December 1987, at Sigmund-Freud-Institut, Frankfurt.

Leuzinger-Bohleber, M. (2003). Transgenerative Weitergabe von Trauma-tisierungen: Einige Beobachtungen aus einer Repräsentativen Katam-nesestudie. In: M. Leuzinger-Bohleber & R. Zwiebel (Eds.), *Trauma, Beziehung und Soziale Realität* (pp. 107–135). Tübingen: Edition Diskord.

Leuzinger-Bohleber, M., & Zwiebel, R. (Eds.) (2003). *Trauma, Beziehung und Soziale Realität*. Tübingen: Edition Diskord.

Leuzinger-Bohleber, M., Henningsen, P., & Pfeiffer, R. (2008). Die psycho-analytische Konzeptforschung zum Trauma und die Gedächtnis-forschung der Embodied Cognitive Science. In: M. Leuzinger-Bohleber, G. Roth, & A. Buchheim (Eds.), *Psychoanalyse, Neurobiologie, Trauma* (pp. 157–171). Stuttgart: Schattauer.

Pillemer, D. B. (2004). Can the psychology of memory enrich historical analysis of trauma? *History & Memory, 16*(2): 140–154.

Plänkers, T. (2001). Über die Fähigkeit zum Dissens. In: B. Schmitz & P. Prechtl (Eds.), *Pluralität und Konsensfähigkeit* (pp. 107–121). Würzburg: Königshausen & Neumann.

Plänkers, T. (2003). Trieb, Objekt, Raum. Veränderungen im psychoana-lytischem Verständnis der Angst. *Psyche—Zeitschrift für Psychoanalyse,* 6: 487–522.

Plänkers, T. (2006). Denken, Sprechen, Nicht-Handeln. Gibt es deutsche Widerstände gegen die Psychoanalyse? *Psychosozial, 29*(105): 21–29.

Plänkers, T. (2008a). Die Verbindung von Trauma und Konflikt: Das Konzept der intrusiven Identifizierung. In: *Karl-Abraham-Institut, Semester-Journal* Winter 2008–09: 15, 29–44.

Plänkers, T. (2008b). Dimensionen des psychischen Raums. Zur Struktur psychischer Triangulierung. In: F. Dammasch, D. Katzenbach, & J. Ruth (Eds.), *Triangulierung. Lernen, Denken und Handeln aus Psycho-analytischer Sicht* (pp. 41–57). Frankfurt: Brandes & Apsel.

Pye, L. W. (1986). Reassessing the Cultural Revolution. *China Quarterly, 108*: 597–612.

Rosenbaum, B., & Varvin, S. (2007). The influence of extreme trauma-tization on body, mind and social relations. *International Journal of Psychoanalysis, 88*: 1527–1542.

Thiel, H. (1997). Dissoziation und multiple Identität als Abwehr gegen die Grenzdiffusion zwischen Phantasie und Handlung: Aus der psychoanalytischen Behandlung einer Inzestpatientin. *Psyche-Zeitschrift für Psychoanalyse,* 3: 239–252.

Van der Kolk, B. A. (Ed.) (1987). *Psychological Trauma*. Washington, DC: American Psychiatric Press.

Varvin, S. (2001). Extreme Traumatisierung und Psychotherapie. *Psycho-analytic Quarterly, 70*: 515.

Varvin, S. (2003a). Auswirkungen extremer Traumatisierung auf Körper, Seele und soziales Umfeld. In: M. Leuzinger-Bohleber & R. Zwiebel (Eds.), *Trauma, Beziehung und soziale Realität* (pp. 137–170). Tübingen: Edition Diskord.

Varvin, S. (2003b). Extreme traumatization: strategies for mental survival. *International Forum of Psychoanalysis*, 12: 5–16.

Weiß, H. (1998). Konstruktion und psychischer Raum. In: G. Kimmerle (Ed.), *Konstruktionen (in) der Psychoanalyse* (pp. 9–36). Tübingen: Edition Diskord.

Winnicott, D. W. (1974). Fear of breakdown. *International Review of Psychoanalysis*, 1: 103–107.

World Health Organisation (2010). *International Classification of Diseases*. Geneva: World Health Organisation.

Wurmser, L. (1990). *Die Maske der Scham* (6. Aufl.). Magdeburg: Klotz, 2010.

Zimering, R., Munroe, J., & Gulliver, S. B. (2003). Secondary traumatization in mental health care providers. *Psychiatric Times*, 20: 4.

# CHAPTER SIX

# The Chinese Cultural Revolution: a traumatic experience and its intergenerational transmission

*Friedrich Markert*

With the unleashing of the Cultural Revolution in 1966, China entered an era of violence and terror in which millions of people were humiliated, persecuted, abused, and killed. The imprint of these experiences is seen not only in the lives of the victims, where it lingers to this day, but also in following generations. I will demonstrate this fact through interviews with a man born in 1930, who was directly affected, and with his son, born in 1968. These interviews also open the door to discussion of the problems of intercultural interpretation.

The interviews were conducted under the aegis of the China Project of the Sigmund Freud Institute (Frankfurt) by a Chinese colleague, and analysed by a group of five psychoanalysts in Germany (see the contribution of Plänkers, pp. 83–120). The following discussion incorporates this work.

### *"It cannot be made good"*

Mr Wang, seventy-three at the time of our two interviews, tells of a life relentlessly pummelled by losses and abuses: separation from his parents at the age of two months; death of a greatly loved grand-mother; political attacks; the loss of his beloved wife; maltreatment and banishment; professional demotion; a forced marriage.

Before the Cultural Revolution, Wang is a policeman. In 1964, he loses his wife, to whom he is devoted, and is still in a state of depres-sive mourning as he comes to the attention of the Cultural Revolution. In August of 1966, the adoptive son of his stepmother denounces him as an alleged property owner.

Not far into his first interview, Mr Wang begins speaking movingly of his sufferings in the Cultural Revolution, beginning in medias res:

> "It was night-time. They dragged me out of bed and started beating me . . . They got a leather strap. . . . They beat me all night long and destroyed everything in the room. The more I tried to defend or to justify myself, the worse the beating got. The shirt I was wearing stuck to my cuts with the blood. They tore the shirt off, got salt from the kitchen and sprinkled it on the wounds. They poured urine into my children's rice porridge."

After that, Mr Wang is locked in a small dark room with ten other sus-pect persons and kept there for twenty days. His three- and seven-year-old daughters, in his sole care since his wife's death, disappear for a time in the general chaos. Their grandmother is not permitted to see to them. Mr Wang finds them only after a long search.

> "It was as though the family had dissolved, it was gone. [Silence.] Dissolved. In the daytime the two children wandered in the streets, they lost themselves. [Sighs.] Nobody was home."

After his release, he is sent to the country for four years of re-education. At first, his children are not allowed to go with him. Soon the authorities force him into marriage with a woman of the poor peasant class, so that he can "learn from her". This second wife is supposed to care for the girls, but neglects and even beats them. Their suffering becomes so obvious that they are finally allowed to return to their old home, to which Mr Wang commutes every day, a lengthy trip, to see to them at night.

> "Often the children sat on the stairs in front of a store near our house and waited for me. I got out of the bus, the children clung to my legs. Tears came into my eyes. My sadness was unspeakable."

Finally, he seeks a divorce, which is refused. In spite of these intentions, a son is born to the couple in 1969, and the marital relationship improves somewhat.

In further conversation, Mr Wang adds that he came close to being labelled a right deviationist during the Anti-Rightist Movement of 1957 (see p. 57), a fate he avoided only by standing before an audience and subjecting himself to a profound self-criticism (see Wurmser, 2010[1990], pp. 96–103, on the subject of shame and shaming in China). Mr Wang says that these terrible experiences are still with him daily:

> "When I remember it, I feel pain, nothing but pain. The memory of this time is unbearable. Often I don't even dare to think about it . . . The place whwere I live now, for instance. When I see the courtyard, enter the building or see the objects, then I remember it. When it snows in winter, then I remember; it's snowing now. On the day that I was exiled, it was also snowing. A big truck, the bundle of sheets, a board, two wooden benches, lots of snow. When it snows, I remember back then. When I arrived, I was white as a snowman and terribly cold. Certain feelings are connected to certain scenes."

In the second interview, he reports how, at the age of two months, he was handed over to his grandparents. He develops a deep relationship especially to his grandmother, whom he experiences as very nurturing. He does not explain why he was sent away from his parents. We learn also that the grandmother favoured him, the eldest grandchild, over his younger brother. Later, when he is an adult, she weeps every time he departs after his weekly visit. When he is twenty-three, in 1953, she dies. Her death deals him such a blow that at her burial he jumps into the open grave to follow her, not wanting to keep on living. The memory of this interment moves Mr Wang so much that he is has froth on his lips.

After his grandmother's death, he is lonely and depressed. Only with his marriage in 1955, at the age of twenty-five, does he once again feel at home. His wife dies in 1964 from breast cancer that was diagnosed too late. Mr Wang speaks of this fact with surprising tolerance and without blaming the doctors. This second death brings another round of existential depression, so bad that he is not permitted to attend the burial and is referred to a psychiatric outpatient clinic.

*Photograph 11.*   Humiliation of Ren Zhongyi, provincial Party Secretary and
First Party Secretary of Harbin, at a mass meeting in the Red Garden Square.
His face smeared with black ink, he is forced to wear a tall paper hat and a
placard around his neck with the incrimination "Black Element". He stands on a
wobbly chair. A cord runs from his hands, behind his back, to the precariously
fitting hat. Harbin, 26 August 1966.

His depressive state of mourning makes it impossible for him to
contemplate a new relationship with a woman, and he avers that,
without the Cultural Revolution, he would never have married again.
At the same time, he sees the son of his second marriage as the
binding element for the entire family. Without this son he would have
divorced.

Looking back at his life, he thinks that he "suffered a lot" and that
his "health is ruined". Because of the Cultural Revolution he never

advanced in his career. Despite his rehabilitation, the things that were done to him "cannot be made good".

## "For a long time, I've thought of the Cultural Revolution as a culture"

Son Wang, thirty-seven at the time of the interview, is born in 1968 as a late addition to a troubled family. His two half-sisters from his father's first marriage are nine and thirteen years older. Wang grows up like an only child, with relatively old parents who quarrel a lot. He learns later that they were forced to marry by political pressure and that his father was under arrest at the time of his birth. Early in the interview, son Wang brings up his experiences in connection with the Cultural Revolution.

> "I came into the world in 1968. It was about 1976 when I began to understand what was going on around me. That year made a deep impression on me. It was the time of the deaths of Chairman Mao and Prime Minister Zhou Enlai. I can still remember the scenes of public mourning. . . . In the evening we went again to Tiananmen Square. We thought these departed statesmen had made basic contributions to the founding of the state and the liberation of China. Their demise shook heaven and earth. Their deaths made gods and spirits weep. The sky was gloomy in those days. The atmosphere was oppressive, the people troubled."

Son Wang says very frankly of his family (he lives in a separate apartment in the parental house), "My family is not quite normal. What do you get from a family in which there is always strife?" Given his own painful experiences, he has lost faith in the family as the "only possible form of living" and has decided not to get married. This decision is met with bafflement and criticism by his family—and also by the interviewer.

> "Last night I was cross-examined at home. I should get married. This was very unpleasant. [The interviewer interposes: "That is because they love you."] If they loved me, they should permit me a happy life. But they don't do that. They say that my pleasure in life is not real. What could I say to that? I could only smile."

He attributes his parents' lack of understanding for his attitudes to a "huge gap between the generations in China". He is glad that modern society is more tolerant and that other living arrangements, not based on the family, are developing in the cities. Asked how he experienced the domestic atmosphere during his childhood, he says that he was raised very strictly and often beaten. Every family member is in conflict with every other, even now.

> "At home we are like hedgehogs. When we're not too close, we feel one another's warmth. When we're too close, we hurt each other with our prickles. I'm on my mother's side, my sisters are on my father's side."

When the interviewer again brings up the subject of women, he reports,

> "Whenever I have a woman friend, my parents interfere. They use the methods of the Cultural Revolution, namely dictatorship. . . . I don't complain, they are after all my parents. I find their methods so ridiculous and pitiful."

He has the feeling of being an object of matchmaking, and thinks of this as "a sort of pimping". His credo is, "Life is like a tree, only healthy, when it can unfold itself."

Asked about the difference between traditional Chinese culture and that of the West, son Wang responds,

> "Psychology, for instance, started in the West. It gets closer to human nature. I think Western culture has a consciousness of Man. We Chinese look at the world differently from Westerners. The older generation imprints the younger one with their ideas. In the West they pay more attention to individuality. Your own experience matters. What others say isn't necessarily true, I have to experience it for myself. . . . For a few thousand years we have let ourselves be pressed into the pattern of traditional culture. As soon as you get indoctrinated, you start living in a predetermined pattern. When a child is born, it automatically becomes like the parents. This is a cultural flaw. A child has its individuality and is different from the parents."

The discussion of the first interview can end with this remark of son Wang's: "For a long time I've thought of the Cultural Revolution as a culture." It is a statement worth thinking about, to which we shall return.

In the second interview, the younger Wang returns to the theme of familial atmosphere and the child-rearing style of his parents. His family was very tradition-conscious; daily life was characterised by material shortage.

> "At first I was left alone at home. Locked in. . . . My sisters came home in the afternoon and set me free. . . . I seldom played with the neighbourhood children. My family felt that they would be a bad influence on me. In childhood, and also later in school, I had difficulty making contact with new people. . . . My mother always told me, a boy should play with other boys, not with girls. For this reason I tried to avoid my sisters. . . . As a child I didn't know what to say to strangers. I got all sweaty and simply went away."

He reports a lot of quarrelling in the family. At the same time, he was spoiled, the subject of exaggerated solicitude, which he did not dare reject, although he experienced it as interfering and controlling. "If you turn it down, they think you want to break with the family"; "If I draw a line, their first thought is that I'm emotionally disturbed." He describes the way he was raised as "a sort of brainwashing".

He says that he needs a lot of time for himself in order to stay in balance. He goes to many films, including American ones, reads books, and listens to music.

Queried as to his relationships with women, he tells of an "online love story" with a Chinese woman on the east coast of the USA and describes his problem thus:

> "The ones I like don't like me. The ones that do like me don't interest me. . . . The other sex and I, we're usually like parallel lines. There are no points of contact."

On the other hand, Mr Wang seems to have formed a trusting relationship to the male interviewer. Later in this interview he says,

> "If I hadn't talked to you about myself, you'd never have believed that I'm unhappy, nobody around me thinks that. . . . If you, Teacher Li, were to say to me some day, "son Wang, come away with me somewhere", I would go with you right away. No problem. I'd follow you."

Asked if he had ever been separated from his family, he tells that he was jailed for 180 days after becoming the target of a denunciation, and references the events of 4 June 1989, when the pro-democracy demonstrations in Tiananmen Square were suppressed by force. He reports that he was frightened and panicky at first, but adds, "Wherever they put me, I have to accept it. What else can I do?"

> "I certainly can't forget that business, but it also wasn't so huge. . . . It didn't do me in. I have nothing to be ashamed of, even today. . . . I wanted to be in on things. I broke the rules of public order. I don't think I was politically motivated or engaged. . . . Just being there was fun."

Taking his leave of the interviewer, son Wang expresses his thanks in fulsome terms, and it seems that he would have liked to take part in further conversations.

> "It was a look back at my childhood. I thank you so much for giving me this chance. I've rarely looked back at the past, because I'm a person who likes to live in the present. This is the first time I've dug these old things up out of myself and aired them in the sunlight. It's good, I feel good."

### Reflections on trauma and transmission

Father Wang, born 1930, tells movingly of his sufferings and traumas during the Cultural Revolution, which still haunt him in the form of flashbacks and nightmares, and also have left their mark in his child-rearing methods. At the age of two months, Father Wang is transferred from his parents to his grandmother, producing, I surmise, a first separation trauma. His parents themselves might have been traumatised by civil war and famine. To the present day in China, there is little awareness of the traumas, individual, familial, and collective, produced by war and civil war. Perhaps this is why the interviewer did not probe these topics.

Mr Wang's grandmother is loving and he becomes deeply attached to her. Her death in 1953, when Mr Wang is twenty-three, is "a heavy blow" to him. At her burial, he jumps into the open grave, unwilling to live on. He falls into a deep, depressive–suicidal crisis, which he re-enacts concretely in the interview. When his "deep emotional relationship" to his grandmother and her death are discussed, he seems confused and foams at the mouth. This exceptional emotional state, which the interviewer does not investigate further, can be understood as the resurfacing of a central loss experience from early life.

Only his marriage in 1955, at the age of twenty-five, brings him out of this serious crisis; it is clear that his wife can provide the missing sense of security. Her death in 1964 of a too-late-diagnosed breast cancer sends him into a new existential depression. Concerned that he might again try to leap into the grave, the authorities keep him away from the funeral. "Crazy" with despair and overwhelmed with unbearable emotions, he must undergo psychiatric treatment.

Two years after Mr Wang's loss of his wife, the events of the Cultural Revolution begin unfolding. We may assume that Mr Wang has not mourned for this loss at all. And suddenly a new drama and trauma sweep over him. The painful experiences that follow double the effect on him, catalysing the reactivation of earlier traumas that had already deeply shaken his grasp of himself and the world. Memories of his earlier feeling states are released, like Russian dolls nestling within each other. Even today, Mr Wang experiences recurring flash memories of the Cultural Revolution, clear signs of a post traumatic stress syndrome. Panic, despair, and deep feelings of powerlessness, along with thoughts of ending it all through suicide, overwhelm him again and again.

It is striking that the questioning did not turn to his experiences in the internal exile period. Apparently, the interviewer thought they were less relevant, or feared being confronted with further traumatic experiences that he himself would find hard to bear.

### "Life is like a tree, only healthy, when it can unfold itself"

Traumatisations such as those suffered by father Wang exceed the psychic processing power of the victim and deeply affect his personality structure, his empathic understanding capabilities, and his ability to relate in marriage and family (cf. the contribution of Plänkers, pp. 83–120). It is to be expected that traumata of the first generation will strongly affect the lives of the following generation. Traumatised parents have limited ability to perform a containment function for their children or to provide them with a sheltered space for their development. The traumatised father is presumably so preoccupied with his own unprocessed traumatic past, and with the connected feelings of existential fear, guilt, shame, hate, and depressive mourning, that he cannot feel his way adequately into the needs of his son, using him rather as a self-object. As a result, the son's process of individuation and separation is largely blocked. That individuation, that separation, are serious threats to a traumatised father, and become associated for the son with fear and guilt. The life-affirming aggression necessary for individuation can hardly be summoned up in the relationship with such a father. A traumatised father is also unable to help the son to separate from his mother. Hence, son Wang has not achieved a sufficient degree of separation, either inner or outer, from his parents.

Son Wang compares the child-rearing style of his parents to "brainwashing"; things were "hammered in" and "drummed in"; he says, "I was frequently beaten." This style makes it clear that the parents themselves identify with the "methods of the Cultural Revolution", perhaps also with a rigid Confucianism, and raised the son according to these methods. So, we can regard the son as abandoned in a sense, not recognised as an individual, rendered powerless by an excess of care, and abused by unwarranted intrusiveness. Although son Wang senses the massive interference, infantilisation, and disregard for personal boundaries that lie behind his parents' solicitude, he is defenceless against these.

It is typical in traumatised parents to see the outer world as threatening. Son Wang grows up rather isolated from his surroundings, because his parents fear that the neighbouring children will spoil him or influence him in bad ways. In this paranoid family atmosphere, son Wang develops social phobias very early, and a schizoid personality as described by Fairbairn (2000).

The identification processes of children who grow up with traumatised parents are extensively described in the literature. Kestenberg labels these identifications "transposition" (1989): unconscious identificatory participation in the past life experience of a traumatised parent. Faimberg (1987, 2009) names it "telescoping", meaning the way the generations come close and even interpenetrate. Identifications are forced onward into the next generation, partially by a process of projective identification, leading possibly to feelings of alienation in the children of traumatised parents.

Son Wang is in a strong counter-identification with his parents: they want to force on him their care and their will; they want him to marry; they want him to think and feel as they do—and he fights back hard. However, a counter-identification always contains a simultaneous identification, which in this case is equally strong. Son Wang does not bring this to consciousness, though, and so does not succeed at either the internal nor the superficial process of separation.

Without a relationship to a woman, Son Wang lives reclusively in his parents' house and seeks refuge in a substitute world of films and books. We asked ourselves if he might be homosexual, but not permitted to admit it and live accordingly. While no longer classed as a mental illness in China (since 2001), homosexuality is still discouraged as a decadent, capitalistic phenomenon.

Even in their private conversation, Wang and his interviewer dismiss his detention for 180 days in connection with the Tiananmen Square massacre as "no longer upsetting". Twenty years after 4 June 1980, the massacre is still taboo in public discussion. Probably, son Wang and his interviewer are conforming to this collective silence.

Son Wang's participation in this demonstration could be understood as identification with his father, who spoke out boldly during the Hundred Flowers Movement of 1956 and then was branded as a rightist deviationist. In the course of the two interviews, son Wang made this general pronouncement: "I regard the cultural Revolution as a 'Culture'." What does he mean by this? Possibly, that a new culture can only begin when youth—and rebelliousness—are recognised and valued alongside the traditional ways.

Denounced and locked up as his father was, son Wang takes no notice of the similarity, also to be understood as identification with the father, remarking, rather, "Psychology is a Western thing."

In a certain sense, the son Wang as a child was already locked up, as if detained. Even now he is as if "in family custody", not having yet managed to separate physically, let alone internally, from his family and from his traumatised father. His process of individuation and separation is seriously stalled. How is it possible to separate, without help, from a traumatised father?

Son Wang makes his interviewer a moving offer, redolent of transference: "If you, Teacher Li, were to say to me some day, 'Son Wang, come away with me somewhere', I would go with you right away." Here, it seems to me, the junior Wang is expressing his deep longing for a father figure who, having the empathic capability to understand him, would free him from his childish dependency on his family.

## East and West: problems of intercultural interpretation

If we have here studied aspects of an Eastern culture with Western attitudes and psychoanalytic eyes, this is partly in order to build a bridge between cultures that seem strange to one another. Levi-Strauss (1973) is of the opinion that engagement with a foreign culture allows us a new, distanced observation of our own; the Zen Buddhists say you cannot talk about a tree limb until you yourself have become the limb.

In order to better grasp the problems of intercultural interpretation, I shall first describe some characteristics of the Chinese lifestyle and worldview. Next, I shall highlight some points of difference with Western attitudes, and go on to point out the similarities and points of agreement that also exist.

## Chinese lifestyle and worldview

The intellectual world of a Chinese person, and with it his or her thinking, feeling, and willing, are primarily marked by the three great spiritual currents of Confucianism, Daoism, and Chán Buddhism, known in Japan as Zen. Confucianism, whose lifestyle and worldview are laid out in the "Analects" of his students and the "Old Writings" edited by the sage himself, was dominant from 136 BCE until 1911, a century ago. As the intellectual mainstream and as the official ideology of the state, Confucianism deeply marked and formed mentalities in all walks of life (cf. Confucius, 1993).

Confucius (551–479 BCE) offers the model of the upright man (*Junzi*), whose most basic virtue is filial piety (*Xiao*). Confucius teaches that this first virtue gives rise to all the others, like human sympathy, morality, and loyalty. Filial piety means the son's duty to respect and care for his parents and to follow in their footsteps. This worldview is permeated by the belief that the family is the nucleus, the centre of all social and political life. Indeed, the family has a towering importance in China. Added to it are beliefs in patriarchy, hierarchy, and tradition.

The joy of study and self-cultivation is as highly valued as the fulfil-ment of duty, the performance of the rites, and the veneration of ancestors. The individual understands himself as part of a social family in which he must take his place, deferring his personal desires. In the nuclear family, too, the Chinese "I" finds its place only within the consciousness of "We", a dependency from which it does not seek to shake free (Gerlach & Haag, 2000).

We can regard the search for harmony, proportion, and the Golden Mean as the mainspring of the Chinese worldview. This pursuit leads to the idea of the accord of Man and Universe, and (with Laozi) to the idea of the accord of Man and Nature. Such visions of harmony yield a Chinese dislike of all kinds of one-sidedness and of extremes. "Both–and" is everywhere preferred to "either/or". One tries to see the mutual dependency of opposites, as crystallised in the doctrine of Yin and Yang, the interaction of two principles, such as active and passive.

The oldest and most honoured book of wisdom, to some extent the Bible of the Chinese, is the *I Ching*. It gives the suffering reader the certainty that everything between heaven and earth is in a state of change. The way to be redeemed from suffering is to accept one's place in the eternal transformation, patiently awaiting what is to come. The person who is considered enlightened and wise does not try to influence processes of heaven and human society, but, rather, bows to the unavoidable fluxes of the world. This might have an affin-ity with Nietzsche's concept of by *amor fati* (cf. the contribution of Wang, pp. 35–56).

To illuminate the differences between Chinese and Western world-views, let us take a closer look at three areas: the relationship of the generations, ways of coping with sorrow, and the understanding of the individual.

## Intergenerational relations

The Chinese character *Xiao*, which can be translated by the word "piety", is composed of the signs for "age" and for "son". Its form captures the hierarchical relationship between father and son. It demands the son's fulfilment of certain duties. He shall care for his elders, devote himself to them, admonish them cautiously when required, and provide them with heirs. He is not to abandon them as long as they live. He is to be constantly solicitous of their health and, so as not to cause them worry, of his own. He is also to honour them before their deaths and after, according to the rites of ancestor veneration. After a father dies, Confucius dictates, it is the son's duty to grieve for three years, balancing the three years of infancy in which he could not have survived alone. As long as the father lives, but also thereafter, the son is to orientate himself by the parental will—though Confucius allows the pious son to admonish his father, in a tender manner, to correct his errors. If the father does not accept the correction, the son must comply all the more reverently with his father's decisions (Xuewu, 1999).

Confucius emphasises reverence as the essential part of a son's duty. A reverent son will produce many children. Not to marry and to remain childless is to break the continuity of sacrifice to the ancestors, a terrible lapse.

The Western ideal is for the son to leave father and mother and become an independent individual. Childish dependency dies and an autonomous person develops, to continue the relationship with his parents on a voluntary basis. In the Chinese world, by contrast, the individuation and separation process takes a more complicated form. Dependency is not allowed to die, but is to be maintained for a lifetime in the form of filial piety. Succession means imitating the father and becoming like him (Rong-Ji, 2008).

According to Sun (1994) the Chinese solution to the generational conflict consists in the capitulation of the young to the old. Only thus can one fulfil his pious duty, *Xiao*. Since harmony is the highest ideal of Chinese culture, a rupture with the parents is forbidden. Sun maintains that no new generation in China can flourish: each is ruined by its parents and passes the same ruin on to its children. Generation by generation, individuality is ground down. If Western civilisation might be described as one of patricide, Chinese civilisation is one of infanticide. Lu Xun (1881–1936), a well-known Chinese author, was similarly convinced that the old had blocked the way of the young and deprived them of air to breathe.

Sun (1994) has this idea: just as the youthful Mao fought the authorities, the Cultural Revolution, decades later, made a frontal assault on many aspects of the deep structure of Chinese society. The revolutionaries wanted to abolish the traditional pressure for harmony, hierarchical thinking, and obedience. In a mighty rebellion of young against old, the culture of child killing was to be "revolutionised". This did not happen. Even today it is rare for a son to speak a direct, clear "No" to his father and mother. Aggressive–destructive feelings exist, of course, but in passivity; conflict between the generations can scarcely be aired. It is perhaps not coincidental that China produced the classic work on sly and concealed aggression titled *Thirty-Six Stratagems*; it describes such tricks as "Hide the Dagger Behind a Smile"; "Lure Your Enemy to the Rooftop and Take Away the Ladder", and "Threaten in the East, Attack in the West" (von Senger, 1999).

The thought that hate can deepen love, if love contains this hatred, is foreign to Chinese theories of harmony. Thus, the separation of son from parents is more difficult, for separation entails the death, the destruction, of the old childish relationship, in order that a new and adult relationship on a voluntary basis can arise.

## Dealing with suffering

Plänkers (2008c, cf. also his contribution here, pp. 83–120) emphasises the need to consider Chinese circumstances if we want to understand how the Chinese ego deals with trauma. It is a sign of great psychic maturity to bear suffering without fighting back. Affliction is to be accepted like a natural event. Thus, the Cultural Revolution was understood as fate and happenstance. This attitude suggests, I think, the basic Stoic attitudes of *apathia* and *ataraxia* in ancient Greece.

Plänkers goes on to say that Chinese readiness to endure suffering is visible even in the character for "endurance of suffering" (the word is *ren*, pronounced in the third tone). The upper part of the ideogram is the sign for "knife", the lower part is the sign for "heart". To endure suffering is, thus, to have a knife in the heart, and the knife may not be drawn out, because this would threaten the control and suppression of emotions. In understanding collective traumatisation through the Cultural Revolution, we must note that Chinese society to date has not acknowledged individual suffering and, thus, has offered no containment, which is the absolute precondition for the personal grieving process. We can well understand what we observed in our research: that both interviewers and subjects went out of their way to avoid stirring up and exploring old traumas.

## The individual

The Western understanding of the child's individuation is a product of the Enlightenment. Enlightenment means looking at traditions critically, conserving what is useful and modifying what is obsolete; reflecting on the self; questioning inherited moral concepts; not simply accepting things because they are old. According to Kant (1724–1804), enlightenment means daring to use your reason and understanding.

In contrast to Confucius, who made the Old his starting point, the Enlightenment turns against every form of blind faith in authority and subservience to tradition. It emphasises individual happiness, seeks personal development, and accords the individual person a right to happiness, self-awareness, and independence. Enlightenment thought takes an emancipatory posture. After happiness, freedom and the unfolding of talents are values held to be grounded in human nature. Freud, who has been called the rationalist of the irrational, is deeply rooted in the Enlightenment tradition. By turning his attention to the psychic life of human beings and to the unconscious resistances to self-knowledge, he pursued the philosophers' quest to illuminate. Psychoanalysis is the Enlightenment psychology *par excellence.*

Descartes (1596–1650), one of the fathers of modern Western philosophy, emphasises the primacy of the subject as against the object, of consciousness as against existence. Thus, he opened the way for psychology and generated a new kind of interest in the subject, something not shared in this form by the Chinese. "Cogito, ergo sum", "I think, therefore I am": the formula gives primacy to autonomy and self-determination. Modern Westerners understand themselves accordingly. Gay (2008) characterises the modern impulse as the attraction of heresy: the pleasure of shocking, of daring something new, unfamiliar, unheard of, in an unconditional exploration of self and subjectivity. If we consider this Western concept essential to the modern era, we can reasonably say that China has not yet arrived in that era.

## Similarities and commonalities

Russell (1922) emphasised the similarities between the Chinese and the Western world. He wrote that Westerners have a theory that the Chinese are inscrutable and full of secret thoughts, impossible for us to understand. He, however, had seen nothing to confirm this opinion.

In his view, the Chinese are not so different from Europeans (cf. Russell 1966[1922], p. 199).

My own experience of China was similar to Russell's. Since 2008, I have been participating in a postgraduate programme called "Group analysis for Chinese psychiatrists and psychologists". Before our first group meeting, I worried that I might not be able to distinguish and remember the faces of individual members. In the event, this problem simply did not exist. The group process, too, had many similarities to what I had experienced in Germany. Psychoanalysis claims to have made certain central discoveries that are of universal meaning, transcending all cultural differences. The Chinese soul also contains an unconscious mind, drives and conflicts among drives, the Oedipus complex, and object relationships that unconsciously serve as guides. The Chinese individual, like the Western one, wants to love and be loved. Just as our Adam and Eve met, loved, and desired each other, so do the Chinese man and the Chinese woman.

I understand my thoughts on intercultural interpretation to be a thesis in need of an antithesis, in order to allow a fruitful dialogue between the worlds. Confucius created an admirable ethical structure that motivated Leibniz (1646–1716) to suggest that the Chinese should send missionaries to Europe. I, too, am convinced that the Western emphasis on the individual meets a challenging antithesis in this Eastern ethic orientated to society, We-consciousness, taking one's place in the community, self-cultivation, self-discipline, and joy in learning. According to Weggel (1997), Confucianism indicates ways in which people must act and react to secure a maximum of harmony in an age of limited space, scarce natural resources, and growing conflicts about the allocation of wealth, for, in Confucianism, the values of conservation far outrank those of development. The increasing contact of cultures can cause recognised values and attitudes to be called into question on both sides. In my opinion, there is a role here for psychoanalysis. Dealing as it does with what is strangest in ourselves and in our own culture, it could also be very helpful in the intercultural dialogue.

### Concluding considerations: Mao and the trauma of the Cultural Revolution

The transgenerational transmission of traumatic experiences produced by the Cultural Revolution was presented using the example of

father Wang and his son, born in 1968. It became clear that the relation of the generations today is still determined by Confucian
thoughts held valid for two thousand years. The construction of a
Communist China changed this as little as did the Cultural Revolution, directed against Confucianism though it was. Rather, we see
that the traumata generated by this reign of terror were "processed"
by the victims in a manner true to the guidelines of Confucian teaching, according to which the unresisting endurance of suffering is a
sign of psychic maturity. At the same time, as son Wang testifies in his
interview, the Confucian demands for filial piety were imposed on the
following generation—in particularly rigid form and with the painful
and damaging methods of the Cultural Revolution thrown in. If son
Wang, none the less, understands the Cultural Revolution as a culture,
he is not speaking of the child-rearing methods he suffered and from
which he suffers still. Rather, his statement shows an identification
with that tendency within the Cultural Revolution that declared war
on the authorities and the desire for harmony, on hierarchic thinking
and the tradition of obedience.

In this connection we should look again at Mao's psychology. We
do not adopt the viewpoint that he was solely responsible for the
Cultural Revolution. Nevertheless, it was Mao himself who spoke out
in favour of freeing individual Chinese from inherited constraints and
advocated their free development. This demand for individuality was
nominally part of the cultural-revolutionary programme—so long as
it was directed only against Confucian ideas of the family and lingering feudal structures in the community. It is this aspect that causes son
Wang, even now, to see something in the revolution that speaks to his
own wishes for a self-determined life.

In truth, Mao fought against "the culture of infanticide", by which
he meant the subjection of the younger to the older generation, and
was in his own youth a rebel, as Böke (2007) vividly describes:

Mao, born 26 December 1893, in the village Shaoshan in Hunan in
central China, started out 100% as a rebel and activist. His father,
whose good commercial instincts had made him a relatively prosperous peasant, had enabled his son to attend primary school. But young
Mao dared to rebel against his father's tyranny, absolutely rejecting
the ruling Confucian ethic. At the age of fourteen, he refused an
arranged marriage; at sixteen, he fled his parents' house, in which
his mother, a gentle-hearted Buddhist, was an inadequate corrective

influence. . . . Mao's attitude was always one of militant solidarity against every kind of repression, combined with pragmatic flexibility in tactics. He began as a man of action, becoming a theorist only later. . . . In his marginal notes in *System of Ethics*, by the German neo-Kantian Friedrich Paulsen, he writes, "There can be no worse crime than there where the individual is constrained, where actions are directed against an individual's nature". He was impressed especially by Tolstoy and the anarchists Bakunin and Kropotkin. (pp. 22–23, translated for this edition)

The adolescent Mao deeply hated Confucianism also because he saw it allied with feudalism and exploitation. Decades later, Mao formed an alliance with the youthful Rebels and shattered the Party that, as Hoffmann notes (1977), he himself had built up through decades of hard work. His purpose was to rein in a Party apparatus that he felt had increasingly become, by the 1960s, a brake on progress; his enemies were bureaucrats.

Yet, Mao's credo that individual development must not be constrained did not prevent him, the "Great Steersman", from behaving like a semi-divine emperor, summoning the people to self-sacrifice and revolutionary enthusiasm at mass demonstrations and in *The Little Red Book*. According to Lifton (1970) the Cultural Revolution was the product of the aged Mao's twofold fear: of his own death, and of the end of "his" revolution (cf. Gänßbauer, 1996). Mao hoped that the Cultural Revolution would secure his "revolutionary immortality". Lifton describes it as Mao's "last throes". The final phase of the revolution, begun in 1973, was a campaign against Confucius (cf. the Party Resolution of 1981, pp. ??–??). At the same time, I think it can be shown that Mao had his own identifications with Confucian ideas.

Like Gänßbauer, I understand the Cultural Revolution as a situation of political extremity with post-trauma consequences, as described movingly by father Wang. His experiences during the period, however, had double the impact because they also catalysed the resurfacing of earlier traumas. As we have seen, the consequences can be observed in the son, an intergenerational transfer (telescoping, according to Faimberg, 1987, 2009).

Looking at the history of China after 1930, the year of father Wang's birth, we see a series of the most various traumatic events. To name a few: from 1927 to 1937, the first Chinese Civil War; from 1937 to 1945, the Second Sino-Japanese War; in 1937, the Rape of Nanking;

from 1945 to 1949, the second civil war, one of the bloodiest in modern history; from 1958 to 1961, the "Great Leap Forward" and the terrible famine it produced. These events, along with western colonialism in the nineteenth century and earlier twentieth century, constitute a heavy human and social mortgage on Chinese shoulders. The country needs empathy and support from the world community. Psychoanalysis, in particular, can be helpful in the task of letting these traumatic experiences be understood: in finding words for what, until now, could be articulated only with difficulty, or not at all.

## References

Böke, H. (2007). *Maoismus: China und die Linke—Bilanz und Perspektive.* Stuttgart: Schmetterling.

Confucius (1993). *The Analects,* R. Dawson (Trans.). New York: Oxford University Press.

Faimberg, H. (1987). Die Ineinanderrückung (Teleskoping) der Generationen: Zur Genealogie Gewisser Identifizierungen. *Jahrbuch der Psychoanalyse, 20*: 114–142.

Faimberg, H. (2009). *Teleskoping. Die intergenerationelle Weitergabe Narzisstischer Bindungen.* Frankfurt: Brandes & Apsel.

Fairbairn, W. R. D. (2000). *Das Selbst und die Inneren Objektbeziehungen: Eine Psychoanalytische Objektbeziehungstheorie.* Gießen, Germany: Psychosozial, Bibliothek der Psychoanalyse.

Gänßbauer, M. (1996). *Trauma der Vergangenheit. Die Rezeption der Kulturrevolution und der Schriftsteller Feng Jicai.* Dortmund: Projekt.

Gay, P. (2008). *Die Moderne. Eine Geschichte des Aufbruchs.* Frankfurt a. M.: Fischer.

Gerlach, A., & Haag, A. (2000). Trennungstraumata in der Chinesischen Kulturrevolution. In: A. Gerlach (Ed.), *Die Tigerkuh: Ethnopsychoanalytische Erkundungen* (pp. 123–141). Gießen: Psychosozial.

Hoffmann, R. (1977). *Maos Rebellen: Sozialgeschichte der Chinesischen Kulturrevolution.* Hamburg: Hoffmann und Campe.

Kestenberg, J. S. (1989). Neue Gedanken zur Transposition: Klinische, therapeutische und entwicklungsbedingte Betrachtungen. *Jahrbuch der Psychoanalyse, 24*: 163–189.

Levi-Strauss, C. (1973). *Tristes Tropiques.* New York: Atheneum.

Lifton, R. (1970). *Die Unsterblichkeits des Revolutionärs: Mao Tse-Tung und die chinesische Kulturrevolution.* Munich: List.

Plänkers, T. (2008). Der Schatten einer Kultur-Revolution. Eltern und Kinder im heutigen China. Unpublished.

Rong-Ji, P. (2008). *Sohnespflicht. Eine Analyse der Familienbeziehungen im alten China*. Saarbrücken: VDM.

Russell, B. (1922). *The Problem of China*. London: Rainbow Bridge Books, 1966.

Sun, L. (1994). *Das Ummauerte Ich: Die Tiefenstruktur der Chinesischen Mentalität*. Leipzig: Gustav Kiepenheuer.

Von Senger, H. (1999). *Die List*. Frankfurt: Suhrkamp.

Weggel, O. (1997). *China im Aufbruch: Konfuzianismus und politische Zukunft*. Munich: Beck.

Wurmser, L. (1990). *Die Maske der Scham* (6. Aufl.). Magdeburg: Klotz, 2010.

Xuewu, G. (1999). *Konfuzius zur Einführung*. Hamburg: Junius.

# Selective chronology of events in the history of the People's Republic of China

*From the founding to the Cultural Revolution (1949–1965)*

1949, October 1
Proclamation of the People's Republic by Mao Zedong.

1951, October
Occupation of Tibet by Chinese troops.

1952
"Five Antis Campaign" in the economic realm, targeting bribery, theft of state property, tax evasion, fraud, and theft of commercial secrets.
"Three Antis Campaign" in the governmental realm, targeting corruption, waste, and bureaucratisation.

1954, September
Initial meeting of the first National People's Congress.
Adoption of the first Constitution of the PRC.

1955
Collectivisation of agriculture and nationalisation of industry and commerce.

1955–56
Campaign against the oppositional clique around Hu Feng. More than 214,000 people are arrested, more than 21,000 sentenced to death, and more than 53,000 die through suicide, torture, or in labour camps.

1956, September
Beginning of the "Hundred Flowers Movement", sanctioning open criticism of state and Party.

1957
Beginning of the "Anti-Rightist Movement"; extensive arrests and dismissals from employment; 550,000 people affected.

1958–1962
"Great Leap Forward"; mass mobilisation for steel production.
Catastrophic famine with ca. 30–40 million dead.

1959, July
At the Lushan Conference of the Party Central Committee, Defence Minister Peng Dehuai is accused of rightist opportunism and relieved of his office.

1960
Publication of the fourth volume of the *Complete Works of Mao Zedong*. Defence Minister Lin Biao exhorts the Army and the nation to study Mao's works.

1962
At the "7000 Cadres Conference", President Liu Shaoqi criticises the "Great Leap Forward" and strives for a course correction. Lin Biao, however, supports Mao Zedong.

1963–1965
Campaign for socialist education and exhortations to "Learn from Comrade Lei Feng".
Class warfare against the "five black categories": landowners, wealthy peasants, counter-revolutionaries, bad elements, and rightist deviationists. Liu Shaoqi and Deng Xiaoping send work groups to the countryside and try to rein in abusive practices in local cadres.

1964, October
First Chinese atomic bomb test.

1965, May
Second Chinese atomic bomb test.

1965, November
Hostile review of Wu Han's play *Hai Rui Was Relieved of Office* in the Shanghai newspaper *Wenhui Bao*. Concerning an official in imperial times who took a critical stance toward the Emperor, the play was interpreted by Mao as directed at himself. The reviewer, Yao Wen-yuan, would be propaganda chief during the Cultural Revolution, and his attack is generally regarded as the Revolution's opening salvo.

## The Cultural Revolution (1966–1976)

1966, March
At an expanded meeting of the Politburo, Mao accuses Wu Han, Liao Mosha, and Deng Tuo of forming an anti-Party clique.

1966, May
Dissolution of the Party Committee for the city of Beijing.

1966, May
Beginning of the Cultural Revolution with the "16 Point Resolution" concerning goals and tasks of the new campaign.
Formation of the Central Working Group of the Cultural Revolution (Chen Boda as Director, Mao Zedong's wife Jiang Qing as Lieutenant Director, Kang Sheng as Adviser).
Dismissal of many supporters of President Liu Shaoqi.
First wall newspaper at Beijing University, by Nie Yuanzi.
Editorial in the *People's Daily* titled "Down with Cow Spirits and Serpent Demons".

1966, June
Nationwide distribution of Nie Yuanzi's wall newspaper at Mao's direction.
Editorial endorsement of Nie Yuanzi in the *People's Daily*.
Liu Shaoqi sends work groups into the institutions.
Attacks on Liu's work groups.

1966, July
The lead editorial in the magazine *Red Flag* supports the attack on the work groups and Liu Shaoqi.

In a wall newspaper, the Red Guards at Qinghua University call for rebellion.

1966, August
Mao Zedong publicly supports the Red Guards, making them a political power. For instance, he receives them in Tiananmen Square.
The conflict between Mao and Liu Shaoqi is evident at the eleventh plenary meeting of the 8th Central Committee.
Chen Boda attacks the work group at Qinghua University, which is led by Liu Shaoqi's wife Wang Guangmei.
Mao Zedong supports the rebellion with his wall newspaper "Bombard the Headquarters!"
The personality cult around Mao Zedong is promoted by Lin Biao.
The "Movement Against the Four Olds" (old ideas, old culture, old customs, and old habits); house searches in Beijing; the spread of Red Guard violence throughout the country.
Mao Zedong und Lin Biao endorse the "Movement Against the Four Olds".

1966, Summer
Red Guards torture more than 300 people to death in a Beijing suburb.

1966, September
Mao again receives the Red Guards in Tiananmen Square.

1966, October
Third reception of the Red Guards by Mao in Tiananmen Square.
Official recognition of the rebellion; intensification of the personality cult centred on Mao.
Jiang Qing and Zhang Chunqiao call on the Red Guards to attack the "capitalist camp".

1966, November
Concentrated attacks on Liu Shaoqi.
The Central Committee calls on the Red Guards to halt the Roving Movement (Da Chuanlian).

1966, December
Persecution of numerous highly situated veteran Party cadres, for instance Peng Zhen, Wan Li, Zhang Wentian, Zhou Yang, Tian Han, Wu Han, Lu Ping, and others.
Lin Biao writes the foreword for the second edition of "Mao's Bible".

Mass demonstration against Liu Shaoqi und Deng Xiaoping by students and docents at Qinghua University.

Arrest and prison maltreatment of Peng Dehuai.

Wall newspaper targeting Propaganda Minister Tao Zhu appears in the Propaganda Ministry.

1967, January

The *People's Daily* and the magazine *Red Flags* issue editorial calls to "Continue the Cultural Revolution".

Jiang Qing persuades Liu Shaoqi's children, Liu Tao and Liu Yunzhen, to denounce their father in a wall newspaper at Qinghua University.

Red Guards invade Liu Shaoqi's residence and attack the President and his wife Wang Guangmei.

Subsequently, other high cadres, Peng Zhen, Luo Ruiqing, Lu Dingyi, and others, are attacked at mass meetings in the Beijing Stadium.

Mao supports the Central Working Group for the Cultural Revolution in its deposition of Tao Zhu, the fourth-ranking member in the hierarchy of the Communist Party of China.

Zhang Chunqiao, Party Secretary in Shanghai, organises "the January Storm", in which workers and students drive the city's Party Committee out of office.

1967, February

The police arrest Liu Shaoqi's son, Liu Yunnuo.

"February adverse current." Jiang Qing gives this name to resistance by the supporters of Liu Shaoqi.

Zhou Enlai calls a meeting of the leading cadres of the Party, government, and the military. Supporters of Mao and Liu come into conflict.

Mao Zedong calls a meeting of the Politburo to condemn the "February adverse current".

Lin Biao reorganises Party structure, replacing the Politburo with the Central Working Group for the Cultural Revolution, and the standing committee of the Central Military Committee with the Operations Department of the CMC.

1967, March

Mao expresses support for Lin Biao und condemns resistance by Liu Shaoqi's supporters.

Mao criticises Liu Shaoqi's book *On the Self-Cultivation of a Communist* as subjective.

The Roving Movement of the Red Guards ends.
Persecution of the so-called "Clique of the 61 Traitors".

1967, April
Red Guards force their way into Liu Shaoqi's office and humiliate him by commanding him to clean, wash, and cook.
Public denunciation of Wang Guangmei before a mass meeting of 300.000 people at the Qinghua University.
Zhou Enlai comes under suspicion of being behind the "February adverse current", is attacked by the Red Guards.

1967, July
Students of the Beijing University of Architecture and Statics set up tents in the government district Zhongnanhai and attack Liu Shaoqi in wall newspapers.
Liu Shaoqi and Wang Guangmei are publicly attacked in the government quarter in an accusation meeting.
The "July 20 Incident" in Wuhan: confrontation between the largest faction of the rebels on one side and the People's Liberation Army and a PLA-supported mass organisation on the other. The Incident is one of the most spectacular acts of resistance against the rebellion involving political and military levels.
Dismissal of Chen Zaidao and Zhong Hua, General Commander and Political Commissar for the military region Wuhan.

1967, August
Liu Shaoqi is physically attacked and attempts to defend himself in reliance on the Constitution of the People's Republic of China.

1967, September
Yao Wenyuan attacks Tao Zhu in the media.
In the government quarter, Liu Shaoqi is confined and mistreated.

1967, December
False accusations and persecution of ca. 84,000 people in Tangshan, with some 3,000 deaths.

1968, January
False charges against Zhao Jianmin (Party Secretary of Yunnan) as a spy. Ca. 14,000 people die in connection with persecution.

1968, April
Editorial in the *People's Daily*: "Never Forget the Class War!"

Beginning of the purge of class ranks, persecution of so-called class enemies in the population.

1968, June
Lin Biao sends Liu Shaoqi to Kaifeng, where he spends his last days.

1968, October
Deng Xiaoping is sent to Jiangxi and then arrested there. Founding of "May 7 Cadre Schools" across the country. Mao Zedong stands fast to the Cultural Revolution and condemns the "February adverse current".
Liu Shaoqi is expelled from the Communist Party of China.

1968, November
Liu Shaoqi becomes ill.

1968, December
Mao initiates the rustication of youth.

1969, January
The first of a total of 12–14 million young students are sent down to the countryside.
Vice Prime Minister and Marshall He Long dies under persecution by Lin Biao.

1969, April
Ninth Congress of the Communist Party of China. Lin Biao is designated the official successor to Mao Zedong.

1969, November
Liu Shaoqi dies and is cremated under a false name.

1970, March
Fourth meeting of the National People's Congress; suggested amendment to the Constitution to abolish the office of President.

1970, August
Second plenary meeting of the Ninth Central Committee.
Mao grows increasingly mistrustful of Lin Biao.

1970, October
Mao criticises Lin Biao's wife, Ye Qun, as well as Wu Faxian and Huang Yongsheng

1970, November
The deposed Defence Minister Peng Dehuai is expelled from the Party and sentenced to life in prison.

1971, January
Campaign against revisionism.
Open criticism of the leader of the Central Working Group of the Cultural Revolution, Chen Boda.
Weakening of Lin Biao's position.

1971, February
Alleged putsch plan against Mao by Lin Biao, his wife, Ye Qun, and his son, Lin Liguo.
Visit to Beijing by US President Richard Nixon.

1971, May
Zhou Enlai falls ill with cancer.

1971, August
Many of the fallen cadres are restored to their positions, for instance Chen Yun, Wang Zhen, Teng Daiyuan.
"Report on the Counter-Revolutionary Actions of the Lin Biao Clique" (Lin Biao, Chen Boda, Ye Qun, Huang Yongsheng, and others are expelled from the Party).

1971, September
Lin Biao is killed in a plane crash in Mongolia, allegedly fleeing after planning a *coup d'état* against Mao.

1971, October
Editorial in the *People's Daily*: "Anarchism is a Counter-revolutionary Instrument of the Pseudo-Marxists".
Zhou Enlai criticises the anarchism of the radical leftists, the "Gang of Four" (Jiang Qing, Wang Hongwen, Zhang Chunqiao, Yao Wenyuan).

1971, November
Zhou Enlai leads an investigation against the Anti-Party Clique of Lin Biao and Chen Boda.
Mao rehabilitates the participants in the "February adverse current" and increasingly reposes his trust in Zhou Enlai.

1971, December
Campaign against Lin Biao.

Zhou Enlai prepares "Work Plan 1972".
Reorganisation in agriculture, industry, and schools.

1972, January
Editorial in the *People's Daily*: "Continue the Revolution, Maximise Production".
Death of Foreign Minister Chen Yi.

1973, March
Deng Xiaoping named Vice Prime Minister.

1973, April
The deposed Defence Minister Peng Dehuai is diagnosed with cancer.

1973, May
Mao Zedong criticises Lin Biao as a Confucian, as an opponent of the Legalists.

1973, August
Editorial in the *People's Daily*: "Confucius—A Thinker from a Slaveholding Society" (allusion to Zhou Enlai).

1974, January
"Address for the New Year" in the *People's Daily*.
Preparation of a new campaign against Lin Biao and Confucius.
Support of this campaign by Mao Zedong.
Jiang Qing mounts a mass meeting in the Beijing Sports Stadium against Lin Biao and Confucius, an allusion to Zhou Enlai.

1974, July
Decree of the central government: "Continue the Revolution, Maximise Production".
Resistance by the "Gang of Four" (Jiang Qing, Zhang Chunqiao, Yao Wenyuan, Wang Hongwen) to reorganisation and development as planned by Zhou Enlai.

1974, October
Mao points to the eight-year duration of the Cultural Revolution and the need for solidarity and stability.

1974, November
The deposed Defence Minister Peng Dehuai dies at the age of seventy-six.

1975, January
Deng Xiaoping becomes interim head of the Central Military Committee.
Jiang Qing tries and fails to form a government.

1976, 8 January
Death of Zhou Enlai. The inhabitants of Beijing mourn him and demonstrate their dissatisfaction with the "Gang of Four".

1976, April
Demonstrations against the Cultural Revolution on the occasion of public mourning for Zhou Enlai in Tiananmen Square.
5 April: Bloody suppression of these demonstrations.

1976, July
Major earthquake in Tangshan.

1976, 9 September
Death of Mao Zedong.

1976, October
Arrest of the "Gang of Four". End of the Cultural Revolution.

# Resolution on Certain Questions in the History of our Party since the Founding of the People's Republic of China

## (Adopted by the Sixth Plenary Session of the Eleventh Central Committee of the Communist Party of China on 27 June 1981)

Note: We reproduce here only Sections 19–26 of the Resolution, concerning the assessment of the Cultural Revolution. (T. P.)

### The decade of the "Cultural Revolution'

19. The "cultural revolution', which lasted from May 1966 to October 1976, was responsible for the most severe setback and the heaviest losses suffered by the Party, the state and the people since the founding of the People's Republic. It was initiated and led by Comrade Mao Zedong. His principal theses were that many representatives of the bourgeoisie and counter-revolutionary revisionists had sneaked into the Party, the government, the army and cultural circles, and leadership in a fairly large majority of organizations and departments was no longer in the hands of Marxists and the people; that Party persons in power taking the capitalist road had formed a bourgeois headquarters inside the Central Committee which pursued a revisionist political and organizational line and had agents in all provinces, municipalities and autonomous regions, as well as in all central departments; that since the forms of struggle adopted in the past had not been able to solve this problem, the power usurped by the capitalist-roaders could

be recaptured only by carrying out a great cultural revolution, by openly and fully mobilizing the broad masses from the bottom up to expose these sinister phenomena; and that the cultural revolution was in fact a great political revolution in which one class would overthrow another, a revolution that would have to be waged time and again. These theses appeared mainly in the May 16 Circular, which served as the programmatic document of the "cultural revolution', and in the political report to the Ninth National Congress of the Party in April 1969. They were incorporated into a general theory—the "theory of continued revolution under the dictatorship of the proletariat"—which then took on a specific meaning. These erroneous "Left" theses, upon which Comrade Mao Zedong based himself in initiating the "cultural revolution", were obviously inconsistent with the system of Mao Zedong Thought, which is the integration of the universal principles of Marxism–Leninism with the concrete practice of the Chinese revolution. These theses must be clearly distinguished from Mao Zedong Thought. As for Lin Biao, Jiang Qing and others, who were placed in important positions by Comrade Mao Zedong, the matter is of an entirely different nature. They rigged up two counter-revolutionary cliques in an attempt to seize supreme power and, taking advantage of Comrade Mao Zedong's errors, committed many crimes behind his back, bringing disaster to the country and the people. As their counter-revolutionary crimes have been fully exposed, this resolution will not go into them at any length.

20. The history of the "cultural revolution" has proved that Comrade Mao Zedong's principal theses for initiating this revolution conformed neither to Marxism, Leninism nor to Chinese reality. They represent an entirely erroneous appraisal of the prevailing class relations and political situation in the Party and state.

1) The "cultural revolution" was defined as a struggle against the revisionist line or the capitalist road. There were no grounds at all for this definition. It led to the confusing of right and wrong on a series of important theories and policies. Many things denounced as revisionist or capitalist during the "cultural revolution" were actually Marxist and socialist principles, many of which had been set forth or supported by Comrade Mao Zedong himself. The "cultural revolution" negated many of the correct principles, policies and achievements of the seventeen years after the founding of the People's Republic. In fact, it negated much of the work of the Central Committee of the Party and the People's Government, including Comrade Mao Zedong's own contribution. It negated the arduous struggles the entire people had conducted in socialist construction.

2) The confusing of right and wrong inevitably led to confusing the people with the enemy. The "capitalist-roaders" overthrown in the "cultural revolution" were leading cadres of Party and government organizations at all levels, who formed the core force of the socialist cause. The so-called bourgeois headquarters inside the Party headed by Liu Shaoqi and Deng Xiaoping simply did not exist. Irrefutable facts have proved that labelling Comrade Liu Shaoqi a "renegade, hidden traitor and stab" was nothing but a frame-up by Lin Biao, Jiang Qing and their followers. The political conclusion concerning Comrade Liu Shaoqi drawn by the Twelfth Plenary Session of the Eighth Central Committee of the Party and the disciplinary measure it meted out to him were both utterly wrong. The criticism of the so-called reactionary academic authorities in the "cultural revolution" during which many capable and accomplished intellectuals were attacked and persecuted also badly muddled up the distinction between the people and the enemy.

3) Nominally, the "cultural revolution" was conducted by directly relying on the masses. In fact, it was divorced both from the Party organizations and from the masses. After the movement started, Party organizations at different levels were attacked and became partially or wholly paralysed, the Party's leading cadres at various levels were subjected to criticism and struggle, inner-Party life came to a standstill, and many activists and large numbers of the basic masses whom the Party has long relied on were rejected. At the beginning of the "cultural revolution", the vast majority of participants in the movement acted out of their faith in Comrade Mao Zedong and the Party. Except for a handful of extremists, however, they did not approve of launching ruthless struggles against leading Party cadres at all levels. With the lapse of time, following their own circuitous paths, they eventually attained a heightened political consciousness and consequently began to adopt a sceptical or wait-and-see attitude towards the "cultural revolution", or even resisted and opposed it. Many people were assailed either more or less severely for this very reason. Such a state of affairs could not but provide openings to be exploited by opportunists, careerists and conspirators, not a few of whom were escalated to high or even key positions.

4) Practice has shown that the "cultural revolution" did not in fact constitute a revolution or social progress in any sense, nor could it possibly have done so. It was we and not the enemy at all who were thrown into disorder by the "cultural revolution". Therefore, from beginning to end, it did not turn "great disorder under heaven" into "great order under heaven", nor could it conceivably have done so.

After the state power in the form of the people's democratic dictatorship was established in China, and especially after socialist transformation was basically completed and the exploiters were eliminated as classes, the socialist revolution represented a fundamental break with the past in both content and method, even though its tasks remained to be completed. Of course, it was essential to take proper account of certain undesirable phenomena that undoubtedly existed in Party and state organisms and to remove them by correct measures in conformity with the Constitution, the laws and the Party Constitution. But on no account should the theories and methods of the "cultural revolution" have been applied. Under socialist conditions, there is no economic or political basis for carrying out a great political revolution in which "one class overthrows another". It decidedly could not come up with any constructive programme, but could only bring grave disorder, damage and retrogression in its train. History has shown that the "cultural revolution", initiated by a leader labouring under a misapprehension and capitalised on by counter-revolutionary cliques, led to domestic turmoil and brought catastrophe to the Party, the state and the whole people.

21. The "cultural revolution" can be divided into three stages.

1) From the initiation of the "cultural revolution" to the Ninth National Congress of the Party in April 1969. The convening of the enlarged Political Bureau meeting of the Central Committee of the Party in May 1966 and the Eleventh Plenary Session of the Eighth Central Committee in August of that year marked the launching of the "cultural revolution" on a full scale. These two meetings adopted the May 16 Circular and the Decision of the Central Committee of the Communist Party of China Concerning the Great Proletarian Cultural Revolution respectively. They launched an erroneous struggle against the so-called anti-Party clique of Peng Zhen, Luo Ruiqing, Lu Dingyi and Yang Shangkun and the so-called headquarters of Liu Shaoqi and Deng Xiaoping. They wrongly reorganised the central leading organs, set up the "Cultural Revolution Group Under the Central Committee of the Chinese Communist Party" and gave it a major part of the power of the Central Committee. In fact, Comrade Mao Zedong's personal leadership characterised by "Left" errors took the place of the collective leadership of the Central Committee, and the cult of Comrade Mao Zedong was frenziedly pushed to an extreme. Lin Biao, Jiang Qing, Kang Sheng, Zhang Chunqiao and others, acting chiefly in the name of the "Cultural Revolution Group", exploited the situation to incite people to "overthrow everything and wage full-scale civil war". Around February 1967, at various meetings, Tan Zhenlin, Chen

Yi, Ye Jianying, Li Fuchun, Li Xiannian, Xu Xiangqian, Nie Rongzhen and other Political Bureau members and leading comrades of the Military Commission of the Central Committee sharply criticised the mistakes of the "cultural revolution". This was labelled the "February adverse current", and they were attacked and repressed. Comrades Zhu De and Chen Yun were also wrongly criticised. Almost all leading Party and government departments in the different spheres and localities were stripped of their power or reorganised. The chaos was such that it was necessary to send in the People's Liberation Army to support the Left, the workers and the peasants and to institute military control and military training. It played a positive role in stabilizing the situation, but it also produced some negative consequences. The Ninth Congress of the Party legitimatised the erroneous theories and practices of the "cultural revolution", and so reinforced the positions of Lin Biao, Jiang Qing, Kang Sheng and others in the Central Committee of the Party. The guidelines of the Ninth Congress were wrong, ideologically, politically and organizationally.

2) From the Ninth National Congress of the Party to its Tenth National Congress in August 1973.

In 1970–71 the counter-revolutionary Lin Biao clique plotted to capture supreme power and attempted an armed counterrevolutionary coup d'état. Such was the outcome of the "cultural revolution" which overturned a series of fundamental Party principles. Objectively, it announced the failure of the theories and practices of the "cultural revolution". Comrades Mao Zedong and Zhou Enlai ingeniously thwarted the plotted coup. Supported by Comrade Mao Zedong, Comrade Zhou Enlai took charge of the day-to-day work of the Central Committee and things began to improve in all fields. During the criticism and repudiation of Lin Biao in 1972, he correctly proposed criticism of the ultra-Left trend of thought. In fact, this was an extension of the correct proposals put forward around February 1967 by many leading comrades of the Central Committee who had called for the correction of the errors of the "cultural revolution". Comrade Mao Zedong, however, erroneously held that the task was still to oppose the "ultra-Right". The Tenth Congress of the Party perpetuated the "Left" errors of the Ninth Congress and made Wang Hongwen a vice-chairman of the Party. Jiang Qing, Zhang Chunqiao, Yao Wenyuan and Wang Hongwen formed a Gang of Four inside the Political Bureau of the Central Committee, thus strengthening the influence of the counter-revolutionary Jiang Qing clique.

3) From the Tenth Congress of the Party to October 1976. Early in 1974 Jiang Qing, Wang Hongwen and others launched a campaign to "crit-

icise Lin Biao and Confucius". Jiang Qing and the others directed the spearhead at Comrade Zhou Enlai, which was different in nature from the campaign conducted in some localities and organizations where individuals involved in and incidents connected with the conspiracies of the counterrevolutionary Lin Biao clique were investigated. Comrade Mao Zedong approved the launching of the movement to "criticise Lin Biao and Confucius". When he found that Jiang Qing and the others were turning it to their advantage in order to seize power, he severely criticised them. He declared that they had formed a "gang of four" and pointed out that Jiang Qing harboured the wild ambition of making herself chairman of the Central Committee and "forming a cabinet" by political manipulation. In 1975, when Comrade Zhou Enlai was seriously ill, Comrade Deng Xiaoping, with the support of Comrade Mao Zedong, took charge of the day-to-day work of the Central Committee. He convened an enlarged meeting of the Military Commission of the Central Committee and several other important meetings with a view to solving problems in industry, agriculture, transport and science and technology, and began to straighten out the work in many fields so that the situation took an obvious turn for the better. However, Comrade Mao Zedong could not bear to accept systematic correction of the errors of the "cultural revolution" by Comrade Deng Xiaoping and triggered the movement to "criticise Deng and counter the Right deviationist trend to reverse correct verdicts", once again plunging the nation into turmoil. In January of that year, Comrade Zhou Enlai passed away. Comrade Zhou Enlai was utterly devoted to the Party and the people and stuck to his post till his dying day. He found himself in an extremely difficult situation throughout the "cultural revolution". He always kept the general interest in mind, bore the heavy burden of office without complaint, racking his brains and untiringly endeavouring to keep the normal work of the Party and the state going, to minimise the damage caused by the "cultural revolution" and to protect many Party and non-Party cadres. He waged all forms of struggle to counter sabotage by the counter-revolutionary Lin Biao and Jiang Qing cliques. His death left the whole Party and people in the most profound grief. In April of the same year, a powerful movement of protest signalled by the Tian An Men Incident swept the whole country, a movement to mourn for the late Premier Zhou Enlai and oppose the Gang of Four. In essence, the movement was a demonstration of support for the Party's correct leadership as represented by Comrade Deng Xiaoping. It laid the ground for massive popular support for the subsequent overthrow of the counter-revolutionary Jiang Qing clique. The Political Bureau of the Central Committee and Comrade Mao Zedong wrongly assessed the nature of the Tian An Men Incident and dismissed Comrade Deng Xiaoping from all his posts inside and outside the Party. As soon as Comrade Mao Zedong passed away in September 1976, the counter-revolutionary Jiang Qing clique stepped up its plot to seize supreme Party and state leadership. Early in October of the same year, the Political Bureau of the Central Committee, executing the will of the Party and the people, resolutely smashed the clique and brought the catastrophic "cultural revolution" to an end. This was a great victory won by the entire Party, army and people after prolonged struggle. Hua Guofeng, Ye Jianying, Li Xiannian and other comrades played a vital part in the struggle to crush the clique.

22. Chief responsibility for the grave "Left" error of the "cultural revolution", an error comprehensive in magnitude and protracted in duration, does indeed lie with Comrade Mao Zedong. But after all it was the error of a great proletarian revolutionary. Comrade Mao Zedong paid constant attention to overcoming shortcomings in the life of the Party and state. In his later years, however, far from making a correct analysis of many problems, he confused right and wrong and the people with the enemy during the "cultural revolution". While making serious mistakes, he repeatedly urged the whole Party to study the works of Marx, Engels and Lenin conscientiously and imagined that his theory and practice were Marxist and that they were essential for the consolidation of the dictatorship of the proletariat. Herein lies his tragedy. While persisting in the comprehensive error of the "cultural revolution", he checked and rectified some of its specific mistakes, protected some leading Party cadres and non-Party public figures and enabled some leading cadres to return to important leading posts. He led the struggle to smash the counter-revolutionary Lin Biao clique. He made major criticisms and exposures of Jiang Qing, Zhang Chunqiao and others, frustrating their sinister ambition to seize supreme leadership. All this was crucial to the subsequent and rela-tively painless overthrow of the Gang of Four by our Party. In his later years, he still remained alert to safeguarding the security of our coun-try, stood up to the pressure of the social-imperialists, pursued a correct foreign policy, firmly supported the just struggles of all peoples, outlined the correct strategy of the three worlds and advanced the important principle that China would never seek hegemony. During the "cultural revolution" our Party was not destroyed, but maintained its unity. The State Council and the People's Liberation Army were still able to do much of their essential work. The Fourth National People's Congress which was attended by deputies from all nationalities and all walks of life was convened and it determined the

composition of the State Council with Comrades Zhou Enlai and Deng Xiaoping as the core of its leadership. The foundation of China's socialist system remained intact and it was possible to continue socialist economic construction. Our country remained united and exerted a significant influence on international affairs. All these important facts are inseparable from the great role played by Comrade Mao Zedong. For these reasons, and particularly for his vital contributions to the cause of the revolution over the years, the Chinese people have always regarded Comrade Mao Zedong as their respected and beloved great leader and teacher.

23. The struggle waged by the Party and the people against "Left" errors and against the counter-revolutionary Lin Biao and Jiang Qing cliques during the "cultural revolution" was arduous and full of twists and turns, and it never ceased. Rigorous tests throughout the "cultural revolution" have proved that standing on the correct side in the struggle were the overwhelming majority of the members of the Eighth Central Committee of the Party and the members it elected to its Political Bureau, Standing Committee and Secretariat. Most of our Party cadres, whether they were wrongly dismissed or remained at their posts, whether they were rehabilitated early or late, are loyal to the Party and people and steadfast in their belief in the cause of socialism and communism. Most of the intellectuals, model workers, patriotic democrats, patriotic overseas Chinese and cadres and masses of all strata and all nationalities who had been wronged and persecuted did not waver in their love for the motherland and in their support for the Party and socialism. Party and state leaders such as Comrades Liu Shaoqi, Peng Dehuai, He Long and Tao Zhu and all other Party and non-Party comrades who were persecuted to death in the "cultural revolution" will live for ever in the memories of the Chinese people. It was through the joint struggles waged by the entire Party and the masses of workers, peasants, PLA officers and men, intellectuals, educated youth and cadres that the havoc wrought by the "cultural revolution" was somewhat mitigated. Some progress was made in our economy despite tremendous losses. Grain output increased relatively steadily. Significant achievements were scored in industry, communications and capital construction and in science and technology. New railways were built and the Changjiang River Bridge at Nanjing was completed: a number of large enterprises using advanced technology went into operation; hydrogen bomb tests were successfully undertaken and man-made satellites successfully launched and retrieved; and new hybrid strains of long-grained rice were developed and popularised. Despite the domestic turmoil, the People's Liberation

Army bravely defended the security of the motherland. And new prospects were opened up in the sphere of foreign affairs. Needless to say, none of these successes can be attributed in any way to the "cultural revolution", without which we would have scored far greater achievements for our cause. Although we suffered from sabotage by the counter-revolutionary Lin Biao and Jiang Qing cliques during the "cultural revolution", we won out over them in the end. The Party, the people's political power, the people's army and Chinese society on the whole remained unchanged in nature. Once again history has proved that our people are a great people and that our Party and socialist system have enormous vitality.

24. In addition to the above-mentioned immediate cause of Comrade Mao Zedong's mistake in leadership, there are complex social and historical causes underlying the "cultural revolution" which dragged on for as long as a decade. The main causes are as follows:

1) The history of the socialist movement is not long and that of the socialist countries even shorter. Some of the laws governing the development of socialist society are relatively clear, but many more remain to be "explored". Our Party had long existed in circumstances of war and fierce class struggle. It was not fully prepared, either ideologically or in terms of scientific study, for the swift advent of the new-born socialist society and for socialist construction on a national scale. The scientific works of Marx, Engels, Lenin and Stalin are our guide to action, but can in no way provide ready-made answers to the problems we may encounter in our socialist cause. Even after the basic completion of socialist transformation, given the guiding ideology, we were liable, owing to the historical circumstances in which our Party grew, to continue to regard issues unrelated to class struggle as its manifestations when observing and handling new contradictions and problems which cropped up in the political, economic, cultural and other spheres in the course of the development of socialist society. And when confronted with actual class struggle under the new conditions, we habitually fell back on the familiar methods and experiences of the large-scale, turbulent mass struggle of the past, which should no longer have been mechanically followed. As a result, we substantially broadened the scope of class struggle. Moreover, this subjective thinking and practice divorced from reality seemed to have a "theoretical basis" in the writings of Marx, Engels, Lenin and Stalin because certain ideas and arguments set forth in them were misunderstood or dogmatically interpreted. For instance, it was thought that equal right, which reflects the exchange of equal amounts of labour and is applicable to the distribution of the means of consumption in socialist society,

or "bourgeois right" as it was designated by Marx, should be restricted and criticised, and so the principle of "to each according to his work" and that of material interest should be restricted and criticised; that small production would continue to engender capitalism and the bourgeoisie daily and hourly on a large scale even after the basic completion of socialist transformation, and so a series of "Left" economic policies and policies on class struggle in urban and rural areas were formulated; and that all ideological differences inside the Party were reflections of class struggle in society, and so frequent and acute inner-Party struggles were conducted. All this led us to regard the error in broadening the scope of class struggle as an act in defence of the purity of Marxism. Furthermore, Soviet leaders started a polemic between China and the Soviet Union, and turned the arguments between the two Parties on matters of principle into a conflict between the two nations, bringing enormous pressure to bear upon China politically, economically and militarily. So we were forced to wage a just struggle against the big-nation chauvinism of the Soviet Union. In these circumstances, a campaign to prevent and combat revisionism inside the country was launched, which spread the error of broadening the scope of class struggle in the Party, so that normal differences among comrades inside the Party came to be regarded as manifestations of the revisionist line or of the struggle between the two lines. This resulted in growing tension in inner-Party relations. Thus it became difficult for the Party to resist certain "Left" views put forward by Comrade Mao Zedong and others, and the development of these views led to the outbreak of the protracted "cultural revolution".

2) Comrade Mao Zedong's prestige reached a peak and he began to get arrogant at the very time when the Party was confronted with the new task of shifting the focus of its work to socialist construction, a task for which the utmost caution was required. He gradually divorced himself from practice and from the masses, acted more and more arbitrarily and subjectively, and increasingly put himself above the Central Committee of the Party. The result was a steady weakening and even undermining of the principle of collective leadership and democratic centralism in the political life of the Party and the country. This state of affairs took shape only gradually and the Central Committee of the Party should be held partly responsible. From the Marxist viewpoint, this complex phenomenon was the product of given historical conditions. Blaming this on only one person or on only a handful of people will not provide a deep lesson for the whole Party or enable it to find practical ways to change the situation. In the communist movement, leaders play quite an important role. This has been borne out by history time and again and leaves no room for doubt. However, certain

grievous deviations, which occurred in the history of the international communist movement owing to the failure to handle the relationship between the Party and its leader correctly, had an adverse effect on our Party, too. Feudalism in China has had a very long history. Our Party fought in the firmest and most thoroughgoing way against it, and particularly against the feudal system of land ownership and the land-lords and local tyrants, and fostered a fine tradition of democracy in the anti-feudal struggle. But it remains difficult to eliminate the evil ideological and political influence of centuries of feudal autocracy. And for various historical reasons, we failed to institutionalise and legalise inner-Party democracy and democracy in the political and social life of the country, or we drew up the relevant laws but they lacked due authority. This meant that conditions were present for the over-concentration of Party power in individuals and for the develop-ment of arbitrary individual rule and the personality cult in the Party. Thus, it was hard for the Party and state to prevent the initiation of the "cultural revolution" or check its development.

## Great turning point in history

25. The victory won in overthrowing the counterrevolutionary Jiang Qing clique in October 1976 saved the Party and the revolution from disaster and enabled our country to enter a new historical period of development. In the two years from October 1976 to December 1978 when the Third Plenary Session of the Eleventh Central Committee of the Party was convened, large numbers of cadres and other people most enthusiastically devoted themselves to all kinds of revolutionary work and the task of construction. Notable results were achieved in exposing and repudiating the crimes of the counterrevolutionary Jiang Qing clique and uncovering their factional setup. The consolidation of Party and state organizations and the redress of wrongs suffered by those who were unjustly, falsely and wrongly charged began in some places. Industrial and agricultural production was fairly swiftly restored. Work in education, science and culture began to return to normal. Comrades inside and outside the Party demanded more and more strongly that the errors of the "cultural revolution" be corrected, but such demands met with serious resistance. This, of course, was partly due to the fact that the political and ideological confusion created in the decade-long "cultural revolution" could not be elimi-nated overnight, but it was also due to the "Left" errors in the guid-ing ideology that Comrade Hua Guofeng continued to commit in his capacity as Chairman of the Central Committee of the Chinese

Communist Party. On the proposal of Comrade Mao Zedong, Comrade Hua Guofeng had become First Vice-Chairman of the Central Committee of the Party and concurrently Premier of the State Council during the "movement to criticise Deng Xiaoping" in 1976. He contributed to the struggle to overthrow the counter-revolutionary Jiang Qing clique and did useful work after that. But he promoted the erroneous "two-whatevers" policy, that is, "we firmly uphold whatever policy decisions Chairman Mao made, and we unswervingly adhere to whatever instructions Chairman Mao gave", and he took a long time to rectify the error. He tried to suppress the discussions on the criterion of truth [that] unfolded in the country in 1978, which were very significant in setting things right. He procrastinated and obstructed the work of reinstating veteran cadres in their posts and redressing the injustices left over from the past (including the case of the "Tian An Men Incident" of 1976). He accepted and fostered the personality cult around himself while continuing the personality cult of the past. The Eleventh National Congress of the Chinese Communist Party convened in August 1977 played a positive role in exposing and repudiating the Gang of Four and mobilizing the whole Party for building China into a powerful modern socialist state. However, owing to the limitations imposed by the prevailing historical conditions and the influence of Comrade Hua Guofeng's mistakes, it reaffirmed the erroneous theories, policies and slogans of the "cultural revolution" instead of correcting them. He also had his share of responsibility for impetuously seeking quick results in economic work and for continuing certain other "Left" policies. Obviously, under his leadership it was impossible to correct "Left" errors within the Party, and all the more impossible to restore the Party's fine traditions.'

26. The Third Plenary Session of the Eleventh Central Committee in December 1978 marked a crucial turning point of far-reaching significance in the history of our Party since the birth of the People's Republic. It put an end to the situation in which the Party had been advancing haltingly in its work since October 1976 and began to correct conscientiously and comprehensively the "Left" errors of the "cultural revolution" and earlier. The plenary session resolutely criticised the erroneous "two-whatevers" policy and fully affirmed the need to grasp Mao Zedong Thought comprehensively and accurately as a scientific system. It highly evaluated the forum on the criterion of truth and decided on the guiding principle of emancipating the mind, using our brains, seeking truth from facts and uniting as one in looking forward to the future. It firmly discarded the slogan "Take class struggle as the key link", which had become unsuitable in a socialist

society, and made the strategic decision to shift the focus of work to socialist modernisation. It declared that attention should be paid to solving the problem of serious imbalances between the major branches of the economy and drafted decisions on the acceleration of agricultural development. It stressed the task of strengthening socialist democracy and the socialist legal system. It examined and redressed a number of major unjust, false and wrong cases in the history of the Party and settled the controversy on the merits and demerits, the rights and wrongs, of some prominent leaders. The plenary session also elected additional members to the Party's central leading organs. These momentous changes in the work of leadership signified that the Party re-established the correct line of Marxism ideologically, politically and organizationally. Since then, it has gained the initiative in setting things right and has been able to solve step by step many problems left over since the founding of the People's Republic and the new problems cropping up in the course of practice and carry out the heavy tasks of construction and reform, so that things are going very well in both the economic and political spheres.

1) In response to the call of the Third Plenary Session of the Eleventh Central Committee of the Party for emancipating the mind and seeking truth from facts, large numbers of cadres and other people have freed themselves from the spiritual shackles of the personality cult and the dogmatism that prevailed in the past. This has stimulated thinking inside and outside the Party, giving rise to a lively situation where people try their best to study new things and seek solutions to new problems. To carry out the principle of emancipating the mind properly, the Party reiterated in good time the four fundamental principles of upholding the socialist road, the people's democratic dictatorship (i.e., the dictatorship of the proletariat), the leadership of the Communist Party, and Marxism–Leninism and Mao Zedong Thought. It reaffirmed the principle that neither democracy nor centralism can be practised at each other's expense and pointed out the basic fact that, although the exploiters had been eliminated as classes, class struggle continues to exist within certain limits. In his speech at the meeting in celebration of the 30th anniversary of the founding of the People's Republic of China, which was approved by the Fourth Plenary Session of the Eleventh Central Committee of the Party, Comrade Ye Jianying fully affirmed the gigantic achievements of the Party and people since the inauguration of the People's Republic, while making self-criticism on behalf of the Party for errors in its work and outlined our country's bright prospects. This helped to unify the thinking of the whole Party and people. At its meeting in August 1980, the Political Bureau of the

Central Committee set itself the historic task of combating corrosion by bourgeois ideology and eradicating the evil influence of feudalism in the political and ideological fields which is still present. A work conference convened by the Central Committee in December of the same year resolved to strengthen the Party's ideological and political work, make greater efforts to build a socialist civilization, criticise the erroneous ideological trends running counter to the four fundamental principles and strike at the counter-revolutionary activities disrupting the cause of socialism. This exerted a most salutary countrywide influence in fostering a political situation characterised by stability, unity and liveliness.

2) At a work conference called by the Central Committee in April 1979, the Party formulated the principle of "readjusting, restructuring, consolidating and improving" the economy as a whole in a decisive effort to correct the shortcomings and mistakes of the previous two years in our economic work and eliminate the influence of "Left" errors that had persisted in this field. The Party indicated that economic construction must be carried out in the light of China's conditions and in conformity with economic and natural laws; that it must be carried out within the limits of our own resources, step by step, after due deliberation and with emphasis on practical results, so that the development of production will be closely connected with the improvement of the people's livelihood; and that active efforts must be made to promote economic and technical co-operation with other countries on the basis of independence and self-reliance. Guided by these principles, light industry has quickened its rate of growth and the structure of industry is becoming more rational and better coordinated. Reforms in the system of economic management, including extension of the decision-making powers of enterprises, restoration of the workers' congresses, strengthening of democratic management of enterprises and transference of financial management responsibilities to the various levels, have gradually been carried out in conjunction with economic readjustment. The Party has worked conscientiously to remedy the errors in rural work since the later stage of the movement for agricultural co-operation, with the result that the purchase prices of farm and sideline products have been raised, various forms of production responsibility introduced whereby remuneration is determined by farm output, family plots have been restored and appropriately extended, village fairs have been revived, and sideline occupations and diverse undertakings have been developed. All these have greatly enhanced the peasants' enthusiasm. Grain output in the last two years reached an all-time high, and at the same time

industrial crops and other farm and sideline products registered a big increase. Thanks to the development of agriculture and the economy as a whole, the living standards of the people have improved.

3) After detailed and careful investigation and study, measures were taken to clear the name of Comrade Liu Shaoqi, former Vice-Chairman of the Central Committee of the Communist Party of China and Chairman of the People's Republic of China, those of other Party and state leaders, national minority leaders and leading figures in different circles who had been wronged, and to affirm their historical contributions to the Party and the people in protracted revolutionary struggle.

4) Large numbers of unjust, false and wrong cases were re-examined and their verdicts reversed. Cases in which people had been wrongly labelled bourgeois Rightists were also corrected. Announcements were made to the effect that former businessmen and industrialists, having undergone remoulding, are now working people; that small tradespeople, pedlars and handicraftsmen, who were originally labourers, have been differentiated from businessmen and industrialists who were members of the bourgeoisie; and that the status of the vast majority of former landlords and rich peasants, who have become working people through remoulding, has been re-defined. These measures have appropriately resolved many contradictions inside the Party and among the people.

5) People's congresses at all levels are doing their work better and those at the provincial and county levels have set up permanent organs of their own. The system according to which deputies to the people's congresses at and below the county level are directly elected by the voters is now universally practised. Collective leadership and democratic centralism are being perfected in Party and state organizations. The powers of local and primary organizations are steadily being extended. The so-called right to "speak out, air views and hold debates in a big way and write big-character posters", which actually obstructs the promotion of socialist democracy, was deleted from the Constitution. A number of important laws, decrees and regulations have been reinstated, enacted or enforced, including the Criminal Law and the Law of Criminal Procedure which had never been drawn up since the founding of the People's Republic. The work of the judicial, procuratorial and public security departments has improved and telling blows have been dealt at all types of criminals guilty of serious offences. The ten principal members of the counter-revolutionary Lin Biao and Jiang Qing cliques were publicly tried according to law.

6) The Party has striven to readjust and strengthen the leading bodies at all levels. The Fifth Plenary Session of the Eleventh Central Committee of the Party, held in February 1980, elected additional members to the Standing Committee of its Political Bureau and re-established the Secretariat of the Central Committee, greatly strengthening the central leadership. Party militancy has been enhanced as a result of the establishment of the Central Commission for Inspecting Discipline and of discipline inspection commissions at the lower levels, the formulation of the Guiding Principles for Inner-Party Political Life and other related inner-Party regulations, and the effort made by leading Party organizations and discipline inspection bodies at the different levels to rectify unhealthy practices. The Party's mass media have also contributed immensely in this respect. The Party has decided to put an end to the virtually lifelong tenure of leading cadres, change the over-concentration of power and, on the basis of revolutionisation, gradually reduce the average age of the leading cadres at all levels and raise their level of education and professional competence, and has initiated this process. With the reshuffling of the leading personnel of the State Council and the division of labour between Party and government organizations, the work of the central and local governments has improved.

In addition, there have been significant successes in the Party's efforts to implement our policies in education, science, culture, public health, physical culture, nationality affairs, united front work, overseas Chinese affairs and military and foreign affairs.

In short, the scientific principles of Mao Zedong Thought and the correct policies of the Party have been revived and developed under new conditions and all aspects of Party and government work have been flourishing again since the Third Plenary Session of the Eleventh Central Committee. Our work still suffers from shortcomings and mistakes, and we are still confronted with numerous difficulties. Nevertheless, the road of victorious advance is open, and the Party's prestige among the people is rising day by day.

## Reference

Central Committee of the Communist Party of China (1981). Resolution on Certain Questions in the History of Our Party Since the Founding of the People's Republic of China. Adopted by the Sixth Plenary Session of the Eleventh Central Committee of the Communist Party of China on June 27, 1981. www.marxists.org/subject/china/documents/cpc/history/01.htm. Accessed 22 May 2013.

# INDEX